Computer Simulation in Management Science

Fourth Edition

Computer Simulation in Management Science

Fourth Edition

Michael Pidd

Management Science Department
The Management School
University of Lancaster

JOHN WILEY & SONS
Chichester · New York · Weinheim · Brisbane · Singapore · Toronto

Copyright © 1984, 1988, 1992, 1998 by John Wiley & Sons Ltd,
Baffins Lane, Chichester,
West Sussex PO19 1UD, England

National 01243 779777
International (+44) 1243 779777
e-mail (for orders and customer service enquiries): cs-books@wiley.co.uk
Visit our Home Page on http://www.wiley.co.uk
or http://www.wiley.com

Reprinted November 1998, April 2001

Other Wiley Editorial Offices

John Wiley & Sons, Inc., 605 Third Avenue,
New York, NY 10158-0012, USA

Wiley-VCH Verlag GmbH, Pappelallee 3,
D-69469 Weinheim, Germany

John Wiley & Sons Australia Ltd, 33 Park Road, Milton,
Queensland 4064, Australia

John Wiley & Sons (Asia) Pte Ltd, 2 Clementi Loop #02-01,
Jin Xing Distripark, Singapore 129809

John Wiley & Sons (Canada) Ltd, 22 Worcester Road,
Rexdale, Ontario M9W 1L1, Canada

Library of Congress Cataloging-in-Publication Data

Pidd, Michael,
    Computer simulation in management science / Michael Pidd.—4th ed.
        p.   cm.
    Includes bibliographical references and index.
    ISBN 0-471-97931-7
    1. Management science—Computer simulation.   I. Title.
    T57.62.P63   1998
    658.4'0352—dc21   97–30971
                                                                  CIP

British Library Cataloguing in Publication Data

A catalogue record for this book is available from the British Library

ISBN 0-471-97931-7

Typeset in 10/12 pt Photina from the author's disks by
Mathematical Composition Setters Ltd, Salisbury.
Printed and bound in Great Britain by Bookcraft (Bath) Ltd, Midsomer Norton, Somerset.
This book is printed on acid-free paper responsibly manufactured from sustainable forestation,
for which at least two trees are planted for each one used for paper production.

*For Sally, whose affection is no simulation and
for Karen and Helen, who take computers for granted
and for whom life is still an experiment.*

Contents

Preface to the Fourth Edition

As in the previous editions, this book is aimed at management science students and practitioners who need to learn how to conduct computer simulation studies. As before, its main focus is on simulation *modelling* and all the material is organised to that end. Since 1992, when I wrote the third edition, progress in computing and in computer simulation has continued apace. Hence, the changes in this edition aim to keep the book up to date, whilst making whatever other improvements seem sensible.

When I started work on the first edition in 1982 I had no idea that I would be working on a fourth edition 15 years later. Much as software and hardware seems to be upgraded every so often, so, it seems, must books. Writing this fourth edition in the last few months I have used three versions of Microsoft Word for Windows—versions 2, 6 and 97; three computers—a DX2, Pentium 100 and Pentium 200; and three operating systems—Windows 3.11, Windows 95 and Windows NT! Such is the pace of change! In the jargon of computer software, this is *Computer Simulation in Management Science 4*. Sadly, most software seems to grow in size at each new version—a temptation that I have avoided with this edition, it being shorter than its predecessor.

A number of people have helped me in producing this fourth edition, by reading the text and by commenting on improvements to the third edition. They include Russell Cheng, Brian Dangerfield, Robert Fildes, David Lane, Doug Love, Ray Paul and Stewart Robinson. As before, John Crookes has stimulated many of my ideas and I'm grateful to him for that. Diane Taylor and colleagues at John Wiley & Sons have also been their usual supportive selves. To all these people, thank you for your help—but I take the blame for any mistakes that remain.

As before, the book is organised around three parts.

PART I: FUNDAMENTALS OF COMPUTER SIMULATION IN MANAGEMENT SCIENCE
There are three chapters in Part I and they provide a general introduction to the principles of computer simulation. Chapter 3, 'Computer simulation in practice', is new and suggests how a simulation study might be conducted. The whole of Part I is deliberately non-technical and makes little or no demand on computing or statistical knowledge, other than the ability to use spread-sheets. It serves as an introduction to those who wish to follow the rest of the book in detail, but is also

aimed at MBA and undergraduate business majors who wish to gain an overview of the subject.

PART II: DISCRETE EVENT SIMULATION

This is aimed at those readers who need to know how to produce valid, working discrete event simulation models. It covers three important aspects of discrete event simulation methods:

1. *Discrete event modelling.* Chapters 4, 5 and 6 introduce the general terminology of discrete event simulation and show, in some detail, how different approaches may be implemented. They assume that such simulations will be developed on personal computers or workstations. Chapter 10 discusses the important issue of model testing and validation, something that is so often squeezed out in practice.

2. *Computing aspects.* Chapters 7, 8 and 9 cover different aspects of computing that are related to discrete simulation. Chapter 7 shows how a three-phase simulation model may be easily implemented in almost any programming language. It uses Turbo Pascal for illustrative purposes and copies of a discrete simulation library in this language and in C, C++ and Visual Basic are available from my World Wide Web page. To find them, use a search engine and search for 'Pidd', 'PiddSim' or 'Computer simulation in management science'. I retain copyright, although the software may be used without charge. Chapter 8 covers the main aspects of visual interactive simulation and of visual interactive modelling systems (VIMS). VIMS are very popular in practice and the chapter highlights their main features. Chapter 9 discusses the discrete event simulation software that is commercially available.

3. *Statistical aspects.* Chapters 12 and 13 are concerned with the statistical aspects of discrete event simulation and form the final section of Part II. They describe how sampling methods can be built into simulation models and how to disentangle the problems of experimentation which follow in their wake. To follow these chapters properly, the reader needs a grounding in basic probability and statistics.

PART III: SYSTEM DYNAMICS

The methods of system dynamics as first propounded by Jay Forrester are, in my opinion, still the most widely used formal simulation methods in management science after discrete event methods. Hence, I have devoted three chapters to the topic and have attempted to provide a general introduction to its methodology in Chapter 14. Chapter 15 discusses the detail of the approach and Chapter 16 describes work carried out by Brian Parker in using the methods to tackle managerial problems.

Lancaster
24 May 1997

Part I

Fundamentals of Computer Simulation in Management Science

1

The Computer Simulation Approach

1.1 MODELS, EXPERIMENTS AND COMPUTERS

Management scientists are not easily separated from their computers and with good reason. Since the 1960s, computers have become smaller, cheaper, more powerful and easier to use by non-specialists. In particular, the development of powerful and cheap portable machines has opened up wide areas of work for the management scientist. Modern computers allow the analyst to explore the whole range of feasible options in a decision problem. These options could be explored without a computer but the process would be very slow and the problem may well change significantly before a satisfactory solution is produced. With a computer, large amounts of data can be quickly processed and presented as a report. This is extremely valuable to the management scientist. One way in which a management scientist uses a computer is to simulate some system or other. This is generally done when it is impossible or inconvenient to find some other way of tackling the problem. In such simulations, a computer is used because of its speed in mimicking a system over a period of time. Again, most of these simulations could (in theory at least) be performed without a computer. But in most organisations, important problems have to be solved quickly. Hence the use of computer simulation in management science.

Computer simulation methods have developed since the early 1960s and may well be the most commonly used of all the analytical tools of management science. The basic principles are simple enough. The analyst builds a model of the system of interest, writes computer programs which embody the model and uses a computer to imitate the system's behaviour when subject to a variety of operating policies. Thus, the most desirable policy may be selected.

For example, a biscuit company may wish to increase the throughput at a distribution depot. Suppose that the biscuits arrive at the depot on large articulated trucks, are unloaded and transferred onto storage racks by fork trucks. When required, the biscuits are removed from the racks and loaded onto small delivery vans for despatch to particular retail customers. To increase the throughput, a number of options might present themselves to the management. For example, they could:

(1)   Increase the number of loading or unloading bays;
(2)   Increase the number of fork trucks;

(3)   Use new systems for handling the goods; etc.

It would be possible to experiment on the real depot by varying some of these factors but such trials would be expensive and time-consuming.

The simulation approach to this problem involves the development of a model of the depot. The model is simply an unambiguous statement of the way in which the various components of the system (e.g. trucks and lorries) interact to produce the behaviour of the system. Once the model has been translated into a computer program the high speed of the computer allows a simulation of, say, 6 months in a few moments. The simulation could also be repeated with the various factors at different levels to see the effect of more loading bays, for example. In this way, the programmed model is used as the basis for experimentation. By doing so, many more options can be examined than would be possible in the real depot—and any disruption is avoided; hence the attraction of computer simulation methods.

To summarise, in a computer simulation we use the power of a computer to carry out experiments on a model of the system of interest. In most cases, such simulations could be done by hand—but few would wish to do so. Now that computers offer significant power for a minimal cost, a computer simulation approach seems to make even more sense in management science.

1.2   MODELS IN MANAGEMENT SCIENCE

Models of various types are often used in management science. They are representations of the system of interest and are used to investigate possible improvements in the real system or to discover the effect of different policies on that system. This is not the place for a detailed exposition of modelling; for this the reader should consult Pidd (1996), Rivett (1994), Miser and Quade (1988) or White (1975). However, some mention of the topic is necessary.

The simplest type of model employed in management is probably a scale model, possibly of a building. By using scale models it is possible to plan sensible layouts of warehouses, factories, offices, etc. In a scale model, physical properties are simply changed in scale and the relationship of the model to the full-scale system is usually obvious. However, such simple scale models do have significant disadvantages.

First, a scale model is concrete in form and highly specific. No one would contemplate using the same scale model for a chemical factory and a school—the two require distinctly different buildings. More subtly, to experiment with a scale model always requires physical alteration of the model. This can be tiresome and expensive.

Second, scale models are static. That is, they cannot show how the various factors interact dynamically. For example, suppose that a warehouse is being designed. One issue that must be considered is the relationship between the internal capacity of the building and the number of loading or unloading bays provided for vehicles. Although it is easy to design a warehouse which always has enough internal space—simply make it too big—this is clearly a waste of money. Given that both the demand for the products and the production level will vary, the art is to design a building which balances the cost of shortages with the cost of over-capacity. Such a balance will vary over time, particularly for seasonal products. No scale model could consider this.

Management scientists tend to employ mathematical and logical models rather than scale models. These represent the important factors of a system by a series of equations which may sometimes be solved to produce an optimal solution. Many of the commonly employed techniques described in management science textbooks are of this form (for example, mathematical programming, game theory, etc.). For computer simulation, logical models are usually required—although in the case of system dynamics (see Chapters 13–15) these are expressed in a mathematical form. The simplest way of thinking about logical models is to consider flow diagrams of various kinds. Industrial engineers often employ flow process charts in method study (Slack *et al.*, 1995) to display the various processes through which products pass in their manufacture and assembly. That is, the charts display the logic of the production process. Such a chart might show that a car body needs to be thoroughly degreased before any painting can begin. Instead of drawing a chart it is possible to represent the logic as a set of instructions. If these directions are clear and unambiguous, then they could be used to show someone how to do the job.

Modern digital computers are logical machines which will obey a sequence of instructions, thus any sequence of instructions can form the basis of a computer program. It is this fact which makes computer simulation possible. At some stage the simulation model, which may initially exist on scraps of paper, in agreed documents or in some formal set of flow diagrams, must be translated into a form which a computer is able to recognise and obey. Once in a computable form, the model may be easily modified so as to permit a wide range of options to be compared in simulation experiments.

1.3   SIMULATION AS EXPERIMENTATION

Computer simulation involves experimentation on a computer-based model of some system. The model is used as a vehicle for experimentation, often in a 'trial and error' way to demonstrate the likely effects of various policies. Thus, those which produce the best results in the model would be implemented in the real system. Figure 1.1 shows the basic idea.

Sometimes these experiments may be quite sophisticated, involving the use of statistical design techniques. Such sophistication is necessary if there is a set of different effects which may be produced in the results by several interacting

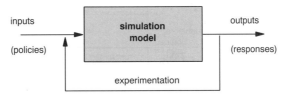

Figure 1.1   Simulation as experimentation

policies. At the other extreme, the experimentation may be very simple, taking the form of 'what if?' questions. Thus, if the simulation model represents the financial flows in an organisation over the next 12 months, typical questions might be:

'What if interest rates rise by 3%?'
'What if the market grows by 5% this year?'

To answer these questions, the simulation is carried out with the appropriate variables of the program set to these values.

An example of a more sophisticated approach can be found in the study described by McCurdy (1977). Although this study was completed over 20 years ago, it clearly illustrates many of the main features of computer simulation in management science. The project was carried out for a motor manufacturer who wished to design a three-storey paintshop for a completely new car. Ideally, such a new paintshop would be all on the same level, but a shortage of land meant that three storeys were necessary. The floors of the paintshop were to be connected by automatic lifts in which the car bodies would be carried. The nature of the process meant that some of them had to be kept physically separate. For example, some of the preparation processes could not be sited next to the ovens because volatile solvents were to be used. Thus, as shown in Figure 1.2, the ground floor was to be two storage areas, one for the unpainted bodies arriving from the bodyshop and the other for painted bodies which had been through the paintshop. These painted bodies would later be required in the assembly area and it was important that they should arrive there in the correct colour sequence. The first floor was to contain all the processes necessary for preparing and painting the bodies and the second floor would house all the ovens through which the bodies passed after each coat of paint.

This outline design meant that each body would undergo a great many vertical and horizontal transfers. Indeed each would require 14 transfers between floors via the automatic lifts. As most people know from their own experience, lifts do break down sometimes. This, combined with the possibility of stoppages in the main process, meant that some buffer storage would be needed—otherwise a breakdown or stoppage anywhere would bring the paintshop to an immediate halt. However, monocoque car bodies take up a great deal of space and can only be stacked on racking. Thus the provision of storage space would be expensive and a limited budget meant that some sort of trade-off between output levels and in-process storage space was inevitable.

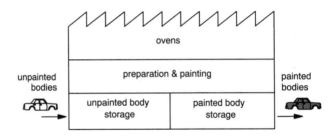

Figure 1.2   The three-storey paintshop

In order to provide this storage, various layouts were possible and therefore several versions of the simulation model were produced—each one representing a possible configuration. These models were then subject to inputs in the form of equipment failure rates, arrival rates of car bodies, size and location of buffer storage, track speeds, etc. In this way the possible dynamic operation of the various layouts was simulated over the equivalent of many real shifts. Great care was taken to ensure that these experiments revealed which of the various factors had caused the changes observed in the simulation. Thus, it was possible to determine the sensitivity of output levels to the various configurations and to different assumptions about reliability and track speeds. From this, a design was developed which met the production targets while avoiding excessive expenditure on idle facilities. In particular, the designers became aware of the way in which each configuration would behave under extreme conditions.

1.4   WHY SIMULATE?

Certainly, computer simulation is no panacea. Realistic simulations may require long computer programs of some complexity. There are special-purpose simulation languages and packaged systems available to ease this task, but it is still rarely simple. Consequently, producing useful results from a computer simulation can turn out to be a surprisingly time-consuming process. In one way, therefore, computer simulation should be regarded as a last resort—to be used if all else fails. However, there are certain advantages in employing a simulation approach in management science and it may be the only way of tackling some problems.

Assuming that a management scientist does not wish to make an instant 'seat of the pants' judgement of a particular problem, various modes of approach are possible. First, it may be possible to conduct experiments directly on the real system. For example, the police may experiment with mock radar speed traps to see if this reduces the number and severity of accidents reported. Second, the analyst may be able to construct and use a mathematical model of the system of interest. For example, Sutton and Coats (1981) describe how mathematical programming techniques are employed to minimise the cost of stainless steel production. A third possibility is to simulate the system.

1.4.1   Simulation versus direct experimentation

Then why simulate when it will be time-consuming and there may be alternative approaches? Considered against real experimentation, simulation has the following advantages:

(1) *Cost*: Although simulation can be time-consuming and therefore expensive in terms of skilled manpower, real experiments may also turn out to be expensive—particularly if something goes wrong!

(2) *Time*: Admittedly, it takes a significant amount of time to produce working computer programs for simulation models. However, once these are written

then an attractive opportunity presents itself. Namely it is possible to simulate weeks, months or even years in seconds of computer time. Hence a whole range of policies may be properly compared.

(3) *Replication*: Unfortunately, the real world is rarely kind enough to allow precise replication of an experiment. One of the skills employed by physical scientists is the design of experiments which are repeatable by other scientists. This is rarely possible in management science. It seems unlikely that an organisation's competitors will sit idly by as a whole variety of pricing policies are attempted in a bid to find the best. It is even less likely that a military adversary will allow a replay of a battle. Simulations are precisely repeatable.

(4) *Safety*: One of the objectives of a simulation study may be to estimate the effect of extreme conditions, and to do this in real life may be dangerous or even illegal. An airport authority may take some persuading to allow a doubling of the flights per day even if they do wish to know the capacity of the airport. Simulated aircraft cause little damage when they run out of fuel in the simulated sky.

(5) *Legality*: Even when not employed by the mafia there are times when an analyst may wish to investigate the effect of changes in legislation. For example, a company may wish to see what the effect would be on its delivery performance of changes in the laws that control drivers' hours of work.

1.4.2   Simulation versus mathematical modelling

What, then, of the other possibility, of building and using a mathematical model of the system? Here too there are problems. First, most mathematical models cannot satisfactorily cope with dynamic or transient effects. For example, the steady-state behaviour of the paintshop was of less concern to the motor manufacturer than the operation of the system after breakdowns. Second, though it is debatable (see Chapter 11) whether this is a good thing, it is possible to sample from non-standard probability distributions in a simulation model. However, queuing theory models permit only certain distributions and therefore cannot cope with many types of problem.

Computer simulation, then, may well be regarded as the last resort. Despite this, it is surprising how often such an approach is needed.

1.5   SUMMARY

Computer simulation methods allow experimentation on a computer-based model of some system. The model is built by carefully describing the ways in which the system changes state and the rules which govern its dynamic behaviour. Modelling is best planned on an incremental and parsimonious basis, with the expectation that the model will need to be enhanced as knowledge about the system develops. Once built, the model is used for experimentation, either interactive or classical or both.

EXERCISES

1. Suppose that a public authority is considering various policies for checking whether goods vehicles are overweight as they arrive at ferry ports. Discuss whether it might be sensible to consider a simulation approach.

2. Spread-sheet packages such as Microsoft Excel™ are widely used on personal computers. Discuss what type of simulation these packages allow.

3. If you were the manager of a factory whose production operations were being simulated by a management scientist, why might you not be convinced that the simulation model was valid even if the production rates output from the simulation were the same as those of your factory?

4. Consider the reasons why simulation approaches often form part of the process of designing new manufacturing systems.

5. Computers are becoming easier to use by non-specialists. Should managers be encouraged to undertake computer simulations themselves or is there still a place for the specialist?

REFERENCES

McCurdy, A. W. (1977) The design of engineering facilities at Rover Triumph, In Littlechild, S. C. (ed.) *O.R. for Managers.* Philip Allan, Oxford.

Miser, H. J. & Quade E. S. (eds) (1988) *Handbook of Systems Analysis: Craft Issues and Procedural Choices.* Wiley, Chichester.

Pidd, M. (1996) *Tools for Thinking: Modelling in Management Science.* Wiley, Chichester.

Rivett, B. H. P. (1994) *The Craft of Decision Modelling.* Wiley, Chichester.

Slack, N., Chambers, S., Harland, C. & Johnston, R. (1995) *Operations Management.* Pitman, London.

Sutton, D. W. & Coats, P. A. (1981) On-line mixture calculation system for stainless steel production by BSC stainless: the least through cost mix system (LTCM). *J. Opl Res. Soc.,* **32**(3), 165–172.

White, D. J. (1975) *Decision Methodology.* Wiley, Chichester.

2

A Variety of Modelling Approaches

2.1 GENERAL CONSIDERATIONS

Before producing a simulation model and thus a computer program, the analyst must decide what will be the principal elements of that model. In doing so, two aspects should be borne in mind. The first is the nature of the system being simulated—obviously, the model needs to be a close fit, a good representation of the system. Needless to say, some modelling approaches are more suited to certain problems than to others. The second aspect is the nature of the study being carried out. That is, what are the objectives of the study, what is the point of the simulation, what results are expected? Considering both of these aspects will allow the analyst to decide what level of accuracy and detail is appropriate for the simulation. There is clearly little point in producing an extremely detailed simulation if only crude estimates are required. The practical decisions that need to be made concern the following, each of which will be considered in this chapter:

- Time handling;
- Stochastic or deterministic durations;
- Discrete or continuous change.

2.2 TIME-HANDLING

One of the advantages of simulation is that the speed at which the experiment proceeds can be controlled. In management science it is usual to speed up the passage of time so as to simulate several weeks or months in a few minutes of computer time. The essence of a simulation is that the state changes of the system are modelled through time. Hence, it is important to consider how time-flow might be handled within the simulation.

2.2.1 Time-slicing

Perhaps the simplest way of controlling the flow of time in a simulation is to move it forward in equal time intervals. This approach is often described as 'time-slicing' and involves updating and examining the model at regular intervals. Thus, for a time-slice of length dt, the model is updated at time $(t + \mathrm{d}t)$ for changes occurring in the interval (t to $(t + \mathrm{d}t)$).

One obvious problem with this approach is that some decision must be taken about the length of the time slice before the simulation is carried out. For example, the activity levels within a supertanker terminal may necessitate a time-slice of one hour, whereas for a civil airport the time slice may be more appropriately set to a half minute or less. Clearly, if the time-slice is too large then the behaviour of the model is much coarser than that of the real system because it is impossible to simulate some of the state changes that occur. If, on the other hand, the time-slice is too small then the model is frequently examined unnecessarily (when no state changes are possible) and this leads to excessively long computer runs.

As a simple example (based on an example in Jones, 1975) consider a workshop with just two machines, A and B. Suppose that the time taken to complete a job on these machines depends on the size of the job. Thus the job times are:

- Machine A: (batch size/50 + 1) days
- Machine B: (batch size/100 + 3) days.

Suppose too that the workshop only takes on jobs which must be processed on both machines and that each job must first pass through machine A as a complete batch and then through machine B as a complete batch. That is, no batch may be started on either machine until the previous batch is completed on that machine. If the workshop expects to receive the four orders shown in Table 2.1, when will the final batch be complete? The expected job times (days) are as shown in Table 2.2. Simulating the workshop using a time-slice of one day leads to the times shown in Table 2.3. Thus job 4 is complete at the end of day 32.

Table 2.1   Job-shop order book

Job number	Batch size	Day order expected
1	200	1
2	400	8
3	100	14
4	200	18

Table 2.2   Expected job times

Job number	Machine A	Machine B
1	5	5
2	9	7
3	3	4
4	5	5

Table 2.3   Job-shop: time-slicing simulation

	Jobs queuing		Jobs in progress			Jobs queuing		Jobs in progress	
Day	for m/c A	for m/c B	m/c A	m/c B	Day	for m/c A	for m/c B	m/c A	m/c B
1	—	—	1	—	17	—	—	3	2
2	—	—	1	—	18	4	—	3	2
3	—	—	1	—	19	4	—	3	2
4	—	—	1	—	20	—	3	4	2
5	—	—	1	—	21	—	3	4	2
6	—	—	—	1	22	—	3	4	2
7	—	—	—	1	23	—	3	4	2
8	—	—	2	1	24	—	—	4	3
9	—	—	2	1	25	—	4	—	3
10	—	—	2	1	26	—	4	—	3
11	—	—	2	—	27	—	4	—	3
12	—	—	2	—	28	—	—	—	4
13	—	—	2	—	29	—	—	—	4
14	3	—	2	—	30	—	—	—	4
15	3	—	2	—	31	—	—	—	4
16	3	—	2	—	32	—	—	—	4

m/c = Machine.

Following Table 2.3 through, on day 1, job 1 arrives and its processing immediately begins on machine A. Nothing new happens on days 2, 3 or 4 until the end of day 5, when machine A has finished job 1. Thus on day 6, machine B starts work on job 1. On day 7 nothing happens. On day 8, job 2 arrives and machine A begins its processing. This is obviously a tedious and inefficient way of simulating such a simple system, for there is little point in examining and attempting to update the model each day — on many days, nothing changes.

2.2.2   Next-event technique

Because many systems include such slack periods of varying length it is often preferable to use a variable time increment. In this case, the model is only examined and updated when it is known that a state change is due. These state changes are usually called 'events' and, because time is moved from event to event, the approach is called the next-event technique.

Consider again the simple workshop. Table 2.4 shows the results of a next-event simulation of this system. Notice that the table is much smaller than that required for a time-slicing approach. The method focuses on the progress of each job as it passes through the workshop. The events are:

- A job arrives;
- Machine A starts a job;
- Machine A finishes a job;
- Machine B starts a job;
- Machine B finishes a job.

Table 2.4 Job-shop: next-event simulation

Job No.	Arrival date	Machine A		Machine B	
		Start	Finish	Start	Finish
1	1	1	5	6	10
2	8	8	16	17	23
3	14	17	19	24	27
4	16	20	24	28	32

Each of these events may occur a maximum of four times during the simulation, once for each job. In fact, as Table 2.4 shows, some of these coincide and the model need only be updated on 16 occasions. By way of contrast, Table 2.3 shows the inevitable 32 updates of a time-slicing approach.

2.2.3   Time-slicing or next-event?

Thus, a next-event technique has two advantages over a time-slicing approach. The first is that the time increment automatically adjusts to periods of high and low activity, thus avoiding wasteful and unnecessary checking of the state of the model. The second is that it makes clear when significant events have occurred in the simulation. Against these, rather more information must be held to control the simulation and simulated time does not flow smoothly. Of course, there are some systems whose events do occur at regular intervals. For example, a superstore may check its stock levels at the same time each day and replenishment may similarly arrive at predictable times. In such cases it is quite adequate to update the model at regular intervals to allow for the intervening changes. Nevertheless, it should be noted that the next-event technique is more general since, if the events in a system occur at regular intervals (once per day, perhaps), the next-event technique will act as if it were a time-slicing approach. The reverse is not true.

2.3   STOCHASTIC OR DETERMINISTIC?

A deterministic system is one whose behaviour is entirely predictable. Provided that the system is perfectly understood, then it is possible to predict precisely what will happen. A cycle of operations on an automatic machine may be deterministic in this sense. Each repeated identical cycle will take the same length of time unless the conditions influencing the cycle times are altered.

A stochastic system is one whose behaviour cannot be entirely predicted, although some statement may be made about how likely certain events are to occur. For example, a lecturer may give the same lecture to several sets of students but the duration of the lecture may vary from occasion to occasion. Statistical statements may be made about the duration of the lecture: for example, that it is normally distributed with a mean of 50 minutes and a standard deviation of 3 minutes. Thus it is highly likely that the duration of the lecture will exceed 48 minutes. However, it is impossible to state precisely how long a particular delivery of the lecture will last unless the lecturer's behaviour can be completely controlled—and that of the class too!

In some senses, the distinction between stochastic and deterministic systems is artificial. It is more a statement of the amount of knowledge about a system or the amount of control over that system exercised by an observer. However, it is important to notice that both stochastic and deterministic simulations are possible.

2.3.1   Deterministic simulation: a time-slicing example

Any simulation model which contains no stochastic elements is usually called deterministic. A simple example was the four-job simulation of the workshop which was featured in Section 2.2. As another example, this time one which can be formulated as a set of difference equations, consider the case of Big Al and his recruitment problems.

After his release from gaol, Big Al, a well-known gangster, decides to rebuild his mob for more assaults on the banks of Bailrigg County. This time he plans a large-scale operation and reckons that he would like to have 50 mobsters working for him within 6 months. He currently has none.

His previous experience in forming a mob suggests that he can recruit at a weekly rate equal to one-quarter of the difference between his ideal mob size (50) and the number currently in the mob. His problem is that mobsters get caught by the cops with depressing frequency. Indeed, Happy Harry, chief of the Bailrigg County cops, boasts that his men will catch 5% of Big Al's active mobsters in each week and they receive gaol sentences of at least 12 months each. Fortunately, 10% of those in gaol escape each week and rejoin Big Al's mob. Big Al himself has other ways to satisfy the needs of the local police and does not expect to be arrested again. How large will his mob size be after 10 weeks?

One approach to Big Al's problem is to use a simple time-sliced simulation based on a two-part set of difference equations. To do this requires some variables to be defined.

Variables

Suppose that any 2-week interval can be represented as starting at time $t - 1$ (the first weekend), with an intervening weekend at time t and a final weekend at time $t + 1$. Variables of two types may now be defined:

(1) Aggregated values at definite time points
Consider the time point t:

   Mob size = MS_t
   Number in gaol = NG_t

(2) Variables which represent rates which are constant over an interval
Consider the interval $t - 1$ to t:

Al's recruitment rate = $REC_{t-1,t}$
The rate at which gangsters are arrested = $ARR_{t-1,t}$
The rate at which gangsters escape from gaol = $ESC_{t-1,t}$

The target mob size is a constant, *TARGET*.

Hence, the following equations can be formulated:

(1) Aggregated values at time t

$$MS_t = MS_{t-1} + (REC_{t-1,t} - ARR_{t-1,t}) + ESC_{t-1,t}$$
$$NG_t = NG_{t-1} + (ARR_{t-1,t} - ESC_{t-1,t})$$

(2) Constant rates over the next week

$$REC_{t,t+1} = (TARGET - MS_t)/4$$
$$ARR_{t,t+1} = MS_t * 0.05$$
$$ESC_{t,t+1} = NG_t/10$$

The system may now be simulated using a simple spreadsheet in which the columns represent the different variables and the rows represent the time points (weekends). The four constants, *TARGET* and the three numerical parameters, can be placed as values on the spread-sheet to make experimentation rather easier.

The number in gaol and the mob size need to be specified for time point 0 (just before the start of week 1) and then the normal spreadsheet-linked computations can be employed. To check the computations by hand, do the following:

Starting with time point 0:

(1)   Write down the values of the mob size (*MS*) and number in gaol (*NG*);
(2)   Write down the rates (recruitment, arrest, escape) over the next interval.

Move time to the next point and repeat until the 10 weeks are over.

The results of the simulation for a 10-week period are shown in Table 2.5 and in Figure 2.1. Table 2.5 is slightly deceptive, for it hides the fact that the rates are

Table 2.5   Big Al's recruitment problem

Week	Recruit rate	Arrest rate	Escape rate	No. in gaol	Mob size
0				0.00	0.00
1	12.50	0.00	0.00	0.00	12.50
2	9.38	0.63	0.00	0.63	21.25
3	7.19	1.06	0.06	1.63	27.44
4	5.64	1.37	0.16	2.83	31.87
5	4.53	1.59	0.28	4.14	35.09
6	3.73	1.75	0.41	5.48	37.48
7	3.13	1.87	0.55	6.81	39.28
8	2.68	1.96	0.68	8.09	40.68
9	2.33	2.03	0.81	9.32	41.78
10	2.05	2.09	0.93	10.48	42.68

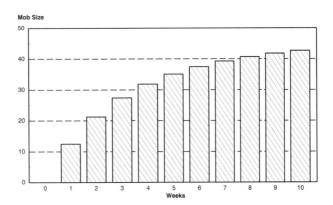

Figure 2.1   Big Al's mob size

actually computed over intervals of length dt, which is 1 week in this case, rather that at the time points 0, 1, 2, etc. Strictly speaking, these rate values should be printed in alternate lines, between the other values. It is clear that Big Al does not reach his target of 50 mobsters within 10 weeks. Indeed, he may have trouble over a much longer period due to the fact that the recruitment rate is a function of the gap between the target and actual mob sizes. To get to 50 he may need to find other incentives.

There is one obvious problem about this model. It uses real values but even gangsters prefer to be treated as integers.

2.3.2   Stochastic simulation

Many systems behave stochastically and must therefore be simulated by a model with stochastic elements. This means that probability distributions are used in such stochastic simulation models. As the simulation proceeds, samples are taken from these distributions so as to mimic the stochastic behaviour. As an example, consider the following replacement problem.

A multi-user computer system includes two disk units which, being mechanical, are prone to failure. If a disk unit fails in service, users lose their files (and their tempers), which need to be restored. Restoration is achieved by copying on to the disk back-up copies of the files held on magnetic tapes. This restoration is inconvenient and so a new operating policy is being considered. At the moment, the disk units are repaired and restored as and when they fail. The proposal is to introduce a joint repair system. Table 2.6 shows the probability of a disk unit failing in the days following its last repair. That is, 5% of the units are expected to fail 1 day after repair or maintenance, 15% after 2 days, etc.

Under the current repair policy, it costs $50/disk to repair and restore a failed unit. The joint repair system would operate as follows. When either unit fails, the failed unit is repaired and restored at a cost of $50/unit. If operational, the other unit will be cleaned at a cost of $25. Cleaning a disk places it in a state equivalent to having been just repaired and restored. Is the new joint repair system cost-effective?

Table 2.6 Probability of disk unit failure

Days since repair or maintenance	Probability of failure
1	0.05
2	0.15
3	0.20
4	0.30
5	0.20
6	0.10
>6	0.00

This question can be answered by a simple stochastic simulation which involves random sampling from the failure distribution of the disks given earlier. Details of sampling methods are given in Chapter 11, but for present purposes a simple method can be used. Figure 2.2 shows a histogram of the disk failure distribution. In Figure 2.3, the data have been rearranged to show the cumulative probability of the various lives. For example, the probability of a disk lasting up to and including 3 days is 0.40 (0.05 + 0.15 + 0.20). Using the cumulative form of Figure 2.3 and random number tables, random samples can be taken from the life distribution by associating a life (in days) with each random number.

An extract from a random number table is shown in Table 2.7, the values range from 00 to 99, and any number in that range has an equal probability of appearing at any position in the table. If these random numbers are divided by 100, so that their range is 0.00 to 0.99, then Figure 2.3 may be used to generate random samples as follows. The first random number in the table is 27 (i.e. 0.27); if this is marked on the vertical axis of Figure 2.3, then the corresponding point on the horizontal axis is 3 days. That is, 3 days is the life associated with the random number 0.27. In general, each life may be associated with a range of random numbers as shown in Table 2.8.

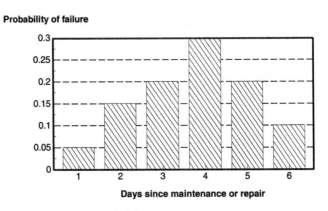

Figure 2.2 Histogram of failure probabilities

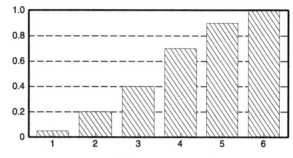

Figure 2.3   Histogram of cumulative failure probabilities

Table 2.7   Some random numbers

27	62	36	30	57	78	22	02	89	22
04	97	43	30	45	12	03	87	16	50
92	26	00	82	58	10	78	44	55	05
21	50	49	83	49	39	25	81	03	99
77	71	43	06	90	09	04	97	07	64
40	39	69	42	63	80	07	85	65	70
60	57	42	97	29	92	84	54	66	91
34	10	78	81	97	99	08	19	15	63
35	37	13	56	88	09	36	40	07	55
04	24	69	52	44	14	61	59	31	50
24	26	29	31	57	17	38	44	03	29
26	63	00	44	64	09	93	15	52	35
91	37	65	32	84	37	80	94	48	46
23	52	10	77	27	40	34	13	73	53
55	89	99	78	50	11	43	43	54	16

Table 2.8   Look-up table linking random numbers and disk life

Life (days)	Associated random numbers
1	0.00–0.04
2	0.05–0.19
3	0.20–0.39
4	0.40–0.69
5	0.70–0.89
6	0.90–0.99

Table 2.9 shows a 50-day simulation of the two policies. In the case of the separate replacement policy, replacements of each of the two units have been simulated until the failure time (the cumulative life) of each is greater than or equal to 50 weeks. For this policy, unit A needed 14 repairs and restores; unit B needed 15. Hence, 29 units were used at a cost of $50/unit, making a cost of $1450 across 50 weeks.

Exactly the same random numbers are used to simulate the second policy, which is also shown in Table 2.9. In this case, the units are considered in pairs. Hence, starting at time zero, the first A unit would last for 3 weeks if allowed to do so, as would the first B unit. In this case, therefore, the first replacement takes place after 3 weeks. The second pair would last 4 weeks (in the case of A) and 3 weeks (in the case of B). Hence the second replacement will take place 3 weeks after the first: that is, after 6 weeks. The simulation continues in this way until the replacement time (the joint cumulative life) is at or greater than 50 weeks. This shows that there were 17 such joint repairs in the period and that, of these 17, nine involved both units in repair and restore (that is, they both failed at the same time—coincidences). The other eight of the 17 involved one unit in a repair and restore, whilst the other need only be cleaned. Hence, there were 26 repairs

Table 2.9   Next-event simulation of the disk repair policies

| | Separate repair | | | | | | Joint repair |
| | Unit A | | | Unit B | | | |
	Random number	Life	Time of failure	Random number	Life	Time of failure	Time of failure
1	0.27	3	3	0.24	3	3	3
2	0.62	4	7	0.26	3	6	6
3	0.36	3	10	0.29	3	9	9
4	0.30	3	13	0.31	3	12	12
5	0.57	4	17	0.57	4	16	16
6	0.04	1	18	0.26	3	19	17
7	0.97	6	24	0.63	4	23	21
8	0.43	4	28	0.00	1	24	22
9	0.30	3	31	0.44	4	28	25
10	0.45	4	35	0.64	4	32	29
11	0.92	6	41	0.91	6	38	35
12	0.26	3	44	0.37	3	41	38
13	0.00	1	45	0.65	4	45	39
14	0.82	5	50	0.32	3	48	42
15	0.58	4	————	0.84	5	53	46
16	0.21	3		0.23	3		49
17	0.50	4		0.52	4		53
18	0.49	4		0.10	2		————
19	0.83	5		0.77	5		
20	0.49	4		0.27	3		

and restores at $50/unit and 8 clean-ups at $25/unit, making a total cost of $1500.

Thus, on the basis of a single simulation, the new policy costs $50 more over a 50-day period. However, it would be wrong to assume that a separate repair policy is therefore more cost-effective. If a different set of random numbers had been used, the result could have been different for both policies and the new policy might appear cheaper. In stochastic simulations, it is important to realise that the results are dependent on the samples taken. Hence it is usual to make several simulation runs, each with a distinct sampling pattern, before drawing any conclusions. Chapter 12 gives details.

The sampling methods employed in stochastic simulations are well developed and documented. Commonly used methods are given in Chapter 11 and most simulation software systems have appropriate sub-routines or procedures ready for use. Thus, distribution sampling should not be a problem in model building. More likely, controlling the sequence of events is the major problem in model building. The interaction of the entities is responsible for the sequence of events, and in the above example these are trivial. But for complex systems a sensible structure is needed. Various common approaches are described in Chapters 5 and 6.

2.4 DISCRETE OR CONTINUOUS CHANGE?

In the job-shop simulation, it was convenient to regard the system as moving from state to state through time. The concern with individual batches was whether their machining was complete or not, rather than with the rate at which the machining was proceeding. The variables which are included in a simulation model can be thought of as changing value in four ways:

(1) *Continuously at any point of time.* Thus, the values are changing smoothly and not discretely and the values taken are accessible at any time point within the simulation.

(2) *Continuously but only at discrete time points.* In this mode, the values again change smoothly but can only be accessed at predetermined times.

(3) *Discretely at any point of time.* In these simulations, state changes are easily identifiable but can occur at any point of time.

(4) *Discretely and only at discrete points of time.* The state changes can only occur at specified points of time.

Historically, computer simulation applications have tended to divide into those employing discrete change and those which allow the variables to change value continuously.

2.4.1 Discrete change

Consider an underground railway in which trains move from station to station, picking up and depositing passengers at each. Viewed from the perspective of discrete change there are a number of obvious system events. For example:

- Train stops at station;
- Doors now open;
- Doors now closed;
- Train starts to leave station.

Thus, to simulate this system using a discrete model, the time taken to travel between stations or to open the doors would either be known deterministically or could be sampled from some appropriate distribution. Thus, for example, when the train starts to leave a station its arrival at the next station could be scheduled by referring to this 'known' journey time. In a discrete simulation the variables are only of interest as and when they point to a change in the state of the system. Chapters 4–7 are devoted to the exposition of methods suitable for discrete simulation.

2.4.2   Continuous change

If the underground railway were to be simulated via a model which allowed continuous change, then the variables would be continuously changing their values as the simulation proceeds. Consider, for example, the train as it travels between stations. If the locomotive is electrically powered, its speed will increase smoothly from rest until it reaches an appropriate cruising rate. The speed does not change by discrete amounts. Thus, if the results of the simulation are to include the state of the system in relation to the continuous variable 'speed', then a continuous change model is needed. These continuous changes could be represented by differential equations which would, in theory, allow the variables to be computed at any point of time.

In considering continuous change models it must be recognised that digital computers operate only with discrete quantities. Hence, changes cannot actually be occurring continuously within a 'continuous' simulation. In system dynamics (see Chapters 13–15) the continuity is achieved by allowing the variables to be inspected or changed at a multitude of fixed points in simulated time.

Continuous simulation 'proper' is not covered in detail in this book because management scientists seem to be more often concerned with systems that can satisfactorily be simulated discretely. More often continuous simulations are the concern of economists in modelling the behaviour of economic systems via sets of differential equations, or the task of engineers designing equipment. Early continuous simulations were mainly carried out using analogue computers. Although these have some appeal for those with an interest in electrical hardware, they tend to be tedious to reprogram and of limited accuracy. Therefore analogue digital simulators, such as CSMP (IBM Corporation, 1970), were developed. Early versions of these simulators employed the block diagram terminology of analogue computers, a description of the block diagram being the 'program' from which digital computers could be programmed to simulate analogue computers. Later versions allow systems to be directly represented as sets of differential equations which are integrated numerically.

2.4.3 Mixed discrete/continuous change

More recently, the vendors of simulation software systems have realised that the separation of discrete and continuous simulation is somewhat artificial. Consequently, a number of simulation software systems now allow the user to program discrete, continuous or mixed models. Recent examples include AweSim (Pritsker and O'Reilly, 1996) and Extend (Krahl, 1996).

EXERCISES

1. Use a spread-sheet program to simulate Big Al's problem as described in Section 2.3.1. Place the constants as values on the spread-sheet and vary these so as to carry out experiments. Use the graphing facilities to see how the mob size builds up.

2. Try using your spread-sheet to model the disk failure problem. This is straightforward in the time-slicing case, but slightly more difficult in the next-event case.

3. Check out your spread-sheet program to see what control, if any, it gives you over the random numbers which are produced. If it does give you proper control, then run the disk failure problem 10 times and try to understand the variation in the results.

4. If you know a computer programming language, write a program to simulate the disk failure problem. Try the time-slicing case first, then the next-event case.

5. Discuss why analogue computers are almost never used in management science despite the fact that many systems do change continuously.

REFERENCES

IBM Corporation (1970) *Introduction to 1130 Systems Modelling Program II (CSMP II).* GH200848-1. White Plains, New York.

Jones, L. (1975) *Simulation Modelling.* Unit 6, Course T341, Systems Modelling. Open University Press, Milton Keynes.

Krahl, D. (1996) Modeling with Extend. *Proceedings of the 1996 Winter Simulation Conference*, Coronada, CA, December. The Society for Computer Simulation, San Diego, CA.

Pritsker, A. A. B. & O'Reilly J. J. (1996) AweSim: the integrated simulation system. *Proceedings of the 1996 Winter Simulation Conference*, Coronada CA, December 1996. The Society for Computer Simulation, San Diego, CA.

3

Computer Simulation in Practice

3.1 PROCESS, CONTENT, PROBLEM AND PROJECT

3.1.1 Process and content

This chapter considers how computer simulation methods may best be put to use in management science. Most of the rest of this book is technical in nature, showing how ideas in computing and statistics can be combined to provide powerful ways to simulate different types of system. Much experience leads the author to believe that technical knowledge and proficiency, although necessary for successful simulation, are not sufficient. One obvious reason for this is that, in operational research and management science (OR/MS), problems do not come neatly labelled as mathematical programming, computer simulation or whatever. Instead, the OR/MS analyst needs to be aware that problem-solving and analysis are more important than the blinkered, if enthusiastic, use of techniques such as computer simulation. In practice, OR/MS is usually judged by its impact on the organisation rather than by technical criteria.

Planning, executing and completing a successful computer simulation study in OR/MS requires more than good computer programming. OR/MS methods were first used in business, commerce and the public sector in the 1950s and analysts have learned that to be successful they must combine two sets of skills. Eden (1989) expresses this in the following neat relationship:

Outcome = Process × Content

It suggests that successful OR/MS depends on the correct deployment of skills related to process and to content. By *process*, is meant the manner in which a study is planned, conducted and completed. Managed properly, the process provides a bridge between the 'technical world' of the analyst and the 'real world' of the organisation. By *content* is meant knowledge related to the system being investigated and the simulation skills being employed to conduct the study. Of course, it is rarely possible to make such a neat distinction between process and content in practice. Nevertheless, the distinction is a helpful one if it serves to focus attention on important issues. The two aspects, argues Eden, need to be properly integrated if an OR/MS study is to be successful. This chapter will explore how these ideas might be deployed so as to increase the likelihood that computer simulation methods are used successfully in OR/MS work.

3.1.2   Problems and projects

A second distinction, related to the one between process and content, is that between a problem and a project. Many OR/MS workers regard themselves as problem-solvers and for a detailed discussion of this, see Pidd (1996). Such a view implies a focus that is sharply directed towards defined goals that may have technical solutions. Thus, some analysts who regard themselves as simulation specialists will happily speak of 'interesting simulation problems' that they have tackled. As faced in OR/MS, problems do not have single correct solutions, for they are not like crossword puzzles. Instead, there may be many different ways of addressing the issues that make up a problem and there may be a range of acceptable solutions. Indeed, it is this fact that makes computer simulation one of the most commonly used tools within OR/MS, for it enables people to explore a whole range of possible solutions and scenarios.

It is important to realise, however, that although OR/MS problems can be solved in a technical sense, this may not be true in an organisational sense. This does not mean that OR/MS projects always end in disaster, it simply means that tackling a problem successfully may provide a way to *handle* the problem rather than actually *solving* it. In many organisations, the same problems crop up time and time again as the organisation, its environment, its competitors, its partners and its customers change. Thus, most organisations face the need to manage stocks of different kinds and may need to explore the market for their goods and services. No project will solve these problems forever more, but good analysis may help the organisation to manage things rather better.

Hence, it is important to realise that OR/MS work within most organisations is managed by a series of projects. A project is, in some ways, an arbitrary thing. The boundaries set and the resources available are rarely determined in a detached or scientific manner but result from forces such as people's opinions, their power and the perceived degree of importance of the work to be done. Hence, although an analyst may dearly wish to be given a whole year to do a 'proper job', it is important to realise that circumstances may dictate that only 3 months are available. If a tailor must cut a coat according to his cloth, so a simulation analyst must learn to do work within defined resource limits.

3.1.3   Two parallel streams

Figure 3.1 shows the need to manage process and content, and problems and projects—all simultaneously. This, needless to say, is not straightforward; but it is similar to the issues that, say, a doctor faces when treating her patients. The doctor must bring her technical knowledge to bear—and most countries have stringent rules to ensure that doctors are technically competent before they are

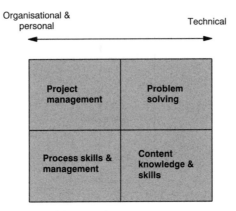

Figure 3.1   Process, content, problems and projects

allowed to practise. However, the doctor must also learn what Miser and Quade (1988), following Schön (1982), term 'craft skills'. The surgeon must learn how to use her instruments and must know when risky interventions are needed. The psychiatrist must learn when to ask very personal questions, even when a patient is clearly distressed. In addition, they both must learn to manage the inter-personal side of their work—bedside manner is very important for doctors (pathologists excepted, perhaps).

This chapter provides introductory coverage of some of these craft issues as they relate to computer simulation. Miser and Quade (1988) devote over 600 pages to this topic, which perhaps gives some idea of its importance and also indicates that the surface can only be scratched here. Nevertheless, the hope is that the novice will gain enough guidance from this chapter to develop a personal style that is successful in its deployment of the craft skills needed for successful integration of process, content, projects and problems.

Figure 3.2 shows that, during a simulation study, the analyst needs to manage the technical work in which she is engaged as well as the project within which the work is being done. The figure shows two parallel loops, one concerned with the project and one concerned with the technical side of the intervention. In a similar vein, Balci (1985) suggests that analysts should realise that simulation studies have life cycles—that is, some activities may need to be carried out several times during a study. This chapter develops a simple model of the technical side of a simulation study based on the one discussed in Pidd (1991). It has three phases, one of which, *modelling*, is concerned with the technical material in the rest of this book. The project side of Figure 3.2 will also be explored. Although the diagram looks rather neat and tidy, the actual experience of carrying out a simulation study is somewhat different. The neat phases shown in the figure overlap with one another and there is often backtracking. Thus, for example, the realisation that the modelling is going wrong (which sometimes it does) may lead to a further attempt at problem structuring.

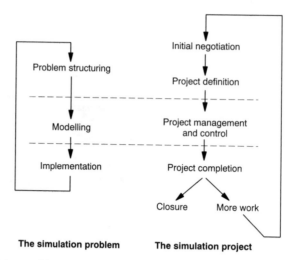

Figure 3.2   Solving problems and managing projects

3.2   THE SIMULATION PROBLEM PART OF THE STUDY

This is the left hand side of Figure 3.2; it covers the technical work carried out during the simulation study and it has three phases, as follows:

- *Problem structuring.*   This is the attempt to take a 'mess' and to extract from it some agreement about the particular problems which might be amenable to OR/MS. The hope is that this process of extraction will not remove all meaning from the 'mess' itself.
- *Modelling.*   This is usually taken as the technical heart of any simulation study and involves the use of statistical and computer methods to analyse the problems defined during problem structuring. The hope is that the modelling will not over-simplify the issues raised during problem structuring.
- *Implementation.*   This is the attempt to put into practice any recommendations that emerge from problem structuring and analysis. It is expected to be a continuing process from which the OR/MS staff will need to withdraw at some stage.

The next sections of the chapter will discuss each of these three aspects in turn, as they relate to computer simulation.

3.3   PROBLEM STRUCTURING

Problem structuring is an attempt to understand the issues which are being addressed in the project in an effort to decide what detailed OR/MS methods will be appropriate. In one sense, therefore, it could be viewed as a mere preliminary to detailed modelling and computer work. However, deciding which are the problems to be tackled and trying to understand their linkages is as challenging a task as the detailed formulation and implementation of simulation models. The challenge in OR/MS is to be good at the full range of activities necessary for successful practice. And that includes problem structuring and implementation skills as well as simulation modelling.

In most cases, the majority of problem-structuring effort takes place at the start of a simulation project. That is, problem structuring is the first phase of the work. How much time will be needed to do this is impossible to specify in general terms—it depends on a number of factors, such as:

- The degree to which this is an entirely new area of work;
- The skills and knowledge of the OR/MS analyst;
- The requirements of the client;
- The time available.

Sometimes, relatively little time needs to be spent in problem structuring, at least in any formal sense. This happens when the work to be done is well established and there is clear agreement about the goals of the study. This may well be the case in organisations that make routine use of simulation methods, for example in designing manufacturing layouts. But even in these studies it is as well to ask some basic questions, even if they take a little time. Writing many years ago, John Dewey (quoted in Lubart, 1994) produced the maxim: 'A problem well put is half-solved'. It seems as if he had in mind the fact that a problem which is poorly posed will be very hard, if not impossible, to solve. Hence, it is best to spend a little time in problem structuring as it may save much anguish later.

Rosenhead (1989) provides a good coverage of the formal methods of problem structuring which have come to be associated with management science. Pidd (1996) also covers some of this material and provides a discussion of problem structuring in the general context of management science modelling. Problem structuring is perhaps best regarded as a period of preliminary data collection, where the data includes qualitative as well as quantitative aspects. An old adage of management information systems is that 'information is data plus interpretation'. In a sense, problem structuring is an attempt to collect and interpret preliminary data so as to learn enough about the problem at hand to know how best to proceed. In parallel, of course, the project side of the study needs to be considered and, at this stage, this involves negotiation with a view to establishing a project definition that can be agreed by all concerned.

3.3.1   Problem structuring as exploration

As mentioned above, there are many formal approaches that are advocated as helpful in problem structuring; the author's experience is that rather simple ideas are often of great value. Two in particular will be mentioned here. The first is that this is best regarded as a process of learning and exploration. Most modern theories of organisational learning (see Kolb, 1983; Argyris, 1983) are cyclic, as is the model of problem structuring shown in Figure 3.3. This represents a view that this exploration proceeds almost in fits and starts as the analyst becomes gradually

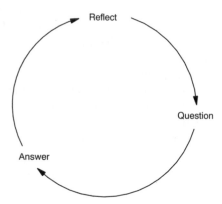

Figure 3.3   Problem structuring as exploration

more comfortable with what may, initially, be new to her. As she learns, so she is able to explore more. The actual learning does not cease, but the priorities of the project side of Figure 3.2 ensure that a halt is called at some stage.

The second, very practical, suggestion about problem structuring, is that six simple questions are often found valuable. These are captured in the well-known verse by Rudyard Kipling from the *Just So Stories* ('The Elephant's Child').

> I keep six honest working men
> (They taught me all I knew);
> Their names are What and Why and When
> And How and Where and Who.

Although all six questions are clearly interlinked, three (What? Why? and How?) relate to the system that may be modelled and three (When? Where? and Who?) provide much of the context. The idea is that the analyst should use these questions, not necessarily in a direct sense, but more as an *aide-memoire* to consider the issues that must be faced in problem structuring.

The result of some of this questioning is likely to be useful data that, when interpreted, provides useful insights. For example, in what eventually became a computer simulation study (Pidd, 1987) a rough and ready analysis of limited data revealed that each 1% increase in the efficiency of a manufacturing plant would contribute an extra £10 000 of profit. This served as a spur to agreeing a more detailed analysis to try and achieve this payoff. Limited preliminary data will also show the scale of the work likely to be needed and this will be useful in agreeing the scale of the projects that might emerge from the problem structuring.

At some stage during the problem structuring, someone must decide whether or not a computer simulation approach is likely to be fruitful. As has been explored in Chapter 1, there are many reasons why simulation approaches are often used. However, it is also true, as discussed in Chapter 1, that simulation projects can be very time-consuming and, if other ways forward are available, then they should certainly be considered.

3.4 MODELLING

Although much of this book addresses the detailed issues involved in developing a simulation model, it is worth touching on the main issues at this point. Figure 3.4 shows that modelling, in computer simulation studies, usually involves four tasks. As with problem structuring, modelling is a learning process that proceeds gradually and in a parsimonious manner. Chapter 4 recommends the use of the 'principle of parsimony' in developing simulation models, which is similar to the idea of stepwise refinement and is further discussed in Pidd (1996). The idea is that a model should be developed gradually, starting with simple aspects that are well understood and moving step-by-step towards a more complete representation. At each stage, the analyst is conducting a partial validation of the model (see later in this section and in Chapter 10) and, finding the model wanting, is adding extra features. As shown in Figure 3.4, there may even be limited experimentation with inadequate models on the way. Often, it is such experimentation that demonstrates that the model needs further development.

3.4.1 Conceptual model-building

Conceptual model-building is an activity in which the analyst tries to capture the essential features of the system that is being modelled. Which features are deemed necessary will depend on two factors. The first is the method by which the system is to be simulated. If discrete simulation (the focus of Part II of this book) is being used, then the aim will be to identify the main entities of the system, and to understand the activity cycle diagrams is a great help in this regard. These and similar tools allow the modeller to map out the main interactions and principal behaviour of the entities in a system that is to be modelled using discrete simulation. Thus, if attempting to simulate an out-patient clinic, the main entities might be doctors, nurses, receptionists, patients and equipment. An activity such as a minor surgical intervention might be governed by conditions such as the availability of a doctor, a nurse, a room and specified equipment.

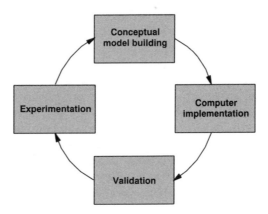

Figure 3.4 Simulation modelling

If system dynamics is being employed (the subject of Part III) then different elements will need to be identified in the system of interest. System dynamics requires the modeller to understand the system in terms of flows (such as patient arrivals) and levels (such as the number of staff needed or the number of patients sitting in the waiting area).

This attempt to capture the essentials of the system is often known as conceptual model building and the resulting model is sometimes known as a *conceptual model*. It may exist as a set of flow diagrams, as a textual description or as a mix of the two. Its specification may form the basis of a contract on the project management side of Figure 3.2. In small-scale studies, such a conceptual model may not exist in any objective form other than in the mind of the analyst, since modern software, especially the use of visual interactive modelling systems (VIMS), means that conceptualisation can occur whilst developing the model at a computer screen.

Alongside the type of simulation approach to be employed, the second factor that affects the aspects to be included in the model is what Zeigler (1976) terms the *experimental frame*. This is the set of conditions within which the simulation model is to be used. As Chapter 10 makes clear, no model can be regarded as valid in any general sense, as models are constructed for particular purposes and these purposes should be captured within a formally described experimental frame. If a model is used within a frame that differs from the original intention, then there can be no guarantee that it will be suitable for the new frame, even if it was ideal for the original one. Thus, a model developed for monthly capacity planning in a factory may be useless for detailed machine and job scheduling. The experimental frame will determine, at least partially, the level of detail at which the system is to be simulated.

3.4.2   Computer implementation

The next box in the circuit of Figure 3.4 is labelled *computer implementation*. If this book had been written before the mid-1980s, this box might have been labelled *computer programming* as that was, until then, the way in which most conceptual models were implemented on computers. However, as much of this book makes clear, many simulations in OR/MS are conducted using what will later be defined as visual interactive modelling systems (VIMS). These are computer packages such as Witness, ProModel and MicroSaint (for discrete simulation) and Stella/iThink for system dynamics. They enable the modeller to develop the computer model by selecting icons from an on-screen palette and linking them together to show the logical interactions that make up much of the model. Chapters 8 and 9 discuss the use of VIMS in discrete simulation and Chapter 14 discusses how Stella/iThink is used in system dynamics modelling and simulation.

These VIMS enable a computer-based model to be developed without recourse to 'proper' computer programming. Instead, the detailed logic and parameters of the system are developed using menus and pull-down forms of the types familiar to users of Windows-type operating systems. VIMS are not suitable for simulating all systems, however. Powerful though they are, they have their limitations and it is still necessary, sometimes, to implement conceptual models by developing computer programs as discussed in Chapter 9. The need to develop a 'proper' computer program arises for a number of reasons, such as the following:

- The simulation involves complex event logic or must include highly specific calculations, e.g. for scheduling purposes.
- The simulation is very large-scale and may need to be maintained for a long period of time. There are many such examples in the defence sector.
- The simulation needs to run very fast, for example in real-time.
- The organisation has no wish to invest in specialist software when it already has considerable expertise in computer programming.

3.4.3 Validation

The third box of Figure 3.4 is labelled *validation* and a detailed account of some of the issues is given in Chapter 10. Validation is the process by which the modeller and the client satisfy themselves that the model, as implemented on a computer, is suitable for use within its defined experimental frame. In the past it was usual to distinguish between validation and verification. Computer programs were verified by checking to see if they were a correct implementation of a model and the model was validated to see if it was appropriate for its experimental frame. However, the use of VIMS muddies the water a little, for in many such cases there is no real distinction between the model and the computer implementation. Hence, in many applications that use VIMS, it is best to think of validating the model and its computer implementation at the same time.

There are many approaches to this validation and extremely thorough accounts of the various techniques available are to be found in Balci (1987, 1994) and Sargent (1982). However, it is important to note that complete validation is never possible. This is because most simulation models are used to investigate things that are not understood. Hence, a model might be developed to simulate part of a hospital and it might be relatively easy to check that it is a valid representation of the way in which the hospital operates at the moment. In many cases, though, such a model will be used to estimate how the performance of the hospital might change under different conditions or under different management policies. A complete validation of the model under these new circumstances will be impossible. Does this mean that simulation approaches are, therefore, a complete waste of time? Not really. When used in this extrapolatory mode they are devices for thinking about how things might be and they need to be subject to the same rigorous analysis as would be any other proposals about possible futures.

3.4.4 Experimentation

The final box of Figure 3.4 is labelled *experimentation* and it refers to the use of the model. The whole reason for building a simulation model is to carry out some experiments on it, and now we consider how such experiments are to be undertaken. Nowadays, most simulations are run either on work-stations or on single-user computers. In both cases, the user has control over the running of the program (how much control will depend on the particular program and the operating system of the computer). Also, the program may display graphics and/or text output on-screen as it runs.

Whatever the form of experimentation, it is as well to be aware that the results of stochastic simulations are more difficult to interpret than those from deterministic models. This is because a stochastic simulation is, in effect, a complex sampling experiment in which samples from various distributions are combined as the model runs. Hence, the sampling processes themselves need to be well controlled so as to reduce the effect of sampling errors. At the very least, the use of pseudo-random numbers allows the experimenter to compare a set of policies, each using approximately the same random samples. Two different types of experimentation may be used—interactive or classical.

As argued earlier, the applications which are best suited to simulation are complicated, highly variable and dynamic. This dynamic behaviour may be represented on-screen as the simulation runs by careful use of icons, diagrams and graphs. The changing state of the entities can be represented by icons which may change position, colour, orientation or size. The icons can be displayed against a back-cloth of some stylised plan of the system being simulated and can be used to give a convincing representation of the system on screen. As an extension, state variables, such as waiting times, queue lengths and throughput, can be displayed in a graphical form and accessed through multiple windows.

Using such devices, the analyst can observe the dynamics of the simulation as it runs. Thus it is possible to see the build-up of queues, the movement of jobs, the delays suffered and the utilisation of the entities without waiting until a simulation run is complete. Of course, such observations can be misleading, because the on-screen behaviour will be a function of the samples taken if there are stochastic elements in the model. If the samples are unrepresentative, then so will be the observed behaviour. Despite this caveat, the ability to view the dynamics as the simulation runs is a real benefit, as it links with the possibility of interacting with the simulation and operating it in a 'gaming mode'.

To provide interaction, the simulation software must permit some way in which the analyst can halt the simulation in its tracks, vary some of the parameters and continue the run under these new conditions. This visual interactive simulation (VIS) (see Chapters 8 and 9) is now the norm in OR/MS and it makes it easier for the analyst to experiment, to see logical errors (where did that crane go just then?) and to convince the client that the simulation is valid.

Sometimes, the VIS approach is not powerful enough, possibly because the system is simply too stochastic or because there are too many entities and variables to display meaningfully on-screen. Thus, some classical form of controlled experiment is needed and which is carefully planned and executed. This is discussed in detail in Chapter 12.

The subject of experimental design is beyond the scope of this chapter, but the basics are simple enough. The experiment must be planned so that the various factors which may influence the results can be disentangled. In this way, the experimenter can determine statistically which factors give rise to which effects and may be able to draw appropriate conclusions about the effect on the system of the policies being simulated. To do this requires the experimenter to consider how long the experiment should be run in order to achieve statistically significant results. It also requires the investigator to be familiar with the appropriate statistical methods.

3.4.5   Implementation

As the old adage has it, 'the proof of the pudding is in the eating'. Within OR/MS, a simulation study is usually conducted because some benefit is sought from doing so. Hence, the issue of implementation cannot be ignored when discussing how simulation projects may be conducted. As with the other parts of the left-hand side of Figure 3.2, it is important to realise that implementation is not something that happens only at a single point in a simulation project—which is what the figure might be thought to suggest.

Broadly speaking, there are two types of implementation that may occur as a result of a simulation study, or indeed of any OR/MS study. The first, and most obvious, might be thought of as a *tangible product*. This occurs when, at some stage in the work (usually at the end) there are clear recommendations about whatever action should or should not be taken as a result of the study. These benefits are usually the official reason for conducting the study in the first place: 'We want to find the best way to organise passengers as they flow through from the plane to the baggage hall via the immigration desks'. The intended result of such a study will be a series of recommendations, based on simulation experiments that suggest how such flows may best be managed. This does not mean that the simulation team have necessarily come up with all the ideas themselves. In most circumstances, the model is used to check the implications of a range of policies suggested by different people. The intended tangible products of the simulation study are often documented in the contract that specifies the conduct of the study.

The second type of implementation might be called *improved knowledge and insight*. It happens when models and model building are used as tools for thinking (see Pidd, 1996). It commonly occurs at two points in simulation studies. The first occurs when problem structuring and asking questions of the 'who, what, where ...' type. It is often the case that the type of data needed to build a model of some system is very similar to the data that would be needed to operate it properly in real life. Thus, a common response when questioning during problem structuring is '... Oh ... that's a good question ... I'm not sure if we know that ... but maybe we should ...' Thus, the problem structuring and model building processes may serve to explicate important features of the system that is to be simulated and the information that emerges may be immediately used in the real world without waiting for the study to end.

The second point at which this often occurs is during experimentation. It is not unusual for these experiments to throw up unexpected results. Sometimes, sadly, these surprises are because the model is invalid, but this is not always so. Forrester (1961) wrote about the 'counter-intuitive behaviour of systems'. By this he meant that our mental models of how things behave may turn out to be wrong when compared with a thorough attempt to model something explicitly. Thus, the spin-off results produced on the way to proper experimentation may allow the participants in the study to develop improved insight. This can be a very valuable benefit, but the relationship of process and content suggested at the start of this chapter is absolutely crucial. The insight will not occur unless the process is properly managed.

3.5   THE PROJECT PART OF THE STUDY

Alongside the technical work in which the analyst must engage is the project by which the work is managed and this section will review some aspects that are particularly relevant to computer simulation studies. The main points are shown on the right-hand side of Figure 3.2 and these will serve as the basis for the discussion here. It should be noted that most large organisations have their own procedures for managing projects and hence the comments made here will need to be interpreted in the light of specific circumstances.

The parties involved will vary greatly and examples include the following, in order of complexity:

(1)   Projects in which an individual is doing the work for him/herself and the person is therefore analyst, project manager and client rolled into one.
(2)   Projects in which there is one or more analyst and a client who takes responsibility for the work.
(3)   Projects in which there is one or more analyst, a client who takes responsibility for the work and other people who serve as day-to-day contacts.
(4)   Large-scale projects that involve teams of people, long time-scales and decision makers who are far removed from the technical work of the study.

Types 1, 2 and 3 are common in business and type 4 is common in some public sector work, especially in defence.

As with the *problem* side of Figure 3.2, so too the *project* side is shown as a cycle. This is because many projects stem from previous efforts, sometimes in the same area, or sometimes because of a reputation made elsewhere. Although both process and content are important on the project side, it is perhaps the case that process may dominate content, whereas the reverse may be true on the problem side of things.

3.5.1   Initial negotiation and project definition

All projects seem to require some terms of reference that specify the expectations of the various parties involved in the study. The idea of the problem structuring on the problem side of Figure 3.2 is to decide, in technical terms, how to go about the study. The idea of these two phases on the project side is to ensure that there is agreement about this and other aspects right at the start of the study. The initial negotiation may, of course, happen before the simulation analyst is involved in the work and this may present a few problems—especially if the problem structuring suggests that simulation may not be appropriate in a particular case.

Hence, where possible, it makes sense to have initial negotiation and project definition occur in parallel to problem structuring. This may mean that the work is done under a two-part contract, the first of which is very short and covers these phases of work. The contract to go on to the rest of the study may thus depend on the outcomes of the problem structuring, the initial negotiations and the project definition.

The aim of these phases is to agree, between all concerned, a number of fundamental aspects of the work to be done. Obvious examples of these aspects are as follows:

(1) A specification of the experimental frame for the modelling work. The experimental frame, discussed above, specifies the conditions under which the model is to be used and the intended purpose of its construction. If this is ignored then it is hard to see how the study can be a success.

(2) An agreement about the time-scale for the work. This can be very problematic since many simulation studies are, by their nature, exploratory. Hence it may not be easy in some circumstances to say, in advance, how long the work will take. Perhaps the best way to cope with this is to agree a series of milestones for the project. These will be specific near the start of the project and the later ones may be re-negotiated as time proceeds. The milestones specify what work will be done and when it will be done. This can be very difficult to specify and it breaks what some cynics feel is a cardinal rule of economic forecasting—never give a number *and* a date, just one or the other!

(3) A specification of the resources needed for the study. As with the time-scale, this can also be tricky when the simulation study is intended to be exploratory. The same way of coping with the difficulty presents itself—use milestones and agree tight specifications for the early ones and negotiate the others as work proceeds. The resources required cover aspects such as costs, manpower, computer hardware and software.

It might be tempting to assume that it is always possible to write a proper requirements specification for a simulation model; however, this is rarely the case. This is another reason why this book argues that the principle of parsimony should drive the modelling process.

In essence, this stage of the project process aims to produce a contract between the various parties so as to support the work and allow its progress to be monitored as work proceeds. The more that these things are considered at the early stages of a project then the less likely it is that unforeseen problems will occur later. However, once again, it must be borne in mind that many simulation projects are not like computer systems development work and attempts to be too bureaucratic should be avoided.

3.5.2   Project management and control

It should be clear from the previous section that there are two key elements in managing and controlling a simulation study. The first is in managing the expectations of the various parties involved in the work. The aim of the initial contract definition is to specify what these are at the start of the work and this presents a useful beginning to the management of the project. However, there is a second aspect, the use of milestones, to cope with the dynamic progress of the technical and other work on the project.

The initial milestones can be specified in the initial contract documents, but it is crucial for all to realise that these milestones may have to be shifted as the project proceeds. There are many reasons for this, such as the following:

- As mentioned earlier, one result of a simulation (and of any OR/MS) study is that there may be spin-offs *en route*. The emergence of these spin-offs may be as valuable as the intended final results of the study and they must be attended to as the work proceeds. Meetings agreed for the milestones may be used to review progress and to consider how realistic the later milestones now seem to be.
- A second problem is that, except in routine applications (such as sometimes occur in manufacturing) the simulation work may involve some novelty and the project hence begins to resemble a research and development effort. Thus, some shifts in the milestones may be inevitable in all but the most straight-forward of work. However, some of these shifts should be positive, when progress is faster than expected.
- A third problem may be due to difficulties with the data that is needed to build the model. This data may not be available as and when it is needed and it may turn out to be faulty in one way or another. This may happen even when the data requirements were specified in the initial contract documents.

For these and other reasons, the use of meetings and reports related to milestones seem to be the key to managing the completion of simulation projects.

It should also be noted that inter-personal skills are vital in managing successful simulation projects. The ways in which the various parties perceive one another play an important part in the assessment of simulation projects and this cannot be ignored. Robinson (1997) discusses this in depth and suggests how some ideas of Total Quality Management, initially developed in the service sector, may be employed to enhance the chance of successful simulation projects.

3.5.3   Project completion

The final stage on the right-hand side of Figure 3.2 is the idea of project comple-tion, which is shown as leading on to either of two routes—closure, or more work. Like any human activity, simulation projects come to an end and it seems important that they do not just dribble out. Instead, an important role in their management is to ensure that the various parties agree that the project is now complete, or that it will lead on to more work.

In a sense, milestones serve a similar purpose. They enable the work so far to be reviewed, they enable those involved to comment on it and to make suggestions and they allow people to decide whether to continue or to cease the work. The difference is that the project completion phase should cover the work in the full glare of the experimental frame that has been agreed for the simulation model. The completion phase may decide that the modeller should play some part in the implementation of the study or that other people will take responsibility for this. If the project was one that resulted in a simulation model which other people will use then this presents one extreme. On the other hand, the final result may be a model that requires considerable technical expertise in its use and maintenance—this is common in the defence sector. Finally, the result may be a set of recommendations and insights that will lead to action by other people.

EXERCISES

1. Find a case study that describes a simulation application and try to understand how the process and content aspects of the project were managed.

2. Find a case study that describes a simulation application and try to decide whether some approach, other than simulation, might have been more appropriate.

3. Find a case study that describes a simulation application and try to understand how the experimentation was planned and controlled.

4. Find a case study that describes a simulation application and try to understand how the model was validated. See if you can uncover its experimental frame from the descriptions that are given.

REFERENCES

Argyris, C. (1983)   Productive and counter-productive reasoning processes. In S. Srivasta (ed.) *The Executive Mind.* Jossey-Bass, San Francisco, CA.

Balci, O. (1987)   Credibility assessment of simulation results: the state of the art. *Proceedings of the Conference on Methodology and Validation*, Orlando, FL, pp. 19–25.

Balci, O. (1985)   *Guidelines for Successful Simulation Studies.* Technical report TR-85-2, Department of Computer Science, Virginia Tech, Blacksburg, VA.

Balci, O. (1994)   Validation, verification and testing techniques throughout the life cycle of a simulation study. In O. Balci (ed.) *Annals of Operations Research*, Vol 23, *Simulation and Modeling.* J.C. Balzer, Basel.

Eden, C. L. (1989)   Using cognitive mapping for strategic options development and analysis (SODA). In J. Rosenhead (ed.) *Rational Analysis for a Problematic World.* Wiley, Chichester.

Forrester, J. W. (1961)   *Industrial Dynamics.* MIT Press, Cambridge, MA.

Kolb, D. A. (1983)   Problem management: learning from experience. In S. Srivasta (ed.) *The Executive Mind.* Jossey-Bass, San Francisco, CA.

Lubart, T. I. (1994)   Creativity. In R. Steinberg (ed.) *Thinking and Problem Solving*, 2nd edn, Academic Press, London.

Miser, H. J. & Quade, E. S. (1988)   *Handbook of Systems Analysis: Craft Issues and Procedural Choices.* Wiley, Chichester.

Pidd, M. (1996)   *Tools for Thinking: Modelling in Management Science.* Wiley, Chichester.

Pidd, M. (1991)   OR/MS method. In M. F. Shutler (ed.) *Operations Research in Management.* Prentice Hall, Hemel Hempstead.

Pidd, M. (1987)   Simulating continuous food plants. *J. Opl Res. Soc.*, **38**(8), 683–692.

Robinson, S. L. (1997)   Service Quality in the Management of Simulation Projects. Unpublished PhD thesis, Lancaster University.

Rosenhead, J. V. (ed.) (1989)   *Rational Analysis for a Problematic World.* Wiley, Chichester.

Sargent, R. G. (1982)   Verification and validation of simulation models. In F. E. Cellier (ed.) *Progress in Modelling and Simulation*. Academic Press, London.

Schön, D. A. (1982) *The Reflective Practitioner. How Professionals Think in Action*. Basic Books, New York.

Zeigler, B. P. (1976)   *Theory of Modelling and Simulation*. Wiley, New York.

Part II

Discrete Event Simulation

4

Discrete Event
Modelling

4.1   FUNDAMENTALS

As the name suggests, a discrete event simulation is one which employs a next-event technique (Section 2.2.2) to control the behaviour of the model. Many applications of discrete event simulation involve queuing systems of one kind or another. The queuing structure may be obvious, as in a queue of jobs waiting to be processed on a machine, or in a stack of aircraft waiting for landing space at an airport. In other cases, the queuing structure may be less obvious, as in the deployment of fire appliances in a large city. In this case, the customers are the fires needing attention and the servers are the fire-fighters together with their associated equipment.

As another example, consider again the car body paintshop described in Chapter 1. The bodies were to pass through a series of processes such as spray booths, ovens and rectification areas. They were to be moved from area to area on lifts, conveyors and other transfer machines until, satisfactorily painted, they reached the painted body store. In some cases (e.g. immediately after a vertical transfer in a lift) the bodies were not to be processed straightaway but were to enter a temporary storage area to wait with other bodies. Because of this part-finished stock, a lift breakdown would not immediately bring the succeeding process to a halt. That is, the stocks are used to de-couple two processes. This stock can be thought of as a queue and, in the simplest case, the queue would operate with a first-in, first-out (FIFO) discipline. The car bodies are waiting for the next process.

Quite a variety of systems can be regarded as having a queuing structure and as such they lend themselves well to discrete event simulation. The purpose of this chapter is to introduce some general terminology that may be used to build models suitable for discrete event simulation. A particular modelling device, the activity cycle diagram, is then introduced as a way of developing the structure of a model.

4.2   TERMINOLOGY

Some of the terminology employed in discrete event simulation is highly varied. Different writers occasionally use the same term to mean different things and this can lead to some confusion. The terminology defined here is fairly standard and is deliberately quite limited to try to minimise confusion. It is divided into two parts. The first set provides labels for the objects which constitute a system to be simulated. The second set defines the operations in which these objects engage over time.

4.2.1   Objects of the system

- *Entities.* These are the individual elements of the system that are being simulated and whose behaviour is being explicitly tracked. Examples might include machines in a factory, patients in a hospital or aircraft at an airport. Within the simulation, the computer program maintains information about each entity and therefore each one can be individually identified. As an entity changes state in the simulation, the computer program keeps track of these state changes. The overall system state is a result of the interaction of the individual entities.
- *Resources* These are also individual system elements but they are not *modelled* individually. Instead, they are treated as countable items whose individual behaviour is not tracked in the computer program. Examples might be the number of passengers waiting at a bus stop or the number of boxes of a product available in a warehouse. Thus a resource consists of identical items and the program keeps a count of how many are available, but their individual states are not tracked.

Whether a system element should be treated as an entity or as a resource is something that the modeller must decide. The decision will depend, mainly, on the purpose for which the simulation is intended. For example, if we need to know how long each passenger takes to complete a bus journey in which different passengers have different trips in mind, then we will treat passengers as entities. If, on the other hand, we are only interested in the number of people on each bus at any time, then we may be able to use a counter such as *NumberOnBus* for this purpose. Section 4.3 gives examples of simulations, some of which treat all elements as entities and some of which use a mixture of entities and resources.

When elements are represented as entities, some software requires further distinctions to be made. Sometimes, the modeller must distinguish between *permanent* and *temporary* entities. Permanent entities are ones that are created at the start of a simulation and which will exist throughout a run. Temporary ones are created and may be destroyed during a run. Temporary entities may often be better modelled as resources.

The other distinction that is sometimes required is between *active* and *passive* entities. This distinction is most common when simulating client–server systems in which entities co-operate in some task or other. One entity is regarded as active—it seizes the other; and the other is regarded as passive—it is seized. This distinction is, of course, wholly arbitrary. In another realm, when two people meet and fall in love, it doesn't really matter which one made the running in the first place!

4.2.2   The organisation of entities

Although entities are individually modelled within a discrete event simulation, it is convenient to think about them in groups, some of which are permanent and some of which are temporary.

- *Classes.* These are permanent groups of identical or similar entities. Bus passengers might be such a class, as might commercial aircraft. The classes can be sub-divided into more detailed sub-classes in some software.
- *Sets.* These are temporary groups of entities and are often used to represent entity states or queues. Thus, those bus passengers currently on bus number 37 could be regarded as being in a set *OnBus37*. Or those waiting in a queue at the depot could be a set *WaitingAtDepot*. Entities move from set to set during a simulation as they change state. Entities within a set may be held in a particular order, such as FIFO, LIFO (last in, first out) or according to some priority scheme, or they may be unsequenced.
- *Attributes.* These are items of information that belong to each entity and they are used for two purposes. First, they are used to distinguish between members of the same class of entity. Thus, the intended route of a bus passenger might be such an attribute, as might the length of time since he/she left home. The second use for attributes is to control the behaviour of an entity. In this sense, attributes may be used instead of sets to represent the state of an entity. Hence, for example, a machine in a factory might have an attribute such as *Condition*. If *Condition* is OK, then the machine may process a job, but not otherwise.

Clearly, there is some redundancy in the above terms. For example, the state of an entity might be represented as its current set membership or as the current value of one of its attributes. Nevertheless it can sometimes be useful to maintain both sets and attributes.

4.2.3   Operations of the entities

As the simulation proceeds, the entities co-operate and thence change state. Some terminology is thus needed to describe these operations and also to describe the flow of time in the simulation.

- *Event.* This is an instant of time at which a significant state change occurs in the system, such as when an entity enters or leaves a set, or some operation begins. Note that it is up to the analyst to define whether an event is significant or not in the context of the objectives of the simulation. In the paintshop, the start or completion of an operation such as rectification may be regarded as an event.
- *Activity.* Entities move from set to set because of the operations in which they engage. Thus the operations and procedures which are initiated at each event are known as activities and these activities are what transform the state of the entities. Thus the activity 'rectification' transforms a body from the state 'awaiting rectification' to the state 'waiting for spray'.

- *Process.* Sometimes it is useful to group together a sequence of events in the chronological order in which they will occur. Such a sequence is known as a process and is often used to represent all or part of the life of temporary entities. For example, a car body arrives, is degreased, hot-dipped, primed, etc.
- *Simulation clock.* This is the point reached by current simulated time in a simulation. Hence in a simulation where the time unit is minutes, the test 'is clock = 240?' might be used to test whether a lunch break is due. If so, appropriate activity could then be initiated in the simulation.

4.3   ACTIVITY CYCLE DIAGRAMS

In a discrete event simulation the various entities interact through simulated time and these interactions can be described in the terms introduced in Section 4.2. In order to build a model suitable for discrete event simulation, it is necessary to:

- Identify the important classes of entity;
- Consider the activities in which they engage;
- Link these activities together.

From this skeleton, the fine detail of the model can be built up.

While considering the topic of simulation modelling, it is as well to bear in mind the 'principle of parsimony'. This requires the analyst to begin model building with the well-understood and obvious elements of the system of interest. Once these are properly modelled and validated, then the more complicated and less well understood elements can be added later. In most modelling there is an overwhelming temptation to dive straight into the complicated features. This temptation is to be resisted.

Activity cycle diagrams are one way of modelling the interactions of the entities and are particularly useful for systems with a strong queuing structure. They were popularised by Hills (1971) and are normally associated with the activity and three-phase approaches described in Chapters 5 and 6. An example of this is HOCUS (Syzmankiewicz, 1984), which is a simulation software system built around the activity cycle diagram concept. However, Mathewson (1974) points out that they are just as useful for other modelling approaches such as event-based methods or process-based methods (see Chapter 6) and hence would seem to be of general value. In most cases they cannot include the full complexity of a system being simulated, but they do provide a skeleton which can be enhanced later.

Activity cycle diagrams make use of only two symbols and these are shown in Figure 4.1. The diagram itself is a map which shows the life history of each class of entity and displays graphically their interactions. Each class of entity is considered to have a life cycle which consists of a series of states. The entities move from state to state as their life proceeds.

An active state usually involves the co-operation of different classes of entity. The duration of an active state can always be determined in advance—usually by taking a sample from an appropriate probability distribution if the simulation model is stochastic. The sampling methods are described in Chapter 11. In a

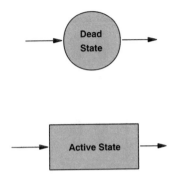

Figure 4.1   Symbols for activity cycle diagrams

queuing system, a service is one such active state because it involves the co-operation of a server and a customer. An appropriate distribution for the service time would provide a way of determining the duration of the active state.

On the other hand, a dead state involves no co-operation between different classes of entity and is generally a state in which the entity waits for something to happen. Dead states are often thought of as sets or queues and the length of time that an entity spends in a dead state cannot be determined in advance. It depends on the duration of the immediately preceding and succeeding active states. For example, in the simulation of the paintshop, the time spent by a car body in the dead state 'waiting for rectification work' depends on when its painting was finished and also on when resources are available to carry out the rectification.

Drawing an activity cycle diagram involves listing the states through which each class of entity passes, and normally these are drawn as alternate dead and active states. The complete diagram consists of a combination of all the individual cycles.

4.3.1   Example 1: a simple job shop

Consider a simple engineering job shop which consists of several identical machines. Each machine is able to process any job and there is a ready supply of jobs with no prospect of any shortages. Jobs are allocated to the first available machine. The time taken to complete a job is variable but is independent of the particular machine being used. The machine shop is staffed by operatives who have to perform two tasks:

(1)   Reset machines between jobs if the cutting edges are still OK;
(2)   Retool those machines whose cutting edges are too worn to be reset.

Thus there are two classes of entity (see Figure 4.2):

(1)   The operative;
(2)   The machines.

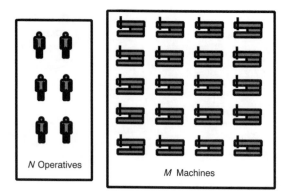

Figure 4.2 Entity classes in the simple job shop

The operative

He is responsible for the two tasks RETOOL and RESET as described above. In addition he may be unavailable while attending to personal needs. Obviously, a real job shop would be much more complicated—however, this example is aimed solely at introducing the concepts of activity cycle diagrams. With this information, the activity cycle for the operative is as shown in Figure 4.3. This shows three active states:

AWAY, RETOOL, RESET.

Obviously, RETOOL and RESET are carried out in co-operation with the machines (the other class of entity) and are therefore active states. Their duration could be obtained by sampling from appropriate probability distributions. The distributions themselves might be obtained by observing the actual times taken by the operative to carry out these tasks. AWAY is also an active state because such a probability distribution could be used to determine its duration and thus it meets one of the conditions for an active state.

When not in any of these active states, the operative is in the dead state WAITING and is available for work of some kind, or is able to attend to his personal

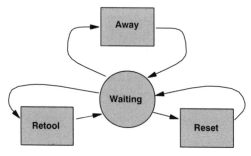

Figure 4.3 The operatives' activity cycle

needs. In practice he may be in this dead state for quite some time or he may merely pass instantaneously through this state between two active states.

Notice, therefore, that the diagram consists of alternate active and dead states. That is, the operative must pass through a dead state when moving between active states.

The machines

These have three active states:

RETOOL, RESET, RUNNING.

The latter active state represents the time when the machine is satisfactorily processing a job. Hence the activity cycle for the machines is as in Figure 4.4.

Following the convention for activity cycle diagrams, the active states have been separated by three dead states. After a machine stops RUNNING (that is, a job is complete) it moves into the dead state STOPPED. From STOPPED it may move to:

- RESET: if its cutting edges are serviceable; or to
- RETOOL: if the cutting edges are too worn.

During a simulation, an attribute may be used to decide whether a machine moves to RESET or RETOOL on each occasion.

After RETOOL, a machine is OK (another dead state) and is then RESET. Now the machine is READY (another dead state) following which it is RUNNING again. In real life, the dead states OK and READY may not exist, as the operative may move smoothly between the three active states. OK and READY are included here for two reasons. First, they maintain the convention of alternate active and dead states. Second, they would allow the model to be enhanced so as to consider, say, two operatives, one of whom is responsible for RETOOL and the other is responsible for RESET.

The two cycles may now be combined into the complete activity cycle diagram shown in Figure 4.5. Note that the dead states are unique to each class of entity. Only the operative can be WAITING and only the machines can be OK, STOPPED

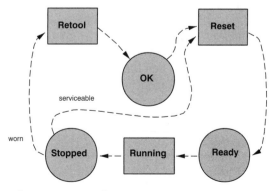

Figure 4.4 The machines' activity cycle

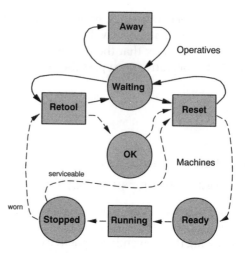

Figure 4.5   The job shop activity cycle diagram

or RUNNING. On the other hand, at least two of the active states involve co-operation between the two classes of entity.

Activity cycle diagrams provide a graphical way of describing the interactions which must be built into the skeleton of the simulation model; that is, they show the logic of the system. Thus, they allow precise specification of the conditions that must hold before state changes can occur. For example, before RETOOL can begin there must be at least one machine STOPPED and in need of a retool and the operative must be available (i.e. WAITING) to do the work. The next example will show in more detail how these diagrams may be used as the basis of a simulation model—this time, of an explicit queuing system.

4.3.2   Example 2: the harassed booking clerk

A theatre employs a booking clerk during the day. The clerk is employed to sell tickets and to answer any enquiries which may arise. Seat bookings are accepted only if the customer turns up in person at the theatre and pays for the tickets. Enquiries can come either from someone there in person or from someone phoning the theatre. The clerk is instructed to give priority to personal customers—after all, they may hand over some cash. Thus, if the phone rings just as a customer arrives in person, then the personal enquirer is served first. Thanks to a sophisticated phone system, incoming calls can queue on a FIFO basis until answered. Phone callers never ring off in frustration.

There are three classes of entity;

(1)   A single booking clerk;
(2)   Personal enquirers;
(3)   Phone callers.

We will consider each of these in turn.

The booking clerk

The booking clerk clearly has two active states:

- SERVICE: serving personal enquirers. Either selling tickets, answering questions or both.
- TALK: speaking to phone callers.

When not engaged in these active states, the booking clerk is in a dead state IDLE. Thus the activity cycle for the clerk is as shown in Figure 4.6. As before, the clerk goes through a sequence of alternate active and dead states. On occasions, the clerk will spend zero time in the dead state between two active states.

Personal enquirers

These are initially OUTSIDE the theatre. They then ARRIVE, QUEUE for service and the SERVICE begins. After the clerk has completed their service, they leave the theatre and are once again OUTSIDE.

First, consider the state SERVICE. This is a co-operative state which requires an enquirer and the clerk if it is to occur. There is therefore no doubt that this is an active state according to the earlier definitions. Second, consider the state QUEUE. As its name suggests, this is the state in which the enquirers wait until they are at the head of the queue and the booking clerk is able to serve them. Thus, as it is not a co-operative state and its duration clearly depends on the duration of the previous customer's service, it is a dead state.

This means that ARRIVAL is an active state, although why this should be so is probably not clear. To understand this, it may be helpful to imagine a machine which somehow transfers personal enquirers one at a time from OUTSIDE the theatre into the QUEUE. It returns for the next enquirer once it has safely placed an enquirer into the QUEUE. This arrival machine takes a finite time to execute this transfer and the enquirers are considered to be in the ARRIVAL state during that time. Hence, the duration of the ARRIVAL state becomes the interval between successive arrivals. In this way, the arrival process may be modelled as an active state provided that the inter-arrival time is determinable. Two obvious ways of doing this would be to use a timetable of arrivals or to take samples from some appropriate probability distribution.

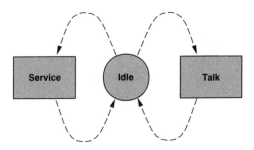

Figure 4.6   The booking clerk's activity cycle

If the inter-arrival times are taken as samples from some probability distribution, then the arrivals are usually controlled by a bootstrapping process. This works as follows:

> If enquirer N arrives at time T, then take a sample from the distribution of inter-arrival times and use the sample as the interval t between customers N and $N + 1$. Thus customer $N + 1$ arrives at time $T + t$.

Clearly, this process must be initiated by a prior determination of the arrival time of the first enquirer. However, once that is done, the method allows successive arrivals to be modelled as active states.

Finally, consider the dead state OUTSIDE. This represents the world outside the theatre from which the enquirers emerge and to which they return after SERVICE. It constitutes the environment of the system being modelled; in effect, the arrivals are quasi-exogeneous events. OUTSIDE is inserted for two reasons:

(1)   To give the personal enquirers the sequence of active and dead states required by the conventions of activity cycle diagrams;
(2)   Because it is normal for all cycles to be closed loops. This is obviously artificial in one sense as the number of potential enquirers is virtually infinite.

The left-hand side of Figure 4.7 shows the resulting activity cycle.

Phone callers

This cycle parallels that of the personal enquirers. This time the arriving 'customers' are phone calls to the theatre which are allowed to queue until the phone is answered. The interval between successive calls is modelled by the active state CALL and the active service state is TALK. The activity cycle is shown in left-hand side of Figure 4.7 and shows that dead states WAIT and ELSEWHERE separate the two active states. As before, ELSEWHERE represents the environment of the theatre from which phone calls emerge.

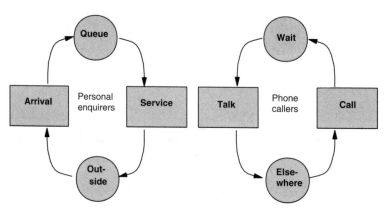

Figure 4.7   The personal enquirers' and phone callers' activity cycles

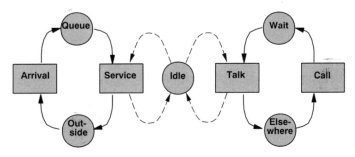

Figure 4.8 The theatre activity cycle diagram

The three cycles may now be combined to form the activity cycle diagram shown in Figure 4.8.

4.3.3   Example 3: the delivery depot

A delivery depot serves two functions. First, goods are received from the factory on large lorries and are held in stock. Second, they are delivered to customers by small vans which collect their loads from the stock held at the depot. At the moment, the depot has two unloading bays for the lorries and four loading bays for the vans. The same labour force is used for loading and unloading, either operation requiring a gang of two men. There are 10 men available at the moment. The owners of the depot wish to know how many loading bays are needed to meet current demand.

To complicate matters, the depot is on a rather awkward site as shown in Figure 4.9. Access to the site is gained from the main road and at the entrance there is a vehicle park in which lorries or vans may wait. To get to either loading or unloading bays, the vehicles must be driven along a narrow access road. Its narrowness means that two lorries cannot pass one another—even if they are travelling in opposite directions. However, there is room for two vans to pass—although not for a van to pass a lorry. At the moment, the site manager

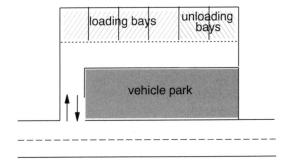

Figure 4.9 The delivery depot: site plan

operates with a rule which ensures that lorries leaving the site have priority over any other vehicles on this road. Second priority is to lorries moving towards the unloading bays.

This system could be modelled in a number of ways. It will be used here to illustrate the use of entities and resources, whereas the previous examples have just used entities. Assume that we wish to study the delays suffered by the vans and lorries to see if delivery performance can be improved. This suggests that vans and lorries should be treated as entities and that it may be possible to treat the rest as resources. Hence, the system might be modelled with the following:

| ENTITY CLASSES | Vans | An unlimited number, arriving and leaving during a simulation run |
| | Lorries | An unlimited number, arriving and leaving during a simulation run |

COUNTABLE RESOURCES	Unloading bays	Two available
	Loading bays	Four available at the moment, but we wish to vary this
	Labour	Five gangs available
	Road in	One available
	Road out	One available

Note that the access road which serves the site has been split into two resources, *roadin* and *roadout*. Lorries fill the entire road when they move and will thus require both *roadin* and *roadout*. Vans need only the *roadin* when they arrive and *roadout* when they leave.

Considering each entity and resource in turn:

- *Lorries.* Since these are to be treated as an entity class, they have their own activity cycle and this is shown in Figure 4.10. The lorries come from OUTSIDE, they ARRIVE and then join a QUEUE in which they wait to MOVE to an unloading bay until both *roadin* and *roadout* are free. Once it is at the unloading bay, *roadin* and *roadout* become free again. Having arrived at the unloading bay, a lorry must wait there until there is a free gang of labour available and, when this condition is met, it may UNLOAD. Once unloaded, the gang of labour is released and the lorry waits in the state EMPTY until both *roadin* and *roadout* are free and it may then LEAVE the site. Once it has left, *roadin* and *roadout* become free again.
- *Vans.* These have a very similar activity cycle to the lorries and this is shown in Figure 4.11. The main difference, apart from the names given to the states, is that ENTER needs only the *roadin* and EXIT needs only the *roadout*.
- *Unloading bays.* These are modelled as a resource, which might be represented as a variable called *unbay* that is initially set to a value of 2, to indicate that both are available at the start of the simulation. As an unloading bay is occupied, the variable *unbay* is decremented by 1 and then incremented by 1 when the lorry leaves the bay.

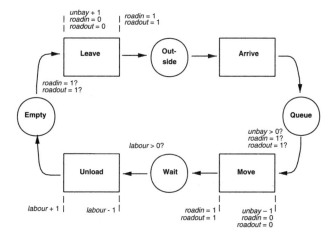

Figure 4.10 The lorries' activity cycle

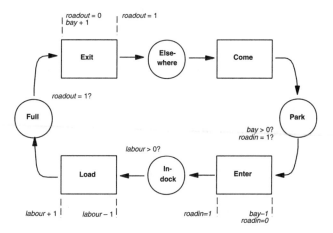

Figure 4.11 The vans' activity cycle

- *Loading bays.* These are rather like the unloading bays, except that they are used by vans. If there are four available at the start of the simulation, then we might represent them by a variable such as *bay* which is initially given the value of 4.
- *Labour.* If labour is also represented as a resource, we might employ a variable such as *labour*, which is given the value 5 initially and then reduced or increased in value as required by vans and lorries.
- *Road in.* These are also resources and might be represented by a variable such as *roadin* that takes a value of 0 or 1. Thus, when the road is free it might have the value 1 and might take the value 0 if it is occupied. Alternatively, *roadin* could be a Boolean variable.

- *Roadout.* These are also resources and might be represented by a variable such as *roadout* that takes a value of 0 or 1. Thus, when the road is free it might have the value 1 and might take the value 0 if it is occupied. Alternatively, *roadout* could be a Boolean variable.

4.3.4   Using the activity cycle diagram

As described so far, activity cycle diagrams are simply a way of showing the interactions between the various classes of entity involved in the system. It would be possible to consider these interactions by the use of lists, but most people find some sort of flow diagram helpful at the early stages of simulation modelling. In drawing these diagrams, the analyst is also forced to consider the events which occur as the system changes state. Initially it is useful to imagine that events occur at the beginning and end of activities. Thus, using the theatre booking clerk as an example, the following changes of state are evident:

SERVICE BEGINS	SERVICE ENDS
ARRIVAL BEGINS	ARRIVAL ENDS
TALK BEGINS	TALK ENDS
CALL BEGINS	CALL ENDS

For instance, when service begins the following changes occur:

- The booking clerk is no longer idle but engaged in service;
- The queue of waiting enquirers is reduced by 1.

Needless to say, the event will only take place if

- There is at least one enquirer in the queue; *and*
- The clerk is free (i.e. idle).

Though eight events are listed above, some of them will always coincide. Consider the active state ARRIVAL which has two associated events ARRIVAL BEGINS and ARRIVAL ENDS. Section 4.3.2 pointed out that arrival processes may easily be modelled by a bootstrapping process and this means that two events will always coincide. That is, the ARRIVAL ENDS event for enquirer N occurs at the same time as ARRIVAL BEGINS for enquirer $N + 1$. Hence, the two can be combined into a single ARRIVAL event. Identical logic allows CALL BEGINS and CALL ENDS to be combined into CALL. In this way, the list of events is reduced from eight to six.

In a discrete event simulation, the simulated time (simulation clock) is moved forward from event to event. At each event, state changes occur and these constitute the behaviour of the model. In the example of the harassed booking clerk, enquirers arrive at irregular intervals, the telephone rings, service begins and ends, phone conversations begin and end and so on. As this happens, queues of phone calls and enquirers build up and run down, the clerk is sometimes busy and sometimes idle, and money is taken for seat tickets. The problem that faces anyone trying to simulate such a system from scratch is to find some way of controlling the state changes.

A particular problem is that, on some occasions, several operations may be due at the same simulation clock time. That is, there are parallel operations to be simulated. An unfortunate characteristic of most digital computers is that they execute instructions serially and not in parallel. That is, parallel simulation events cannot be made to occur at the same real time. This problem is handled by making the simulation program perform a two-stage process as follows:

(1) The program moves the simulation to the time of the next state change(s). The simulation clock is then held at that time.

(2) Any operations now due at that time are performed in some sort of priority order. For example, the harassed booking clerk must serve personal enquirers in preference to answering the phone. Once all the possible operations are complete, the program returns to the first stage.

Thus, serial operations in the program are used to simulate parallel processes.

Various different ways of modelling the operations of the system exist and the four main methods are described in Chapters 5 and 6. All have in common the fact that the operations are broken down into a set of basic building blocks. The nature of the blocks varies between the four methods, but in all cases each block becomes a segment of computer program. The job of sorting out priorities and of sequencing the operations therefore becomes one of ensuring that the segments of program are executed in the right order. In this way, the question of 'who' does 'what' and 'when' is easily managed.

4.4   ACTIVITY CYCLE DIAGRAMS: A CAVEAT

Activity cycle diagrams are most useful for systems that can be easily regarded as having a queuing structure. In fact this includes a surprisingly large number of systems which need to be simulated. The dead states are used to represent the queues and entities are assumed to pass from queue to queue via active states. Some commercial software makes use of this structure and notation, for example, the HOCUS package (Syzmankiewicz, McDonald and Turner, 1988) and the CAPS program generator (Clementson, 1991). The commercial success of such software indicates the utility of the activity cycle concept.

Nevertheless, there are systems which do not easily fit the activity cycle notation—although enthusiasts would argue that they can be made to fit. One such type of system is where the interruption of an active state may occur before it reaches its scheduled termination. As a rather brutal instance of this, consider the simulation of a battle tank which is hit whilst the missile launcher is being targeted. The interrupted active state 'targeting' is shortened by a hit from some other entity—a missile in flight.

Another type of system not conveniently represented by activity cycle diagrams is one in which the important entities are not the temporary ones which pass around the system. Consider, for example, a T junction on a road system. Vehicles arrive and form queues, but the main resources are the various sections of the road junction over which the vehicles pass, and it is the state of these road sections which is important—as well as whether particular queues exist in the junction.

Attempts to draw activity cycle diagrams of such road junctions usually succeed, but at the cost of a hideously over-complicated view of the system.

Systems which do not easily fit the activity cycle concept are best modelled directly as a set of possible state changes, as shown in the next two chapters. Chapter 5 considers in outline how to do this for a T junction.

EXERCISES

1. Draw an activity cycle diagram for the following system.

    A barber's shop employs two barbers, each of which has his own barber's chair. Both barbers work between the hours of 9.00 am to 5.00 pm and both take a 60-minute lunch break at 12.00 noon. Customers arrive at random at the shop and are served by the first available barber. If neither is free then the customers sit in the waiting area in one of the five chairs provided and read the appropriate literature. There being no shortage of barbers, customers who arrive and find the waiting area full do not remain to wait for a seat. The length of time taken to cut a customer's hair varies randomly.

2. What revisions would you need to make to the activity cycle diagram produced for Exercise 1 if each customer has a preferred barber?

3. Draw an activity cycle diagram for the following system.

    Trucks laden with feed grain for export arrive at a dock. At the entrance to the dock, each load of grain is sampled and, if the quality is unacceptable, the truck leaves immediately still laden. Time taken to sample a load varies randomly, as does the size of a load. Accepted loads are driven to one of three conveyors which transfer the grain to a suitable silo, of which five are available. The silos have a finite capacity and if no space is available, the trucks must wait. Periodically, ships arrive at the docks and receive grain from the silos, no ship taking grain from more than a single silo.

4. Modify the diagram drawn for Exercise 3 so that no trucks are accepted into the port if all three conveyors are in use or if all the silos are full.

5. What events would you need to consider if you were to simulate the system described in Exercise 3?

6. Consider a T junction at which all normal turns are permitted. What system events would you need to consider if you were to simulate this system?

7. The Management Board of the Lancaster People's Hospital is concerned about its accident and emergency service, which operates 24 hours per day, 7 days per week. A recent audit showed that patients were waiting a long time (over 30 minutes) before seeing any member of staff and that some patients spent over 3 hours in the clinic. These times breach Government Guidelines. A recent study of the clinic suggested a new mode of operation. There would be three grades of staff; doctors, nurses and specially trained nurse-practitioners. Patients, who arrive at random, would be seen as quickly as possible by a specially trained nurse-practitioner who would classify the patient into one of three groups:

    ● Needs to see a doctor.
    ● Needs only to see a nurse.
    ● No treatment needed.

    Once classified, the patients would wait for a doctor or nurse, as appropriate, or would leave the clinic.

Patients who see a doctor will then need dressings to be applied to wounds and these will be applied by the first available nurse. Having seen a doctor, they rejoin the nurse queue for this purpose. After the application of a dressing, they leave the clinic. Patients who are sent by the specially trained nurse-practitioner to see a nurse wait for the first available nurse. The nurse may decide that the patient needs to see a doctor or needs no further treatment. Patients sent by a nurse to see a doctor must wait for the first free doctor and are then treated as if sent to the doctor by the specially trained nurse-practitioner.

The Board are thinking of employing two doctors, two nurses and a single specially trained nurse-practitioner on each shift. Meal breaks are covered by staff from elsewhere in the hospital but the Board would like to know if these would be sensible manning levels. They would like to meet the following service targets:

- Arriving patients should expect to wait less than 5 minutes to see a specially trained nurse-practitioner.
- Patients whom the specially trained nurse-practitioner decides needs treatment by a doctor or a nurse should expect to spend no more than 30 minutes in the clinic after arriving.

They also believe that, of the patients who arrive at the clinic:

- 30% will be sent by a specially trained nurse-practitioner to see a nurse, 40% to see a doctor, and the rest will need no treatment.
- 10% will be sent by a nurse to see a doctor.

There is plenty of space for patients to wait for a doctor or nurse and enough consultation rooms can be made available for up to 10 staff, whether specially trained nurse-practitioners, nurses or doctors.

Develop an activity cycle diagram that may be used as the basis of a discrete simulation model of this accident and emergency department.

REFERENCES

Clementson, A. T. (1991)   *The ECSL Plus System Manual.* Available from A. T. Clementson, The Chestnuts, Princes Road, Windermere, Cumbria, UK.

Hills, P. R. (1971)   *HOCUS.* P-E Group, Egham, Surrey, UK

Mathewson, S. C. (1974)   Simulation program generators. *Simulation,* **23**(6), 181–189.

Syzmankiewicz, J. (1984)   *A Description of the HOCUS Simulation System.* P-E Information Systems, Egham, Surrey, UK.

Syzmankiewicz, J., McDonald, J. & Turner, K. (1988)   *Solving Business Problems by Simulation.* McGraw-Hill, Maidenhead.

5

The Three-phase
Approach

5.1 INTRODUCTION

5.1.1 A range of possible approaches

Chapter 4 showed that many systems may be modelled by discrete event methods and that many important features of such models can be captured in an activity cycle diagram. There are commercial software packages that will take the description of such a diagram and automatically generate a computer-based model from it. However, it seems important to understand rather more of the detailed inner workings of discrete event simulation models. Otherwise, we are at the mercy of the software vendors. Also, it is much easier to appreciate some of the foibles of commercial software if we understand what is going on inside their black boxes.

There are many different ways in which a model description, such as that captured in any activity cycle diagram, may be organised in a computer program. This chapter will describe the three-phase approach that was first presented by Tocher (1963). Chapter 6 will describe three other approaches that have been used. However, it should be noted that there are many possible variations and hybrid approaches.

In the early days of discrete event simulation it was realised that two parts of a model could be separated. These were the *simulation executive* (sometimes known as the control program) and the *logic of the particular application* being simulated. The executive could be written once and then could be used with any application. Whenever a new application was to be simulated, it could be written in terms that could be controlled by this pre-written executive. Each of the four approaches to be discussed in this chapter and the next imply particular forms for the executive. Each executive requires that the logic of the application be captured in a way that suits its expectations.

5.1.2 Simulation executives

A simulation executive controls the activities and events in which the entities and resources engage. It does this by maintaining, at the very least, a simulation *clock*, and a *calendar*. The simulation clock denotes the time within the simulation, which will not be related to real-time unless this is a real-time simulation. As time within the simulation proceeds, so the clock variable increases in value. The calendar is rather like a diary into which future commitments are entered. As with a diary, once the simulation clock reaches a time for which the calendar contains an entry, then the simulation executive must do something. The executive is, thus, a form of automaton whose job is to maintain control of the entities and resources.

This control can be considered under two headings. First, the executive must see to the correct *scheduling* of activities and events. This means that it must ensure that they happen at the right time. Thus, for example, if a shop is due to open at 9.00 am, the executive must make sure that this happens. The executive must also ensure that any conditional activity happens at the right time. Conditional activity is not so much dependent on the passage of time as on the availability of resources. Thus, for example, the service of a customer cannot begin unless the customer is waiting to be served and there is a server ready to serve.

Secondly, the executive must make sure that activity occurs in the correct *sequence* within the simulation. Some of this sequencing is a mirror of the world that is being simulated. For example, engineering parts must be ground before they are polished. Other aspects of sequencing are slightly more subtle and are related to the nature of digital computers. Although most computers are capable of some parallel operations, they are at heart sequential machines. Hence, most computer programs consist of a sequence of steps. For example, in Pascal, we can write something like the following:

```
x := 0;
x := x + 1;
Write ℓn (x);
```

and we would expect the computer to put the variable x to 0, then to increment it and then to write its value on an output device. We would, therefore, be puzzled if the value of 0 were to be written out. In a discrete event simulation, we often must simulate systems which actually do have activities that occur simultaneously and in parallel.

For example, in the harassed booking clerk example introduced in Section 4.3.2, if there were more than a single clerk, then it is perfectly possible for one clerk to be serving a personal enquirer and another to be answering the phone. If one of these activities has a higher priority (say, talking to personal customers since they may spend money) then the executive might need to ensure that a phone conversation only begins if there are no personal enquirers waiting to be served. Thus, the executive must be able to cope with simulating parallelism on computer systems that are essentially sequential and must do so in the correct sequence. In many ways, this is similar to the need for a multi-tasking computer operating system to control several computer programs at the same time.

5.1.3   Application logic

The way in which the application logic is expressed depends on the way in which the simulation executive is implemented. This chapter discusses how application logic must be expressed for a three-phase executive. Chapter 6 considers the way in which it could be expressed to suit three other forms of executive: activity-based, event-based and process-based. Any application that is suited to discrete event simulation can be expressed in any of these four ways, although it will become clear later that some are more convenient than others. This book takes the view that a three-phase approach is, on balance, the preferred option.

5.2   Bs AND Cs

The three-phase approach rests on the realisation that there are two ways in which activity may start within a discrete simulation.

5.2.1   Bs

Some operations have a starting or finishing time that can be predicted in advance. These can therefore be scheduled as if they were appointments being entered into a diary. These are known as *Bs*. Originally they were known as B activities, which was an abbreviation for *Book-keeping* activities or *Bound* activities, the term '*bound*' indicating that they were bound to happen at some specified time, and the term '*book-keeping*' that they might used for keeping regular records (for example of queue lengths). Some people refer to B events instead, and to avoid confusion they are called *Bs* here.

Because these Bs can be directly scheduled, then the simulation executive can precisely control when they will occur by ensuring that they are executed when the simulation clock reaches the correct time. Hence, each B must have an entry in the event calendar which serves as a reminder to the executive to take some action. A suitable analogy for this would be a central heating controller in which the start time for the heating is set at, say, 6.30 am. When the clock of the controller reaches 6.30 am, it triggers the central heating system into life.

As a general rule, to which there are some exceptions, any state which is represented by an active state on an activity cycle diagram ends with a B. For example, consider the activity cycle diagram for the harassed booking clerk in Figure 3.9, reproduced here as Figure 5.1. The active state *Service*, once started, must come to an end. If we know the time at which it started then we can schedule when it will end. If the duration of this state is deterministic (e.g. it always takes 10 minutes) then the known duration can be used to make an entry in the event calendar. If the duration is stochastic, then a sample from a probability distribution (as in Section 2.3.2) can be used to find its duration and this may then be used to create an entry in the event calendar. Hence, we can consider *EndOfService* to be a B. Similarly, *EndOfTalk* will also be a B.

The usual effect of a B is to release resources and entities. Hence, when the *EndOfService* B is executed, the activity cycle diagram shows that the clerk who had been carrying out the Service is released back into an Idle state. The customer is released back into the Outside world. The *EndOfTalk* B operates similarly. Thus,

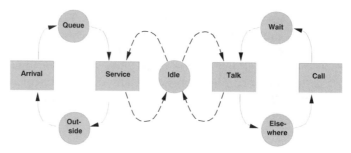

Figure 5.1   The harassed booking clerk activity cycle diagram

when either of these Bs is executed, it frees a clerk to engage in another task, should there be customers waiting.

5.2.2   Cs

Operations that are not Bs are regarded as *Cs*. This was originally an abbreviation for *Conditional* activity or *Co-operative* activity, the idea being that such activity is not dependent on the simulation clock but must wait until the conditions are right or until some other entity is ready to co-operate in the task. As with Bs, some people refer to C events instead, and so the term C will be used here.

The simulation executive has no direct say in when these Cs will occur, for this will depend on the states of the entities and resources in the simulation. Obviously the executive has some indirect control, since the main effect of the Bs (which it does control) is to release entities and resources. This means that, as a general rule, states which are depicted as active states on an activity cycle diagram begin with a C. Thus, in general, active states begin with a C and end with a B, as shown in Figure 5.2. There is one important exception to this rule and this will be discussed in Section 5.2.3.

As with Bs, this rule can be illustrated by the active states for *Service* and *Talk* in the harassed booking clerk activity cycle diagram in Figure 5.1. From the diagram it is clear that two conditions must be met before a personal service can begin. That is, there must a clerk in an Idle state and there must be a personal enquirer waiting

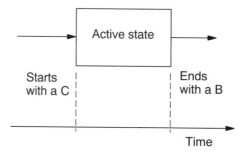

Figure 5.2   Bs and Cs in active states

for service in the Queue. Only if both of these conditions are met can the Service begin. This means that *BeginService* is both co-operative (it involves a personal enquirer and a clerk) and conditional (the clerk must be Idle and the enquirer must be in the Queue). Hence, *BeginService* is a C. The effect of this C is to engage resources and entities, unlike Bs, which release them. Thus, the clerk is no longer in an Idle state and the enquirer is taken from the Queue. The two remain together for some period, which, as discussed in Section 5.2.1, may be computed. At the end of this period, the active state *Serve* is over. Hence when a C is executed, it must ensure that the executive is informed that a B must be executed at some time in the future. Hence, one effect of the C *BeginService* is to tell the executive to schedule an *EndOfService* at some definite time in the future. By a similar argument, the active state *Talk* begins with a C which could be given the name *BeginTalk*.

The section of computer program that represents a C has a two-part structure. First there is a *test-head*, which indicates the conditions that must be satisfied if the actions that follow are to be executed. For example, the *BeginServe* C might look as in Table 5.1. If the tests fail, then the actions are not executed.

5.2.3   The exception to the general rule

The rule shown in Figure 5.2 does not hold in one special case. This is for those active states that generate new entities into the system. The most common of these are Arrival states, of which there are two, *Arrive* and *Call* in Figure 5.1. This can be a little confusing and it arises because such states are really inter-arrival states. That is, when an entity is in this state it is on its way to arriving in the system. Some people find it helpful, in this context, to imagine a machine of some type that produces these entities one at a time. Thus, it takes the machine a finite gestation period to produce the next entity. The entity sits in this state until its gestation is over and it can enter the system.

These arrival-type processes are often known as boot-strapping processes, since another way to imagine them is to consider arrivals fastened to one another by variable length boot-laces. As one entity arrives, it falls into the system and jerks the next one to its feet by pulling on its boot-laces and dragging it into life. Thus, new entities are boot-strapped into the system.

The effect of this is that these states need not be represented by a C at the start and by a B at the end. If they were to be so represented, then the effect would be as

Table 5.1   Test head and actions for the *BeginServe* C

Test-head	If (there is a clerk in Idle) and (a personal enquirer in the Queue) then
Actions	Take personal enquirer from Queue Take clerk from Idle Compute Service time Schedule B2: *EndOfService*

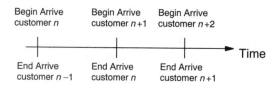

Figure 5.3   Bootstrapping arrivals

shown in Figure 5.3. This is a one-dimensional graph with time as the axis. It shows that for the arrival of customer n, the start of this state (its C) coincides with the end of the same state (a B) for customer $n-1$. Similarly, the end of arrival for customer n (its B) coincides with the start of arrival (the C) for customer $n+1$, and so on. Instead of using C–B pairs, these inter-arrival states may be represented by just a single B, since the actual arrival of one customer causes the next one to begin its journey into the system.

5.2.4   Bs and Cs in the harassed booking clerk problem

It may be helpful to summarise the ways in which Bs and Cs are used to represent a discrete event system by using the harassed booking clerk problem as an example. Its activity cycle diagram shows that it has four active states: *Arrive*, *Serve*, *Call* and *Talk*. These can be decomposed into 4 Bs and 2 Cs as follows:

- *B1: Arrive*—in which the next personal enquirer arrives at the booking office and joins the queue.
- *B2: EndOfService*—in which a personal Service is complete, releasing the personal enquirer back into the world Outside and putting the clerk back into an Idle state.
- *B3: Call*—in which the next phone call Arrives, causing the phone to ring or being added to the Calls waiting.
- *B4: EndOfTalk*—in which a phone conversation is complete, releasing the caller and putting the clerk back into an Idle state.
- *C1: BeginService*—which will begin if a clerk is Idle and there is a personal enquirer in the Queue. The effect of this C is to engage the server and the personal enquirer and to tell the executive to schedule the *EndOfService* (B2) after some known time.
- *C2: BeginTalk*—which will begin if a clerk is Idle and there is a phone Call waiting. The effect of this C is to engage the server and the phone caller and to tell the executive to schedule the *EndOfTalk* (B4) after some known time.

5.3   A SIMPLE ROAD JUNCTION

Although activity cycle diagrams are a useful step on the way to modelling a discrete event system as a set of Bs and Cs, they are not essential. Indeed, there are systems in which their use actually makes things more complicated rather than simpler. As indicated at the end of Chapter 4, one such case is a simple road junction, for example the T junction shown in Figure 5.4. This shows a road junction in a country (such as the UK, Japan or Australia) in which vehicles drive on the left-hand side of the road.

If this is an unsignalled junction in which U-turns are banned, then there are six possible routes through the junction and the usual priorities would be as follows:

(1)   Routes A to B, B to A and B to C.
(2)   Route C to A.
(3)   Route A to C.
(4)   Route C to B.

To keep things simple, assume that all drivers obey the traffic regulations. This means that queues may form at the junction from any of the three arrival points. If the vehicle is not controlled by traffic lights, then the vehicle at the head of each queue is waiting for particular sections of the road to become free. These are shown in Figure 5.4 as sections I, II, III and IV. They need not all be the same size, but are safe zones—that is, a car is safe to move out if no other vehicle is currently passing through those zones. The sections are resources and the vehicles are entities which compete for the scarce resources.

Vehicles can arrive from points A, B or C. Thus, if we are interested only in this single junction, these are entity generation processes which may be modelled as straightforward Bs. For example, the inter-arrival times may be governed by probability distributions and a vehicle, on arrival, joins a notional queue. The queue is notional because, in the case of priority 1 routes (A to B, B to A and B to C), the way through should never be blocked and therefore the vehicle should spend zero time in the queue.

Moving through the junction is also an active state, but this time is one that should be modelled by a C–B pair. Hence, each move should include a C, which starts the move if the required road sections are free. For example, moving safely from C to B may require all four sections I, II, III and IV to be free. The end of each move is thus a B, and its effect is to free the road sections that are occupied in the C that started the move.

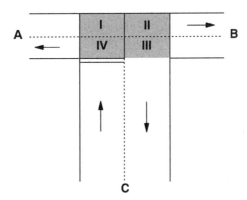

Figure 5.4   A simple road junction

Thus, the legal movement of the traffic through this junction could be modelled as the following nine Bs and 6 Cs:

B1:	Arrive from A	C1:	Start move A to B
B2:	Arrive from B	C2:	Start move B to A
B3:	Arrive from C	C3:	Start move B to C
B4:	End A to B	C4:	Start move C to A
B5:	End B to A	C5:	Start move A to C
B6:	End B to C	C6:	Start move C to B
B7:	End C to A		
B8:	End A to C		
B9:	End C to B		

There is no need to draw an activity cycle diagram to model this junction as Bs and Cs. Indeed, to do so would make the task harder.

It is important to notice that the priority of routes through the junction can be preserved by the sequence in which the Cs are attempted by the simulation executive. As will become clear in the next section, a three-phase executive attempts each of the Cs in turn. If, for example, route C to B is attempted last, then it cannot be executed if any other vehicle is using any of the road sections that it needs. It will therefore have the lowest priority. If route A to B were to have the highest priority, then it should be attempted first amongst the Cs.

5.4   THE THREE-PHASE APPROACH

Although it is not necessary to know the detailed inner workings of a simulation executive in order to write a working simulation program, some understanding may help to improve that program. This section takes a look at the inner workings of three-phase simulations, showing how the executive manages its scheduling and sequencing tasks. Figure 5.5 is a flowchart that shows how a three-phase executive operates. As might be expected, this executes a repeated cycle of three phases, known as A, B and C to make them memorable.

Section 4.2 explained that the objects of a system may be modelled as entities or as resources, the difference being that the behaviour of entities is individually tracked. In a three-phase simulation, this may be achieved by keeping at least three pieces of information about each entity as follows:

- *The time cell.*   This is the time when it is next due to change state, if this is known. It is only meaningful if the entity is committed to some B in the future.
- *The availability.*   This is a Boolean field that shows whether the entity is committed to some future B. If this is TRUE then the entity is uncommitted and its time cell is meaningless. If it is FALSE, then the time cell indicates when the entity will next change state.
- *The next activity.*   Like the time cell, this is only meaningful if the availability is FALSE, and it indicates the B in which the entity is due to engage at the time shown by the time cell. It is meaningless if the availability is TRUE.

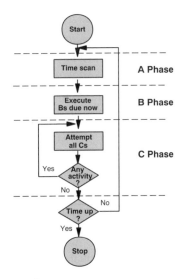

Figure 5.5   A three-phase executive

Thus, at the core of a three-phase simulation is a set of records, one to each entity. The executive manages the entities and their involvement in Bs and Cs by controlling the information held in these records. The records may have many more than three fields if necessary, and certainly the use of entity attributes would add extra fields to each record.

5.4.1   The A phase

The A phase is also known as the *time scan* and is analogous to someone checking his diary to see when his next appointment is due. In this time scan, the executive examines its event calendar to see when the next event is due and it moves the clock to that point. The clock is now held constant until the next A phase. Using the three-part entity record described above, the executive searches for any entity record with the minimum time cell and which has an availability field set to FALSE. This search can be accomplished in a variety of ways and a simple example will be shown in Section 5.5.

Because there may be several Bs due at this new clock time, the executive must also make a note of which of the non-available entities have this new clock time as their time cell. These form the *DueNow* list.

5.4.2   The B phase

Once the *DueNow* list has been formed, the executive must ensure that the correct Bs are executed. This is done by working systematically through the *DueNow* list and examining the record for each entity that is on that list. For each such entity, in turn, the executive does the following:

- Remove the entity from the *DueNow* list.
- Put its availability field to TRUE.
- Execute the B that is shown in the next activity field.

Note that executing the B may cause this same entity or another entity to be committed to this or some other B in the future.

5.4.3   The C phase

For the C phase, the executive maintains a light touch. It merely causes the Cs to be attempted one after the other. It does this by looking at each C in turn to see if the conditions in its test-head (see Section 5.2.2) can be satisfied. If they can, then the actions are executed. As was explained at the end of Section 5.3, the order in which these are attempted determines their priority. If there are two Cs that require the same entities or resources (e.g. in the harassed booking clerk problem, both Cs need an idle clerk) then the first to be tested gets the first pick. Thus, a later C will be pre-empted by one that is higher up the list.

In most cases, the effect of a C is to engage resources and entities, but there are exceptions to this rule and it is possible that a C later in the list may free resources and entities needed by a higher priority C. This could cause deadlock. To avoid this, the Cs are repeatedly scanned, whilst holding the clock constant, until all test-heads are failed. The executive then returns to the A phase.

5.5   THE HARASSED BOOKING CLERK—A MANUAL THREE-PHASE SIMULATION

As introduced earlier, the harassed booking clerk problem has four Bs and 2 Cs that are described in Section 5.2.4. They are as follows:

- B1: Arrive
- B2: EndOfService
- B3: Call
- B4: EndOfTalk

- C1: BeginService
- C2: BeginTalk

There are three classes of object in the simulation (personal enquirers, phone callers and the clerk) and, although the obvious structure is to use entities to model each, this will not be done here. Instead, the personal enquirers and phone callers will be modelled as resources and another concept, the *arrival machine*, will be used to generate new arrivals into the system. As there are two such resources, two arrival machines are needed, and each such machine will become an entity in the simulation. There are, therefore, three entities in the simulation:

(1)   Personal enquirer arrival machine.

(2)   Phone call arrival machine.

(3)   Clerk.

Clearly, if we wished to simulate a system in which there were more than a single clerk, then each would need to be represented by an entity. The records of each entity can be maintained as in Table 5.2 below which are some important status variables. This shows that the initial conditions for the simulation are as follows:

- The single clerk is idle (therefore its availability is TRUE).
- The first personal enquirer is due to arrive at time 4 and the first phone call is due at time 6 (suppose that these were set as the result of samples from suitable probability distributions).
- The time is zero and thus the simulation clock is zero.
- No personal enquirers or phone calls have arrived.
- All queues (*Queue* and *Wait*) are empty.

5.5.1   The first A phase

During the A phase, the executive must find when the next event is due, must move the simulation clock to that time and must place all entities due to engage in a B at that time into the *DueNow* list. After the first A phase, therefore, the situation is as in Table 5.3. This shows that the next event is due at time 4. Thus the *Clock* value is now 4. The only entity due to engage in a B at this stage is entity 1, the personal enquirer arrival machine. Thus the *DueNow* contains only entity 1.

Table 5.2   Initial conditions

Entity	Time cell	Availability	Next Activity
(1) Personal enquirer arrival machine	4	FALSE	Personal arrival
(2) Phone call arrival machine	6	FALSE	Phone call
(3) Clerk	0	TRUE	

Status variables: *Clock* = 0; *Queue* = 0; *Wait* = 0; *PersIn* = 0; *PhoneIn* = 0.
DueNow is empty.

Table 5.3   Time 4: end of A phase

Entity	Time cell	Availability	Next Activity
(1) Personal enquirer arrival machine	4	FALSE	Personal arrival
(2) Phone call arrival machine	6	FALSE	Phone call
(3) Clerk	0	TRUE	

Status variables: *Clock* = 4; *Queue* = 0; *Wait* = 0; *PersIn* = 0, *PhoneIn* = 0.
DueNow 1.

5.5.2 The first B phase

During the B phase the executive must execute the Next Activity of those entities that are on the *DueNow* list. In this case, there is just one such entity, the personal enquirer arrival machine. This is due to engage in the B that represents a personal arrival. In this case it brings the first personal enquirer into the system and schedules the next such arrival to occur after 5 minutes, that is, at time 9. The first personal enquirer is placed in the *Queue* and *PersIn*, the counter for personal arrivals, is incremented as shown in Table 5.4. Note that the method maintains a very strict separation between Cs and Bs. Even though we (and therefore the executive) know that the clerk is idle, the service does not start in the B phase, instead, the first arrival is placed in the queue.

5.5.3 The first C phase

During the C phase, the executive must attempt each C in turn by checking if the conditions in the test-heads are satisfied. In this simulation, there are two Cs, both of which have two conditions. *BeginService* requires the clerk to be idle and a personal enquirer to be in the queue. *BeginTalk* requires the clerk to be idle and a phone call to be waiting. If the agreed priority is that *BeginService* is to be preferred to *BeginTalk*, then it must be attempted first. Since the clerk is idle and there is a single personal enquirer in the queue, the test-head of *BeginService* is satisfied and the actions can be executed. The result of that is shown in Table 5.5. This shows

Table 5.4 Time 4: end of B phase

Entity	Time cell	Availability	Next Activity
(1) Personal enquirer arrival machine	9	FALSE	Personal arrival
(2) Phone call arrival machine	6	FALSE	Phone call
(3) Clerk	0	TRUE	

Status variables: *Clock* = 4; *Queue* = 1; *Wait* = 0; *PersIn* = 1, *PhoneIn* = 0.
DueNow is empty.

Table 5.5 Time 4: end of C phase

Entity	Time cell	Availability	Next Activity
(1) Personal enquirer arrival machine	9	FALSE	Personal arrival
(2) Phone call arrival machine	6	FALSE	Phone call
(3) Clerk	9	FALSE	*EndService*

Status variables: *Clock* = 4; *Queue* = 0; *Wait* = 0; *PersIn* = 1, *PhoneIn* = 0.
DueNow is empty.

that some sampling process led to a duration for the personal service of 5 minutes, therefore it is due to end at time 9. Thus, the availability field of the clerk is now FALSE, the time cell is now 9 and the next activity is *EndService*. As the personal enquirer has been taken from the queue, the variable *Queue* is now reduced to zero. The second C, *BeginTalk*, cannot succeed since the clerk is no longer idle. Repeating the C scan leads to no further activity.

5.5.4   A second A phase

The second A phase results in the situation shown in Table 5.6. It shows that the next event is found to be due at time 6, and that it will involve entity 2, the phone call arrival machine. Hence, the *DueNow* list contains the number 2 and clock is moved to 6.

5.5.5   The next B and C phases

The next B phase involves the phone call arrival machine whose next activity is to schedule the arrival of the second phone call. Suppose that the sample taken for this interval is 3 minutes, meaning that the second phone call is due at time 9. Hence, after the B phase, the situation is as shown in Table 5.7. Notice that the phone call that arrives at time 6 is placed into the queue *Wait* and the counter for the number of arrivals so far, *PhoneIn*, is incremented.

Table 5.6   Time 6: end of A phase

Entity	Time cell	Availability	Next Activity
(1) Personal enquirer arrival machine	9	FALSE	Personal arrival
(2) Phone call arrival machine	6	FALSE	Phone call
(3) Clerk	9	FALSE	*EndService*

Status variables: *Clock* = 6; *Queue* = 0; *Wait* = 0; *PersIn* = 1, *PhoneIn* = 0.
DueNow 2.

Table 5.7   Time 6: end of B phase

Entity	Time cell	Availability	Next Activity
(1) Personal enquirer arrival machine	9	FALSE	Personal arrival
(2) Phone call arrival machine	9	FALSE	Phone call
(3) Clerk	9	FALSE	*EndService*

Status variables: *Clock* = 6; *Queue* = 0; *Wait* = 1; *PersIn* = 1, *PhoneIn* = 1.
DueNow is empty.

The C phase at time 6 results in no change to the table, since both *BeginService* and *BeginTalk* fail because the clerk is not idle at this time.

5.5.6   The third A phase

The third A phase finds that the next event is due at time 9 and that there are 3 entities due to engage in Bs at that time. Thus, it moves the clock to 9 and adds entities 1, 2 and 3 to the *DueNow* list. This results in the situation shown in Table 5.8.

5.5.7   The third B phase

The third B phase involves all three entities. Suppose that this results in the next personal enquirer being due at time 12 and the next phone call at time 15. The result of the *EndService* B is to release the clerk, whose availability field is now TRUE. Hence the situation is as shown in Table 5.9. Note that there are now two phone calls and one personal enquirer waiting. Changing that situation must wait until the C phase.

   The simulation may be continued in this manner until it has run long enough for the experiments for which it is being used. Chapter 7 shows how the approach can be implemented in any general-purpose computer programming language.

Table 5.8   Time 6: end of C phase

Entity	Time cell	Availability	Next Activity
(1) Personal enquirer arrival machine	9	FALSE	Personal arrival
(2) Phone call arrival machine	9	FALSE	Phone call
(3) Clerk	9	FALSE	*EndService*

Status variables: *Clock* = 9; *Queue* = 0; *Wait* = 1; *PersIn* = 1, *PhoneIn* = 1.
DueNow = 1, 2, 3.

Table 5.9   Time 9: end of B phase

Entity	Time cell	Availability	Next Activity
(1) Personal enquirer arrival machine	12	FALSE	Personal arrival
(2) Phone call arrival machine	15	FALSE	Phone call
(3) Clerk	9	TRUE	*EndService*

Status variables: *Clock* = 9; *Queue* = 1; *Wait* = 2; *PersIn* = 2, *PhoneIn* = 2.
DueNow is empty.

EXERCISES

1. Write down the logic of the Bs and Cs that would be necessary for a three-phase simulation model of the T junction as described in Section 5.3.

2. Write down the logic of the Bs and Cs that would be necessary for a three-phase simulation model of the delivery depot described in Section 3.3.

3. Write down the logic of the Bs and Cs which would be needed for a three-phase simulation model of the following system.

   Trucks arrive randomly at a weigh-bridge in a port, having travelled by ferry from another country laden with various goods. The weigh-bridge is used to check whether the vehicles are overloaded before they are allowed to travel on the roads. Trucks queue for the weigh-bridge after leaving the ferry. If they are found to be overloaded then they are moved to another area in the port where the surplus load is removed and the drivers are interviewed by the police. They may then leave the port where they rejoin those trucks whose loads were within the regulations.

4. Write down the logic of the Bs and Cs which would be needed for a three-phase simulation model of the following system.

   The Morecambe Bay Hovercraft Company (MBHC) is anxious to make its new service more efficient before the Cross-Bay Tunnel opens. They wish you to study the operation of their Hest Bank Shore terminal. Hovercraft land at the Shore terminal after their flight from Humphrey Head at intervals which are more or less according to a timetable, the variation in landing times being due to obvious factors such as weather and problems at the Humphrey Head terminal. If the slip-way is free then the craft floats onto it and lands. Any vehicles and passengers then disembark and, in the meantime, the passenger cabin is cleaned.

   When all vehicles and passengers have disembarked, and when the cabin is clean, the vehicles and passengers who wish to travel to Humphrey Head are loaded. High vehicles are loaded first, followed by all other vehicles of less than 1.6 metres in height. Foot passengers board the craft whilst the vehicles are being loaded. When all vehicles and passengers are loaded, the doors are closed and the flight to Humphrey Head can begin.

   At the moment, MBHC operates only a single slipway at Hest Bank and is wondering whether to double its capacity by adding an extra slipway. The extra capacity would be used to add extra flights on this route. They might be able to add extra flights without doubling the capacity—but there is a risk that customers might sometimes face long delays and also that an incoming flight may not be able to land. There is plenty of spare capacity at Humphrey Head.

5. Write down the Bs and Cs that would be needed to simulate the accident and emergency department described in exercise 7 of Chapter 4.

REFERENCE

Tocher, K. D. (1963)   *The Art of Simulation*. English Universities Press, London.

Event, Activity and Process-based Approaches to Discrete Simulation

6.1 GENERAL IDEAS

Chapter 4 showed how many systems can be modelled as discrete event simulations using tools such as activity cycle diagrams. Chapter 5 took these descriptions and showed how they can be broken down into the basic building blocks of three-phase simulations, Bs and Cs. This chapter extends the treatment of simulation modelling to cover three other approaches that are used. Although each of them will be presented in a relatively pure form here, it must be noted that there are ways in which the approaches can be combined with one another.

Experienced simulation modellers will already have their own preference for one of these approaches and it is not the aim of this chapter to show one to be superior to the others. Given that three-phase simulation dominates several chapters in this book, it should be no surprise to realise that this is the author's preference.

Another point that should be re-iterated, is that any system that can be modelled by one approach can also be expressed in one of the others. Sometimes, however, one approach somehow seems more convenient to cope with one type of system and when this is the case, this chapter will point this out. Each of the approaches assumes a particular world-view that prescribes how a model should be developed and expressed. Although a novice might wish to proceed otherwise, there is much anecdotal evidence to support the view that world-views are helpful rather than a hindrance. Therefore, novices should avoid the temptation to sit immediately with a computer and hammer away at the keys in a common-sense manner. The result is likely to be a model which is difficult to program and a program that is a headache to debug.

As Figure 6.1 shows, a three-part structure tends to be found in many discrete simulation programs. The three parts are: the *simulation executive*, which controls the running of the entire simulation; the *model logic*, which is the expression of the activities in which the entities of the system engage; and *a set of general tools*, which offer support for tasks such as debugging, input:output and random sampling. Each of the three approaches to be discussed in this chapter implies its own unique form of simulation executive and each requires the model logic to be expressed in a different way. It is the task of the system provider to write the

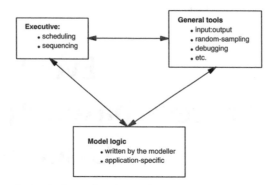

Figure 6.1   Three-part structure of discrete simulation programs

executive and to prescribe how the model logic should be expressed. It is the job of the analyst or modeller to use the rules about logical expression to formulate a model of the system that is to be simulated.

To ease the task of description, the three approaches will be described by comparing them to the three-phase approach that was introduced in Chapter 5.

6.2   THE EVENT-BASED APPROACH

This approach was probably the most commonly used during the 20 years from 1960, partly because it was embedded within one of the most widely used simulation programming languages, SIMSCRIPT, which originated in the work of Markowitz *et al.* (1963) at the RAND Corporation and has since been developed by CACI into SIMSCRIPT II.5 (Russell, 1987). Later versions of SIMSCRIPT encourage modellers to use the process-based approach, described later in this chapter, rather than an event-based approach. For this and other reasons, event-based approaches have fallen from favour since 1980.

Whereas the basic building blocks of a three-phase model are Bs and Cs, in an event-based model the atomic parts are known as *event routines*. An event routine is a set of statements, in some programming language, which capture the entire set of logical consequences that can flow from an event. An event, as in three-phase approaches, is a state change that occurs at an instant of time.

6.2.1   Events in the harassed booking clerk problem

To illustrate what this means, consider the harassed booking clerk problem that was introduced in Section 4.3.2. This had a clerk with two tasks, serving personal enquirers and answering the phone when it rang, with both personal enquirers and phone calls allowed to queue for service. The activity cycle diagram for this system, shown in Figure 3.9, has four active states: *Arrival* (of personal enquirers), *Call* (arrival of a new phone call), *Service* (of a personal enquirer by the clerk) and *Talk* (a phone conversation by the clerk). In event-based terms, this system may be reduced to four events as follows:

(1)   *Arrival*: the arrival of a personal enquirer.
(2)   *Call*: the arrival of a new phone call.
(3)   *EndOfService*: the end of a service.
(4)   *EndOfTalk*: the end of a phone call.

This contrasts with the need for four Bs and two Cs in the three-phase approach: why should this be?

   The reduction is possible because each of the event routines can include both a B and one or more Cs within its statements. This is because the event routine needs to capture *all* possible consequences of the state change. As an example, consider what happens at the end of a personal service. In the three-phase approach, this was modelled by a B in which the clerk was returned to an idle state and the personal enquirer was released into the world outside. The start of the next personal service was handled, in a three-phase approach, by a C, *BeginServe*, which allowed a service to start if the conditions in its test head were satisfied. These were that the clerk is idle and that there is a personal enquirer waiting in the queue. The B and the C were entirely separate and their linkage was managed dynamically by the executive.

   In an event-based approach, the B and C should be combined into a single *EndOfService* event routine. In this, the clerk must check to see if there are any other personal enquirers waiting in the queue, if so, then the next personal enquirer ($n + 1$) is taken from the queue and the next service begins. If the queue is empty, the clerk must then check to see if any phone calls are waiting. If they are, then a phone call must be taken from the phone queue and a phone conversation is started. If there are no personal enquirers waiting and no phone calls waiting, then the clerk can be released into idle. Thus, the *EndOfService* event routine must include the three-phase B *Arrival* and must also include the two three-phase Cs, *BeginServe* and *BeginTalk*.

   Hence, using a form of pseudo-code, the *EndOfService* event routine could be expressed as follows:

Release PersonalEnquirer *n* into the world
If (Queue > 0) then
      Take Personal Enquirer *n* + 1 from the queue
      Compute the *ServiceTime*
      Schedule the *EndOfService n* + 1 to occur after *ServiceTime*
Else if (PhoneQueue > 0) then
      Take next Phone Call from the phone queue
      Compute the *TalkTime*
      Schedule the *EndOfTalk* for this call to occur after *TalkTime*
Else Release Clerk to Idle.

   A similar logic must be applied to the event routine for the *Arrival* of a personal enquirer. In the three-phase simulation, this B simply placed personal enquirer *n* into the queue, computed the time to the arrival of personal enquirer *n* + 1 and then scheduled this next arrival. As with the *EndOfService* event routine, the *Arrival* event routine is rather more complex because the event routine is responsible for sorting out all the possible consequences of the arrival. In the three-phase approach, the executive sorts out the consequences dynamically as the simulation runs. Hence, the *Arrival* event routine could be written as pseudo-code, as follows:

Compute time to arrival of personal enquirer $n + 1$
Schedule *Arrival* of personal enquirer $n + 1$
If (Queue = 0) and (the clerk is idle) then
    Take clerk from idle
    Engage Personal Enquirer n
    Compute the *ServiceTime*
    Schedule the *EndOfService n* to occur after *ServiceTime*
Else add personal enquirer n to the queue.

As in the case of the *EndOfService* event routine, this is more complicated than the corresponding B that would be used in the three-phase approach.

6.2.2   Event-based executives

In an event-based approach, the simulation executive can be rather simpler than the one needed for a three-phase simulation. This is because the executive is only concerned with scheduling the event routines and has no sequencing tasks to perform. The sequencing is managed explicitly by each event routine. Hence, in the case of the *EndOfService* event routine described in the previous section, the priority of personal service over phone conversations is handled explicitly within the logic of the event routine. This means, inevitably, that should we wish to change this logic—to see, for example, what the effect would be of different priorities—then we must dig into the program code of the event routine to do so. In a three-phase simulation, we need only swap the order in which the executive attempts the Cs in the C phase.

An event-based executive has just two phases, in contrast to the three needed by a three-phase approach. The bare bones of such an executive is shown in Figure 6.2. It assumes that the executive maintains an event calendar into which references to event routines (known as event notices) are entered when a future event is scheduled. Thus, the executive knows which events are due to occur next. The processing of an event-based simulation is managed as follows:

(1)   Examine the event calendar to find when the next event is due and move the simulation clock to this time. Move all event notices that are scheduled for this new clock time onto a current events list.
(2)   Holding the clock constant, perform each of the event routines whose notices are in the current events list.

This cycle is repeated until the simulation is over.

The event-based simulation of the harassed booking clerk should run rather faster than the three-phase version. This is because there is no need to attempt a full scan of all the Cs at every event time. Instead, all of the logical consequences are held in the appropriate event routine. The snag, of course, is that for

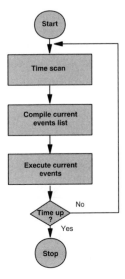

Figure 6.2 An event-based executive

complicated systems it can be very difficult to ensure that all possible consequences are accounted for within the event routine. This problem is particularly acute when a model is enhanced in some way. Thus, the event-based approach is not really in accord with the 'principle of parsimony' advocated throughout this book. This principle suggests that simulation models, and their computer programs, should be developed and enhanced gradually. An approach that makes this difficult can hardly be recommended.

6.3   THE ACTIVITY-BASED APPROACH

This approach, like the strict event-based approach, is not much used nowadays and was the original basis of the three-phase approach described in Chapter 5. It is often misunderstood, especially in the USA, where many people imagine that a strict activity-based approach is the same as a three-phase one. As will be clear by the end of this section, this confusion is understandable, but is to be avoided. The approach was developed in the UK and appeared in the early simulation programming language, CSL (Buxton & Laski, 1962) that was developed by Esso in co-operation with IBM. Its main beauty is its simplicity, but this is bought at a price—the simulation programs written this way tend to be rather slow in execution.

6.3.1   Activities

As in the case of the event-based approach, the harassed booking clerk problem of Section 4.3.2 will be used to explain how this approach operates. The basic building block of the approach is an *activity* which has exactly the same structure as a C in a three-phase approach. That is, a C has a test-head followed by a set of actions. In the harassed booking clerk simulation, there would be six such activities, as follows:

- *Arrive*
- *EndOfService*
- *Call*
- *EndOfTalk*
- *BeginService*
- *BeginTalk*

That is, the Bs and the Cs all become activities. In the case of the three-phase Cs, the activities are unchanged as activities in the activity-based approach. Thus, as in Section 5.2.2, the *BeginServe* activity is as shown in Table 6.1.

However, what would be Bs in a three-phase approach need to acquire test-heads in a strict activity-based approach. The only conditions that govern the start of these activities are whether the simulation clock has reached the time for which these activities are scheduled. Hence, the three-phase Bs acquire test-heads that check whether the simulation clock has advanced far enough to cause these former Bs to be executed. As an example, the *Arrive* activity would look as shown in Table 6.2. The other activities that would be represented as Bs in a three-phase simulation would have a similar structure. Hence, the activities are very simple, but do not take advantage of the fact that the executive can know when some activities are due to happen. Instead, the executive is, as in the event-based approach, a rather crude two-phase control program.

Table 6.1 The *BeginServe* activity

Test-head	If (there is a clerk in Idle) and (a personal enquirer in the Queue) then
Actions	Take personal enquirer from Queue Take clerk from Idle Compute service time Schedule *EndOfService*

Table 6.2 The *Arrive* activity

Test-head	If the Clock has reached the time at which the arrival of personal enquirer n is scheduled then
Actions	Add personal enquirer n to the Queue Computer time to arrival of personal enquirer $n + 1$ Schedule Arrival of personal enquirer $n + 1$

6.3.2 Activity-based executives

An activity-based executive can be simpler than that needed in a three-phase simulation. It has only to ensure that it detects the time at which the next activity is due to happen and it uses a repeated scan of the activities to decide what will happen at that time. An activity-based executive need not even maintain an event calendar; all it needs to do is check the time cells of each entity record and find the minimum time cell. It is, of course, perfectly possible to implement such an executive with an event calendar. Such a calendar would consist only of the times at which events are due and would not contain information about what those events are. Figure 6.3 shows a flow-diagram of such an executive and it has two phases, which are as follows:

(1) Check the time cells (or event calendar) to find the time of the next event. Move the simulation clock to this time.
(2) Repeatedly scan through the activities, trying each test-head to see if that activity is now due or able to occur. Continue the scan until no more activities are executable at that time.

This cycle is repeated until the simulation is over.

The original attraction of an activity-based approach was its simplicity, and it certainly supports the parsimonious modelling advocated in this book. However, there is a price to pay—the simulations will run much slower than will their event-based counterparts. This is because, at each event time, the executive must conduct a repeated scan of all the activities even though it could know that not all of them are due at that clock time. This was the reason for the development of the three-phase approach, in which the activities are separated into Bs and Cs and then only the Cs (of which there will be fewer) are scanned. In a three-phase

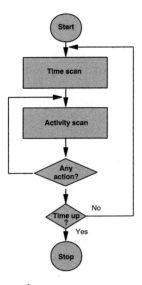

Figure 6.3   An activity-based executive

approach, the Bs are handled rather as if they were event routines, but with no need to follow through all possible logical consequences.

6.4   PROCESS-BASED APPROACHES

Process-based approaches are, perhaps, the ones in most frequent use around the world, although this may not be obvious to the user of simulation software. This section of the chapter refers to process-based approaches, in the plural, since there are a number of variations on this theme. The basic process-based approach is recommended as the best approach when using SIMSCRIPT II.5 (Russell, 1987) which, despite its antiquity, is still widely used.

To model a system using activity- or event-based approaches, the analyst must consider the process (or life cycle) of each entity class and must then break this down into more fundamental parts. For an event-based simulation, the process is divided into independent event routines, each of which defines all the possible logical consequences of an event. For an activity-based simulation, the analyst must define the list of unique activities and the executive sorts out the dynamic linkages between activities. Process-based simulations differ from this atomisation in that they take the whole process of an entity as the basic logical building block of a simulation model.

A process is defined as the sequence of operations through which an entity must pass during its life within the system. Tracing through all the loops of an activity cycle diagram will define the processes of the various entity classes which make up the diagram. Each class of entity has its own process and each entity created as a member of that class will inherit this process. The life of an entity is traced by checking its progress through its process. Thus a process-based executive needs to know the whereabouts of each entity in its process and needs some way of stopping and starting the entity's movement through its process.

Thus a process-based simulation model consists of a set of processes, at least one for each active entity class in the simulation. During the simulation, entities will be created as members of these classes. When an entity is created, it takes the process of its class as a template for its future life and the system then keeps track of how far the entity has moved through its process. A process-based executive has the job, at each time point in the simulation, of moving each existing entity as far through its process template as possible, the progress of an entity being halted temporarily by one of two conditions:

- *Unconditional delays.*   These occur when the progress of an entity is halted for a time period which can, in principle, be determined in advance. Thus, the delay is conditional only on the passage of simulated time. Once the appropriate simulated time has elapsed, then the entity can be re-started in its progress through its process. When two entities co-operate to perform a task whose duration can be determined, e.g. by sampling, then this might be modelled as an unconditional delay for these two entities.
- *Conditional delays.*   These occur when an entity's movement through its process is halted until specific conditions in the simulation are satisfied. Thus,

the entity must remain at this conditional delay point in its process until told to move on. For example, a customer may remain in a queue until reaching the head of the queue and until the server is free.

6.4.1 Processes in the harassed booking clerk problem

When defining a process for an entity class, the analyst must give some thought to the points at which an entity may be delayed. These are usually known as re-activation points. As an example, consider a possible process for personal enquirers in the harassed booking clerk problem. One approach might be to define this process as follows, allowing the process for customer n to begin with its actual arrival at the booking office:

- Personal enquirer n arrives;
- Compute time of arrival of personal enquirer $n + 1$;
- Create process for personal enquirer $n + 1$;
- *Delay* personal enquirer $n + 1$ until due to arrive;
- Personal enquirer n, *wait until* (at head of queue) and (clerk free);
- Engage clerk;
- Take personal enquirer n from queue;
- Compute service time n;
- *Delay* personal enquirer n until service time has elapsed;
- Release clerk to idle;
- Release personal enquirer n.

This process contains two unconditional delays and one conditional delay. The unconditional delays are indicated by the italicised word *Delay* in which the progress of the entity through its process pauses until some simulated time interval has elapsed. This is equivalent to scheduling a B or an event routine for some time in the future. The conditional delay is marked by the italicised term *wait until*, which indicates that the entity's progress is blocked until certain conditions are met—in this case, that the enquirer has reached the front of the queue and the clerk is free to serve them.

A similar process description could be formulated for phone calls, and their interaction could be managed by their competition for the clerk—a scarce resource.

6.4.2 Process interaction

It would also be possible, though not recommended in this case, to write a process template for the clerk which would operate alongside the templates for the two types of customer. Then, instead of managing the interaction of the processes by their competition for a scarce resource, the interaction would have to be explicitly managed. This would mean that one process might create and operate upon the conditional and unconditional delays of another. Such simulations create what are known as *process interaction* models, which are more complicated than the simple process-based approach described here. It would be equivalent to insisting that all objects in the system are treated as entities, rather than treating some as entities and some as resources.

The first proper process-based simulation system was SIMULA (Dahl & Nygaard, 1966; Hills, 1973) which originated in Scandinavia as an extension to the Algol family of languages. SIMULA never achieved widespread acceptance within the simulation community, possibly because of its base in Algol, but it had an enormous effect in the wider world of computer software. SIMULA promoted the idea that a system could be divided into classes, each of which had its own process. It also promoted the idea that classes could inherit properties from previously defined classes. Thus SIMULA was the precursor of object-oriented programming, as found in systems as diverse as SmallTalk and C++.

The GPSS family of computer software (Gordon, 1979) uses a much less flexible transaction flow approach which has some similarities to the process interaction approach of SIMULA. Rather than being concerned with processes which interact with one another, GPSS considers transaction flows which may have limited interaction. A description of GPSS is given in Chapter 9. As mentioned earlier, another widely used simulation programming language, SIMSCRIPT II.5 (Russell, 1987) can also be used in a process-based mode. SIMSCRIPT is more versatile than GPSS but less so than SIMULA.

6.4.3   A process-based executive

Although, in theory, a process is simply a list of chronologically ordered operations, it should be clear from the preceding description that things are not so simple. The executive needs to know at what points an entity may be halted in its process for either a conditional or an unconditional delay. Thus each process must contain re-activation points at which they hand control of an entity back to the executive. A simple process-based executive might maintain a record for each entity which contains two fields as follows:

(1)   Its re-activation time (if known).
(2)   Its next re-activation point (i.e. where it is in its process).

The executive might then maintain two lists of these records.

(1)   *Future events list.*   This is a chronologically sequenced list of the records of those entities whose progress is unconditionally delayed. Thus, this list is sequenced by the re-activation time of the entities whose records are in the list. Only entities whose re-activation time is ahead of the current simulation clock time would appear in this list.
(2)   *Current events list.*   At any time in the simulation, this list contains the records of two types of entity. First there are those that have been unconditionally delayed and whose re-activation is due at the current simulation clock time. For example, a personal service may be due to end now. Second, the list includes the records of all those entities that are subject to conditional delays.

These two lists then permit a simulation executive to operate with a three-phase cycle at each simulation clock time as follows (and as shown in Figure 6.4):

(1) *Future events scan.*   The future events list is used to determine the time of the next event. This is easily found if the future events list is sequenced chronologically. The simulation clock is advanced to this new time.

(2) *Move between lists.*   Those entities on the future events list whose re-activation time equals the new clock time are moved from the future events list to the current events list.

(3) *Current events scan.*   The executive must now make repeated events to move each entity on the current events list further through its process. Thus, each entity on the list will be moved on if conditions permit (e.g. if the server is now free and the entity is at the head of the queue). Those entities that have been moved will either complete their process or will be halted due to a conditional or unconditional delay. If the delay is unconditional, then their records are moved to the future events list. The executive notes their next re-activation points in the records of these entities.

6.4.4 Process-based versus three-phase approaches

Given that a process-based executive distinguishes, in effect, between two types of event (unconditional and conditional) and given that a three-phase approach uses Bs and Cs for this purpose, does this mean that the two approaches are, at heart, the same? Certainly it means that they share two common advantages. First, they avoid programs that are slow to run (as in a strict activity-based approach due to the need to scan all activities). Second, they avoid the need to think through all

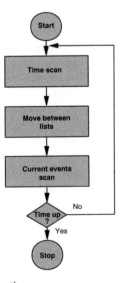

Figure 6.4   A process-based executive

possible logical consequences of an event (as in the event-based approach), which should make at least initial program construction somewhat simpler.

However, there is one very important difference that may not be obvious. In a three-phase simulation, the B phase is completed for all due-now entities before the C phase is attempted for any entity. This is to avoid possible deadlock in which an entity needs a resource or other entity that must be free before it can proceed. In general, Bs release these entities and resources, although occasionally this may happen in a C and therefore the C scan is repeated as in Figure 5.5. There is therefore, in a three-phase approach, an explicit separation of the two phases. In this way, the simultaneous and parallel activity of the real world is translated into the sequential procedures of a digital computer.

By contrast, in a process-based approach, each entity in turn is taken as far through its process as possible: that is, until it reaches an unconditional delay, or until it reaches a conditional delay whose conditions are not met. Hence, an entity may complete some activity (equivalent to a B) and may move immediately to attempt to start something else (equivalent to a C) without waiting for any other entity to complete its B. Thus, there is no explicit separation of B and C phases in a process-based approach. In essence, the process-based executive lies dormant until asked to do something by an entity, whereas a three-phased executive maintains a much more active control over each entity.

Any discrete simulation model that contains parallel and simultaneous activities that are to be run on a computer which is essentially serial in operation must have some strategy to avoid deadlock. In a three-phase approach, this is managed by repeated C scans in the C phase. In a process-based approach, the modeller must ensure that any possible deadlock is explicitly managed in the development of each process template. This is straightforward for simple models, such as that of the harassed booking clerk, but can be very tricky with models in which there is much interaction across many processes. This problem is particularly acute when a complex model is developed in a parsimonious way as advocated here. As each enhancement is made to the model, the process-based modeller must think about possible deadlocks. The three-phase modeller is freed from such worries.

What then is the attraction of process-based approaches? The first is that they are closest to the approaches that might be taken by novice modellers. Many people, faced with the need to consider how entities interact within a simulation model, will imagine themselves acting as one of those entities. 'Now let me see, first I arrive, then I wait until it's my turn to be served, and, oh yes, until the clerk is free. Then I suppose I talk to the clerk for a while, who might need to phone someone for information. Then, I suppose, the clerk can serve someone else, or might even answer the phone, when I'm finished.' This is clearly a very helpful way to think about these things and it provides a good starting point for modelling. However, it can helpful to atomise a model somewhat further into its Bs and Cs, because this finer fragmentation makes things rather easier when the model grows complicated.

For all of these reasons, the author takes the view that a three-phase approach is preferable when dealing with simulations of some complexity, although for simple systems, it matters little which approach is chosen. In many cases, the approach that must be taken is determined by the computer software being used. If it relies on a process-based executive, then the modeller must use such an approach. If it relies on a three-phase executive, then that approach must be used.

EXERCISES

1. Using an event-based, activity-based or process-based approach, develop a description of the modules needed to simulate a modified version of the harassed booking clerk problem in which clerks have dedicated tasks—some answer the phone, whilst others attend to personal callers.

2. Using an event-based, activity-based or process-based approach, develop a description of the modules needed to simulate the barber's shop described in exercise 1 of Chapter 4.

3. Using an event-based, activity-based or process-based approach, develop a description of the modules needed to simulate the grain dock described in exercise 3 of Chapter 4.

4. Using an event-based, activity-based or process-based approach, develop a description of the modules needed to simulate the T junction described in exercise 6 of Chapter 4.

5. Using an event-based, activity-based or process-based approach, develop a description of the modules needed to simulate the Morecambe Bay Hovercraft Company described in exercise 4 of Chapter 5.

6. Using an event-based, activity-based or process-based approach, develop a description of the modules needed to simulate the accident and emergency department described in exercise 7 of Chapter 4.

7. A common problem in computer simulation is deadlock, which occurs when more than one entity is waiting for the same resource to be released. In this regard, consider how the three-phase approach compares with the approaches discussed in this chapter.

8. Using the three-phase executive developed in Chapter 7 for guidance, use a programming language with which you are familiar to develop an event-based, activity-based or process-based executive. Use this to simulate the harassed booking clerk problem.

REFERENCES

Buxton, J. N. & Laski, J. G. (1962)   Control and simulation language. *Computer J.*, **5**.

Dahl, O. & Nygaard, K. (1966)   SIMULA—an Algol-based simulation language. *Comm ACM*, **9**, 671–678.

Gordon, G. (1979)   The design of the GPSS language. In N. R. Adam & A. Dogramaci (eds) *Current Issues in Computer Simulation*. Academic Press, New York.

Hills, P. R. (1973)   *An Introduction to Simulation Using SIMULA*. NCC Publication 5-Ss, Norwegian Computing Centre, Oslo.

Markowitz, H. M., Hausner, B. & Karr, H. W. (1963)   *SIMSCRIPT: A Simulation Programming Language*. RAND Corporation, RM-3310-pr. Prentice-Hall, Englewood Cliffs, NJ.

Russell, E. C. (1987)   *SIMSCRIPT II.5 Programming Language*. CACI, La Jolla, CA.

Writing a Three-phase Simulation Program

7.1 INTRODUCTION

Chapter 5 introduced the basic ideas of three-phase simulation. These were that the activity within such a model is divided into Bs, which can be controlled by the executive; and Cs, which depend upon the entity states within the model. This chapter takes these ideas further and shows how they can be used to develop a three-phase simulation in almost any general purpose programming language. For the sake of illustration, the program code in this chapter will be shown in Turbo Pascal, but the same ideas have been used by the author to develop three-phase libraries in BASIC, VISUAL BASIC, C, C++ and Java, as well as in Turbo Pascal. With the exception of the original versions of BASIC, all of these languages allow a programmer to split the overall program into independent units or modules. This makes it much easier to test programs as they are developed and also eases the task of developing libraries for other people to use.

Apart from the original BASIC program, full copies of all of these libraries, in a range of programming languages, are available on the Internet. To find them, use an appropriate search engine and look for *PiddSim*. The libraries are stored in a compressed format using the ZIP system and therefore, once downloaded, they need to be unzipped using software that is compatible with the UNZIP system. Readers are welcome to use this software with no restriction other than some form of acknowledgement. The author accepts no liability whatsoever in any country for any uses to which these three-phase libraries are put.

The chapter begins by explaining the basic structure of such a three-phase library and then develops each part gradually, using Turbo Pascal as the exemplar. Turbo Pascal has one or two strange quirks which create occasional disadvantages for programmers developing libraries for other people to use, and these will be pointed out as appropriate. What should become clear is that developing a straightforward three-phase simulation library is well within the capability of anyone with average programming skills. There is no need to be a qualified rocket scientist to do this.

7.1.1 The basic structure of the library

Fishman (1973) was perhaps the first person to point out that a basic discrete event simulation program has a three-part structure. Even commercial simulation software, which may be sold at high prices, has a similar organisation. The structure is shown in Figure 6.1, reproduced here as Figure 7.1, and its elements are as follows.

(1) *Simulation executive.*   The nature of these executives has been discussed in Chapters 5 and 6. Their main task is to ensure that the entities and resources of the model engage in appropriate activity at the correct simulation time. The executive acts like a puppeteer, pulling the strings that make the entities and resources co-operate so as to display the behaviour which characterises the system being simulated. Without the executive to pull the strings, nothing would happen. The executive is, therefore, in complete control over what happens within the simulation. Thus it is sometimes known as the control program. The executive which will be developed in this Chapter is for three-phase simulation, but the basic design of other executives is very similar.

(2) *Model logic.*   This is not really a part of the library, since this is the simulation model as written by the modeller, whereas the executive is written by the system provider. The model logic describes how the entities and resources are used to mimic the dynamic activity within the system being simulated. It must be expressed in such a way that it can be controlled by the executive and can communicate with it. In this chapter, the model logic will be expressed in three-phase terms, using Bs and Cs to represent the activities.

(3) *General tools.*   The third component, which is the second part provided by the system provider, is a set of general tools that may be used by the executive and by the model logic. This covers obvious aspects such as input:output, plus features such as debugging aids, random sampling functions, graphical displays and other desirable features. In many cases, this library will be much larger than either the executive or the model logic. Its size and features will be wholly dependent on the facilities that form part of the language in which the library is to be written and on the computer operating system being used.

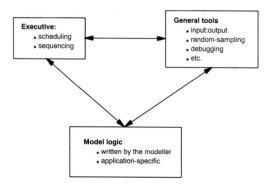

Figure 7.1   Three-part structure of discrete simulation programs

The library developed here is clearly not a commercial system, but it has many of the same features, albeit in a rudimentary form. The general tools component of most commercial systems is much better than that provided here, although there is no particular reason why readers should not extend this library to meet their own needs. Over the years, quite a number of simulation projects have used this library as the simulation engine for the work. These have included applications in the motor industry, food manufacturing, emergency planning and retailing. Versions used were written in Turbo Pascal, C, C++ and BASIC.

7.2   INSIDE THE EXECUTIVE

Section 5.4 showed how a three-phase simulation could be controlled by creating a record, with three fields, for each entity within the simulation. In many ways, this three-part record *is* the entity so far as the executive is concerned. The executive must continually monitor and interact with these entity records and thus they must be linked into some form of data structure. The simplest way to do this is to link them into an array, the control array. They could, of course, be linked in some dynamic form such as a linked list, tree or heap, but not all languages provide the pointers that are needed to create proper versions of these dynamic data structures. For an example of the ways in which a three-phase executive could use dynamic data structures in Turbo Pascal, see Pidd (1989).

7.2.1   The control array

The idea of this control array is shown in Figure 7.2. Each row of the array is devoted to an entity, with the columns denoting the fields of each record. To make the system more usable, the three fields discussed in Chapter 5 have been extended to five as follows:

(1)   *Name.*   This is a *String* variable that is used to give a name to each entity so that it can be displayed on an output device.
(2)   *Avail.*   This is a Boolean field which indicates whether the entity is available.
(3)   *TimeCell.*   This is an integer or long integer that holds the time at which the entity is next due to change state, if the Avail field is false.
(4)   *NextAct.*   This field points to the activity in which the entity is scheduled to engage in next, if the Avail field is false. How this field is implemented is entirely dependent on the programming language being used.
(5)   *Util.*   This integer or long integer field holds the total utilisation of the entity within the simulation, up to and including its next state change.

The precise implementation of the record is obviously dependent on the programming language being used. This is especially the case in the *NextAct* field, since this must point to the next B, if any, for which the entity is committed in the future. It is fundamental to three-phase simulation that each B or C should be based on its own program module (whether this be a function, procedure, method

	Name	Avail	TimeCell	NextAct	Util
PersEnq					
PhoneEnq					
Observer					
Clerk 1					
Clerk 2					
Clerk 3					
Clerk 4					

Figure 7.2 The *Details* array

or whatever term is used by the language). In the case of C, C++ and Turbo Pascal, the *NextAct* field can be used to point directly to the address of the function or procedure for that B. In BASIC and VISUAL BASIC, things are not so simple and a work-around must be devised. The principles of this work-around are shown in the first two editions of this book, Pidd (1984, 1988).

To illustrate the use of this library, a slightly enhanced version of the harassed booking clerk problem of Section 4.3.2 will be used. Figure 7.2 shows a control array, in which there are seven entities: *PersEnq* (the personal enquirer arrival machine); *PhoneEnq* (the phone call arrival machine); *Observer* (an imaginary entity whose job is to note performance statistics at regular intervals); and *Clerk 1..Clerk 4* (the four clerks employed in the booking office). In Turbo Pascal, the entity record could be written as follows:

```
EntDetails = Record
               Name: String;     {Entity name for listings}
               Avail: Boolean;   {Indicates whether occupied}
               TimeCell: Integer;
                                 {Time cell}
               NextAct: BAct;    {Next B activity, if one due}
               Util: Integer;    {Utilisation so far}
             End;
```

where BAct is a user-defined procedural type which, in Turbo Pascal, requires a compiler switch {$F+} to force far calls. It points to the machine address of the procedure that embodies the B in which the entity will next engage. If C or C++ were used, then this field would be a function pointer. If a dialect of BASIC is used, then a work-around of some kind is needed. The control array is based on the *EntDetails* record, and the following variable may be defined in Turbo Pascal:

```
Var Details : Array[1..MaxEnt] of EntDetails;
```

where *MaxEnt* is a constant which defines the maximum number of entities that the simulation system will manage. There are two limitations to bear in mind when setting a value for *MaxEnt*. The first is the limit imposed by many compu-ters, which is that an array is limited to 64 kbytes in size for most PC compatibles. The second is the speed of operation of the simulation, which will involve the executive searching through the *Details* array. The control array approach works very well with up 100 entities; thereafter some form of dynamic data structure may be needed. Hence, *MaxEnt* should probably be set to a value of 100.

7.2.2   Other executive control variables

Several other variables are used by the executive to control the running of the simulation in addition to the *Details* array. It is crucial that the values of none of these variables, including the *Details* array is changed by accident. With many programming languages this is hard to avoid as they do not permit data hiding. Most object-oriented programming languages, for example C++, do provide this protection. In other languages it is important that the programmer is disciplined enough not to change these variables which have to be given global scope. That is, they need to be accessible in all modules of the program. In the Turbo Pascal implementation, these variables are as follows:

```
Var Details : Array[1..MaxEnt] of EntDetails;
    CArray : Array[1..MaxC] of Procedure;
    NumCurrEnts : Integer;    {Used in APhase & BPhase}
    Clock, PrevClock : Integer;{Current simulation time}
    RunDuration : Integer;    {Length of run}
    NumEnts : Integer;        {Number of entities}
    NumCs : Integer;          {Number of C Activities}
    CurrEntArray : Array[1..MaxEnt] of Integer;
                              {Entities due now}
    CurrEnt : Integer;        {Entity involved in current B}
    CStarted : Boolean;       {Used in CPhase for repeat scans}
```

CurrEntArray

The manual three-phase simulation of Chapter 5 used a list, known as *DueNow*, to control the B phase of the simulation. The idea was that this list is empty at the start of the A phase and that, during the A phase, pointers are added to the list for each entity that is due to change state at the next event time. This same idea is used in the array-based three-phase executive described in this chapter. In this case, an array *CurrEntArray* is used to hold this information.

When the A phase finds that an entity is due to engage in a B at the next event time, it adds an integer to the next empty cell of this *CurrEntArray*. The integer value is the row number of the *Details* array that corresponds to the entity. For example, if the first entity found to be due to change state in this way is the phone call arrival machine, then the value 2 (see Chapter 5) would be entered in the first cell of *CurrEntArray* during the A phase.

NumCurrEnts and CurrEnt

Two other global variables that are required and which must be protected are *NumCurrEnts* and *CurrEnt*. These are both integers and are used as follows. *NumCurrEnts* is zero at the start of the A phase and, at the end of the A phase, holds a value that corresponds to the number of entities which are scheduled for a B at this next event time. For example, if the A phase found that the phone call arrival machine, clerk 2 and the observer were all due to change state at time 50, then at the end of the A phase (and therefore at the start of the B phase) *NumCurrEnts* would have the value 3.

CurrEnt is also an integer variable and is used by the executive to control the B phase of the simulation. During the B phase, the executive works down the *CurrEntArray*, one cell at a time. It takes the value from the cell, goes to the appropriate row of the *Details* array, uses the row number as *CurrEnt* and then executes the *NextAct* shown in that row of *Details*. *CurrEnt* should never, ever, be altered during a B or C.

Clock, PrevClock and RunDuration

The executive must keep track of simulation time and the library uses the integer or long integer variable *Clock* for this purpose. Why is an integer variable used, when time in the real world is continuous? The main reason is that all models are approximations (see Pidd, 1996, for a discussion of such approximations in models) and that sensible modellers use these approximations to their advantage. Using integer time will make a model run quicker than one based on floating point (real valued) time. There are two reasons for this. The first is that the computer arithmetic is faster. The second is that most data collections on which simulations are based stem from a sample of values. Thus the integer approximation is perfectly adequate, given the ways in which the data will be aggregated. In addition to *Clock*, it can be useful (although not essential) to use an extra global integer to store the previous event time. This variable will be called *PrevClock*.

The *RunDuration* variable is used by the executive to store the planned length of the simulation run. Thus, at the end of each C phase, it compares the current *Clock* value with *RunDuration* to see if the simulation run is complete or whether it should work through a further sequence of A, B and C phases.

Controlling the Cs

Finally, three variables are used to control the C phase of the simulation. *CArray* holds the addresses of the Cs which form the simulation and they are held in their priority sequence. Thus *CArray[1]* will be attempted before *CArray[2]* during a simulation run. In the Turbo Pascal implementation, the cells of the arrays hold pointers to the appropriate procedures, much as the *NextAct* field of the *Details* array holds pointers to the Bs. During the C phase, the executive works down the *CArray*.

NumCs holds the number of Cs that make up the simulation and is used to control the C phase of the simulation. *CStarted* is a Boolean variable that becomes *true* if a C is started successfully during the C phase, having been *false* at its start. It forces a re-scan of the Cs if it is *true*, so as to avoid the deadlock problems discussed in Chapter 5.

7.3   THE THREE PHASES

This Section shows how the data structures just defined are used to ensure a safe simulation using the three-phase approach discussed in Chapter 5 and shown in Figure 5.5. Each phase will be discussed in turn.

7.3.1   The A phase

During the A phase, the executive must examine the records of all entities and, from those which are not currently available, must find the ones with the smallest time cells. This time cell value is used to update the simulation clock to the time of the next event, this clock being held constant until the next A phase. The identities of those entities that are due to engage in Bs at this new event time are held in a temporary list, *CurrEntArray*, that is emptied at the start of each A phase. Figure 7.3 shows how this is implemented in the approach described here.

The Turbo Pascal code for the A phase is shown in Figure 7.4. It should be possible for anyone familiar with a standard programming language to follow what is happening. The first steps are to put *NumCurrEnts* to zero and to put *Minm*, which will be used to search for minimum time cell, to some very large value. The A phase procedure then works down the *Details* array, entity by entity, *NumEnts* being the number defined in this simulation. During this scan it checks whether the *Avail* field of the entity is false and, if so, it compares the value of its *TimeCell* with the current value of *Minm*. If *TimeCell < Minm*, it puts *NumCurrEnts* to 1, or if *TimeCell = Minm*, *NumCurrents* is incremented by 1, otherwise the entity is ignored. The value of *Minm* is then updated and the number of the entity involved is placed in the appropriate cell of the *CurrEntArray*.

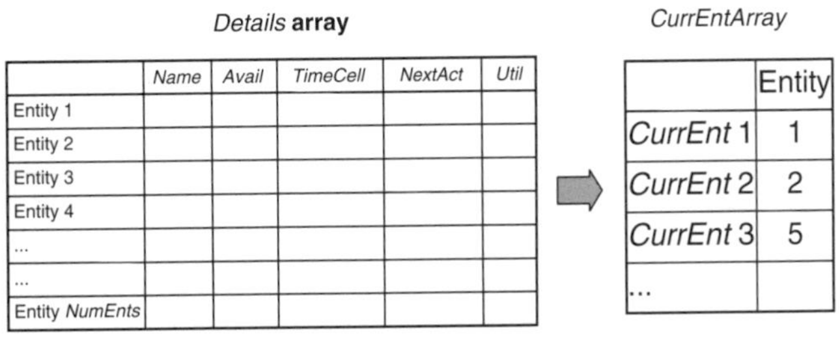

Figure 7.3   The A phase: finding the due now entities

```
Procedure Aphase;
{Time scan by examining the Details array of records. Checks all entities
for which Avail is false. For these, finds those with the smallest timecells
and puts the number of the entity into the CurrEntArray}
Var Entity, Minm : Integer;
Begin
NumCurrEnts := 0;
Minm := MaxInt;
For Entity := 1 to NumEnts do
    With Details[Entity] do
        If Not Avail then
            Begin
            If Timecell <= Minm then
                Begin
                If TimeCell < Minm then NumCurrEnts := 1
                    Else NumCurrEnts := NumCurrEnts + 1;
                Minm := TimeCell;
                CurrEntArray[NumCurrEnts] := Entity;
                End;
            End;
If Minm = MaxInt then Error('Error in A phase, Minm still = MaxInt');
If Minm < 0 then Error('Seems to be a mistake in A phase, Minm -ve');
PrevClock := Clock;
Clock := Minm;
End;
```

Figure 7.4   The A phase: Turbo Pascal code

The A phase ends with some sensible checks to make sure that nothing strange is happening—which could be the case if the modeller has, foolishly, altered one of the global control variables in another module. Finally, it resets the values of *Clock* and *PrevClock* ready for the B phase.

7.3.2   The B phase

This is similarly straightforward and is shown graphically in Figure 7.5 and as a Turbo Pascal listing in Figure 7.6. The aim of the B phase is to complete all the Bs that have been scheduled for the current clock time, before moving on to work with the Cs at this clock time. This reduces the possibility for deadlock, since most Bs release resources and entities, if only temporarily.

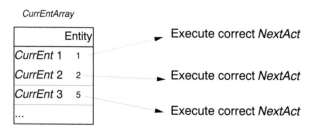

Figure 7.5   The B phase: executing the due now Bs

```
Procedure Bphase;
{Works through the CurrEntArray. For each entity number stored in
CurrEntArray,
executes the B activity indicated for that entity. Executed after A phase
and before C phase}
Var Loop : Integer;
Begin
If TraceOn then
    Begin
    Writeln(TraceFile);
    Writeln(TraceFile, 'Time now .. ', Clock:5);
    End;
ShowEntDetails;
For Loop := 1 to NumCurrEnts do
    Begin
    CurrEnt := CurrEntArray[Loop];
    With Details[CurrEnt] do
        Begin
        Avail := True;                 {Release CurrEnt}
        NextAct;                       {Do this B Activity}
        End;
    End;
End;
```

Figure 7.6   The B phase: Turbo Pascal code

The first Section of the *BPhase* procedure in the Turbo Pascal listing of Figure 7.6 is used when debugging a simulation. It writes the current simulation *Clock* time to a specified output file for later interrogation. It then uses a hidden procedure, *ShowEntDetails*, to write a copy of the *Details* array to this same trace file. It does this writing to the trace file if a Boolean variable, *TraceOn*, is currently true. This part of the procedure is not essential, but it can save a lot of heartache when debugging a simulation program.

The main Section of the procedure then follows. As might be expected, it works down the *CurrEntArray*, line by line. It uses the value stored in the appropriate cell of this array to go to the correct row of the *Details* array and from this to call the appropriate procedure for whatever B is scheduled for the entity in question. It also sets the entity in question free, by putting its Boolean *Avail* field to true. This means that the entity is now available for committal to some other B, should that be required, and it means that the entity will not be picked up in the next A phase, should that happen before the entity is re-committed.

7.3.3   The C phase

Figure 7.7 shows the Turbo Pascal code for the C phase, which is the simplest of all the three phases. It involves a repeated scan of the *CArray*, attempting each C in turn and continuing until there is no more successful C activity at this clock time. The *CStarted* flag is used for this purpose.

```
Procedure Cphase;
{Try each C activity in turn}
Var Loop : Integer;
Begin
Repeat
      CStarted := False;
      For Loop := 1 to NumCs do CArray[Loop];
Until Not CStarted;
End;
```

Figure 7.7   The C phase: Turbo Pascal code

7.4   USING THE THREE-PHASE LIBRARY: THE HARASSED BOOKING CLERK

As introduced earlier, the harassed booking clerk problem has four Bs and two Cs that are described in Section 5.2.4. They are as follows:

- B1: Arrive
- B2: EndOfService
- B3: Call
- B4: EndOfTalk

- C1: BeginService
- C2: BeginTalk

Each of these Bs and Cs will be a separate block of code which communicates with the general tools (see Figure 7.1) and the executive, but not directly with other Bs or Cs. As the problem is a simple one, each B and C can be contained within a single Turbo Pascal procedure. It makes sense to put the Bs and Cs in a separate program module. Thus, in the case of Turbo Pascal, the model logic would form a separate Turbo Pascal unit, which holds the relevant procedures.

The version of the harassed booking clerk used here has two important differences from the version used in Chapters 4 and 5. The first is that there is more than a single clerk, in fact the number of clerks is a variable, *NumClerks*, that the user may set at run-time. The second is that there is an extra entity, *Observer*, as shown in Figure 7.2, which will be used to take regular observations of queue lengths. These will be made at intervals defined by the user at run-time and stored in the variable *ObsInterval*.

7.4.1   Personal enquirers and phone calls arrive

As shown above, each of these is modelled with a separate B, and the Turbo Pascal listing for these is given in Figure 7.8. Given that the problem is, at heart, a simple queuing system with two types of customer who have many similarities, it should not be surprising that their procedures are very similar. The B for personal enquirer arrival will be discussed here and the comments made apply also to the B for the arrival of phone calls.

```
Procedure Arrive;
{Arrival of personal enquirer}
Var Time : Real;
Begin
Inc(PersIn);    {Increment number of arrivals}
Time := NegExp(PersArrTime, 1);
Inc(PersQ);         {Increment queue length}
Display('Personal enquirer No. ' + Int2Str(PersIn,3) + ' arrives, queue = '+
             Int2Str(PersQ,3) + ' next due after ' +
             Int2Str(Round(Time),3));
Schedule(PersEnq, Arrive, Time); {Schedule next personal arrival}
End;



Procedure Call;
{Arrival of phone call}
Var Time : Real;
Begin
Inc(PhoneIn);   {Increment number of calls}
Time := NegExp(PhoneArrTime, 2);
Inc(PhoneQ);        {Increment queue length}
Display('Phone enquirer No. ' + Int2Str(PhoneIn,3) + ' arrives, queue = '+
             Int2Str(PhoneQ,3) + ' next after ' +
Int2Str(Round(Time),3));
Schedule(PhoneEnq, Call, Time);   {Schedule next phone call}
End;
```

Figure 7.8   The schedule procedure: Turbo Pascal code

The first step in the B is to keep track of the number of arrivals so far by incrementing a variable *PersIn* which is set to zero at the start of the simulation. The next line is used to compute the interval before the next arrival will occur and it uses a function *NegExp()* to do this. This generates a sample from a negative exponential distribution using a method discussed in Chapter 11, Section 4.1. The third line notes that the arrival is added to the queue by incrementing the variable *PersQ*. Note that this version of the program makes no attempt to distinguish between individual customers; were it to do so, then it might be necessary to represent the customers as proper entities. The *Display()* procedure of the next line causes information about this B to be sent to the trace file (see the discussion of the B phase in Section 7.3.2 above) if *TraceOn* is true. Finally, the next arrival must be scheduled and this is done by calling the *Schedule* procedure, shown in Figure 7.9, which is part of the executive.

The *Schedule* procedure is used by the executive to update the row of the *Details* array that belongs to an entity. Although the *Details* array could be updated directly, this is not a good idea if accidental damage is to be avoided. The procedure has three parameters: the *Entity*, the *Activity* (the B in which it will next engage) and the *RTime* (the time for which this B is being scheduled). Thus, the *Schedule* procedure updates the fields of the entity record, using an rounded integer of *RTime* for the time data. The *Avail* field is set to false, to show that the entity is now committed for a B at some time in the future.

```
Procedure Schedule(Entity : Integer;
                   Activity : BAct;
                   RTime : Real);
{Commits specified entity to Activity after RTime}
Begin
With Details[Entity] do
     Begin
     NextAct := Activity;
     TimeCell := Clock + Round(RTime);
     Avail := False;
     Util := Util + Round(RTime);
     End;
End;
```

Figure 7.9   The *Arrival* and *Call* Bs: Turbo Pascal code

```
Procedure EndServe;
{End of personal service. CurrEnt is clerk who is released}
Begin
Inc(PersOut);    {Increment number of completed services}
Display('End of personal service:' + Int2Str(PersOut,3) +
           ' freed Clerk:' + Int2Str(CurrEnt,2));
End;
```

```
Procedure EndTalk;
{End of phone conversation. CurrEnt is clerk who is released}
Begin
Inc(PhoneOut);    {Increment number of completed conversations}
Display('End of phone conversation:' + Int2Str(PhoneOut,3) +
                  ' freed Clerk: ' + Int2Str(CurrEnt,2));
End;
```

Figure 7.10   The *EndServe* and *EndTalk* Bs: Turbo Pascal code

7.4.2   The end of personal service and phone calls

These two activities are also modelled by Bs and the Turbo Pascal code for these is shown in Figure 7.10. As in the case of the Bs in Figure 7.8, the two shown in Figure 7.10 are very similar and the one relevant to personal enquirers, *EndServe*, will be discussed here. The procedure is simple, with only two lines. The first line increments the number of personal enquirers who will leave, *PersOut*, by one—so as to keep track of the number of satisfied customers. The next line uses the *Display()* function, as discussed in Section 7.4.1. Note that the entity involved in this B, which is stored in the variable *CurrEnt*, is made available in the B phase, by having its *Avail* field set to true before its *NextAct* is called (see Section 7.3.2).

7.4.3   Observations

As mentioned earlier, this version of the harassed booking clerk includes an extra entity, the *Observer*, which is used to take regular observations of the queue lengths as the simulation proceeds. The observation interval is specified by the user at the start of the simulation run in the *Initialisation* procedure of the simulation (see Section 7.4.5). The Turbo Pascal code for the *Observe* B is shown in Figure 7.11. It uses two arrays, *PersRec[]* and *PhoneRec[]* in which to store the queue lengths that are current at the simulation clock time that the B is executed. The meaning of the program code should be self-evident.

7.4.4   The Cs

There are two Cs and they are very similar. Figure 7.12 shows the code for the *BeginServe* C. That for the phone conversations, *BeginTalk*, is very similar, with references to personal enquirers being replaced by references to phone calls. The procedure must allow for several services to begin at the same time and thus the

```
Procedure Observe;
{Collect time series of queue lengths}
Begin
PersRec[Obs] := PersQ;
PhoneRec[Obs] := PhoneQ;
Inc(Obs);
Schedule(Observer, Observe, ObsInterval);      {Schedule next observation}
Display('Recording, Personal queue = ' + Int2Str(PersQ,3) +
                  ', phone queue = ' + Int2Str(PhoneQ,3));
End;
```

Figure 7.11   The *Observe* B: Turbo Pascal code

```
Procedure BeginPersService;
{Serve first customer in the queue of personal enquirers}
Var Time : Real;
    Clerk : Integer;
Begin
Clerk := FirstClerk-1;
While (PersQ > 0) and (Clerk < LastClerk) do
      Begin
      Inc(Clerk);
      If Details[Clerk].Avail then
         Begin
         CStarted := True;
         Dec(PersQ);
         Time := NegExp(PersServeTime, 3);
         Schedule(Clerk, EndServe, Time);
         Display('Start of Personal service with Clerk:' + Int2Str(Clerk,2));
         End;
      End;
End;
```

Figure 7.12   The *BeginPersonalService* C: Turbo Pascal code

test-head is formed, in Turbo Pascal, by a *while .. do* loop. Thus, the code inside the loop will only be executed whilst the queue exists ($PersQ > 0$) and whilst some of the clerks have yet to be tried. If this test is successful then the clerk is examined to see if it is available, if it is, then the service can begin. As with the Bs that control arrivals, the service time is taken from a negative exponential distribution and the *Schedule()* function is used to commit the relevant clerk to the B *EndServe*.

7.4.5   Initialisation and finalisation

To allow for experimentation and analysis, the simulations must be controlled and parameterised. This is done by two procedures: *Initialisation*, which is called before the first A phase, and *Finalisation*, which is called when the run is complete.

In the *Initialisation*, all variables used in the model must be explicitly set to whatever initial values are required. Thus, all counters (such as *PersIn*) must be set to zero and any activity which is in progress at the start of the simulation must be set in train. All entities and Cs required by the simulation need to be declared in the initialisation, which means ensuring that the *Details* array has the correct number of rows and that each row contains the correct information. Thus, if entity number 1 is the personal enquirer arrival machine, and if the first personal enquirer is due at time 5, this information must be placed in the *Details* array in the *Initialisation*.

The *Finalisation* is used to collect the results of the simulation and to put them in some suitable state for analysis. This might mean writing them to the screen or to a file that could be analysed, say, with a common spreadsheet such as Microsoft Excel.

7.4.6   The main simulation loop

The executive exercises overall control of the simulation via a loop that proceeds until *Clock* is greater than or equal to *RunDuration*. The self-explanatory Turbo Pascal code for this is shown in Figure 7.13.

```
Begin        {Main program}
Initialisation;
While Clock <= RunDuration do
     Begin
     Aphase;
     Bphase;
     Cphase;
     End;
Finalisation;
End.
```

Figure 7.13   The main simulation loop: Turbo Pascal code

7.5   ADDING GRAPHICS AND INTERACTION

As described so far, the simulation program will be an adequate representation of the harassed booking clerk system and, if properly coded and linked, should compile and run quite satisfactorily. However, nowadays many programs run on computer systems that offer high quality graphical output via windowing systems. Therefore, many people expect to be able to see output from a simulation as it runs and wish to be able to interact with the program. This section shows how this can be achieved.

As such, Turbo Pascal is not an inherently graphical language, neither is it particularly well-suited to operating systems that present a graphical user interface (GUI). It has been extended by its developers, Borland International, into the Delphi system, which provides a way to write Pascal programs that make full use of the Microsoft Windows environment. Were these facilities to be used, then the control loop of the executive shown in Figure 7.13 would need to be altered to that shown in Figure 7.14. This has three extra procedures after the basic A–B–C loop of the executive as follows.

UpDateScreen is a procedure that the modeller must develop which displays output on the screen in whatever graphical windows are required. *ScreenDelay* is a procedure that slows down the run-time output if this is needed to make it easier to read. Many computers run so quickly that the output, especially for a complicated system, may be impossible to take in at full speed. Thus it can be useful to be able to control that speed and this procedure has that purpose. The third procedure is *CheckInterrupt* and this is used to detect whether the user of the simulation wishes to interrupt its running, to abort the run, to ponder over what is visible on the screen, or to allow some adjustment to some of the resources in the model. If the latter mode of interaction is being used, then the simulation can become a form of game in which the user attempts to find the level of resources and entities that provide the best system operation. For example, in the harassed booking clerk, the user might observe that queues are too long with two clerks and may experiment, on the fly, with three or four clerks.

This interaction and its link to run-time displays are the basis of visual interactive simulation and modelling, which are the subjects of the next chapter.

```
Begin       {Main program}
  Initialisation;
  While Clock <= RunDuration do
        Begin
        Aphase;
        Bphase;
        Cphase;
        UpDateScreen;
        ScreenDelay;
        CheckInterrupt;
        End;
  Finalisation;
  End.
```

Figure 7.14   The main simulation loop with graphics and interaction: Turbo Pascal code

The VISUAL BASIC equivalent of the Turbo Pascal three-phase library, available on the Internet, makes use of the in-built visual features of VISUAL BASIC to create a 'proper' visual interactive simulation.

EXERCISES

1. Modify the harassed booking clerk program so as to give priorities to phone callers rather than to personal enquirers.

2. Modify the harassed booking clerk problem so as to have dedicated clerks—some to serve personal enquirers and some to answer the phones. Use this simulation model to decide which system is best, dual-purpose or single-purpose clerks.

3. Modify the harassed booking clerk problem so as to have phone callers waiting for a limited period of time only. (*Hint*: when a call arrives, keep track of when it will ring off and create a new B which will remove it from the queue if it is not answered by the time the caller becomes frustrated.)

4. Develop a three-phase simulation program of the T junction described in exercise 6 of Chapter 4.

5. Develop a three-phase simulation program of the Morecambe Bay Hovercraft Company described in exercise 4 of Chapter 5.

6. Develop a three-phase simulation program of the accident and emergency room described in exercise 7 of Chapter 4.

REFERENCES

Fishman, G. S. (1973) *Concepts and Methods of Discrete Event Digital Simulation*. Wiley, New York.
Pidd, M. (1984) *Computer Simulation in Management Science*, 1st edn. Wiley, Chichester.
Pidd, M. (1988) *Computer Simulation in Management Science*. 2nd edn. Wiley, Chichester.
Pidd, M. (1989) Simulation in Pascal. In M. Pidd (ed.) *Computer Modelling for Discrete Simulation*. Wiley, Chichester.
Pidd, M. (1996) *Tools for Thinking: Modelling in Management Science*. Wiley, Chichester.

8

Visual Interactive Simulation and Modelling

8.1 BASIC IDEAS

8.1.1 Changes in computing methods

When discrete simulation methods were first developed, the process of programming a computer and of getting the results from the program was a laborious and highly skilled task. Until the mid 1970s, most computers were large and expensive and were operated mainly in batch mode. Thus someone writing a simulation program would have to develop the program on coding forms, have the program punched on to cards, have someone else feed the cards to the computer and then wait for the results. Often as not it was impossible to achieve more than one or two runs each day on most commercial computers. The results, when they appeared, were usually printed onto wide computer paper by a line printer.

Nowadays, most simulations are developed in a very different computing environment. Users take for granted that programs and data can be directly entered into the computer from a keyboard or with help of a device such as a mouse. They also assume that they will have direct control over their own computing via a multi-user system, networked work-stations or a personal computer. They are also accustomed to seeing the results of computer programs reported and manipulated on a display screen rather than handed over as a pile of printout. Inevitably, these technological changes have altered the methods of discrete simulations and they affect the analyst as well as the user.

8.1.2 Graphics

One area in which this is obvious is the common use of graphical displays on personal computers. Until the emergence of micro-computers in the late 1970s, graphical display devices for computers were expensive and were used only by specialists. Nowadays, users of personal computers take for granted that their machines will include colour graphics displays of a reasonable resolution. The personal computer market is dominated by IBM PC compatibles and, to a lesser extent, the Apple MacIntosh range, both offering excellent graphical facilities. UNIX work-stations are now cheap and most often even graphical higher resolution and it seems clear that graphics resolutions will continue to improve on most computers over the next few years. Much business software for these computers makes very effective use of the displays to present the results of analyses. Part of the success of modern spreadsheets, such as Lotus 1-2-3™ and Microsoft Excel™ is due to the way in which numerical results can be displayed in excellent graphic forms with minimal effort. Well designed displays can be used to convey complicated ideas in a way that would require many words.

Most discrete computer simulations are nowadays written on personal computers and workstations. Also commonly, they are written as delivered software for use by the client directly rather than by the analyst on the client's behalf. That is, the modeller may deliver the model rather than an analysis based on the model, and the client may take his/her own control over the analysis. It is thus very sensible to use the graphical displays that are available.

Three benefits come from using dynamic graphical display in simulations, the first two of which accrue to the client of the study. First, when properly designed, a graphical display can give a very good idea of the logical behaviour of the simulation program. Thus, in a simulation of a flexible manufacturing system, the display may clearly show automatic guided vehicles moving from cell to cell. It may also show the cells changing state as jobs are completed. In this way, the client—who may be the owner or designer of the system being simulated—may quickly gain an idea of whether the model logic is correct. There is less need for the user to take on trust that the simulation is a valid representation of the system. This logical clarity also makes it possible to think of developing simulation programs in co-operation with the client. The developing display will give the client some idea of whether the developing model is sensible.

The second advantage will also benefit the user of the simulation, for even with no ability to interact with the program the graphics are an aid to effective experimentation on the model. It is often easy to spot that a particular experiment is fruitless by watching a dynamic graphical display. For example, a simulation of a warehouse may display, amongst other things, the queue of vehicles waiting to be unloaded. If this queue is seen to grow too large, then it is clear that more resources must be supplied if the queue is to be kept to acceptable lengths. There may be no need to complete a full run of the simulation once such undesirable behaviour is noted. Instead, the run can be aborted and other possibilities may then be simulated. This is much quicker than having to wait for a finished printout before learning that the experiment is unprofitable.

There is, of course, the danger that this may lead to ill-considered experimentation. It could be argued that, because batch computing was slow, the analyst was likely to be careful about which experiments were likely to be worthwhile. This risk of lazy experimentation must be faced: however, the solution to the problem lies in better analysis and not in abandoning the use of graphics. As can be seen, there are clear benefits from the use of graphics. The use of graphics does not remove the need for carefully planned experimentation. Far from it. There is still a need for the sort of statistical methods described in Chapter 12. Graphics may be of use to reduce the potential set of feasible experiments.

The third advantage accrues to the programmer. Unlike many types of computer program, the main concerns in a simulation program are often logical variables rather than numeric variables. That is, in a discrete event simulation, the state of the system results from the states of the individual entities and the important variables are the ones which represent and link these logical states. If the analyst is to be confident that the system is being modelled correctly, then he/she must carefully follow through all the logical consequences of state changes in the system. This can be done by following a trail of text printed out from each activity—as is provided by the trace file in the harassed booking clerk program of Chapter 7. However, dynamic interactions are best seen dynamically. That is, it is easier to spot errors of logic when entities are seen to change state wrongly on a properly designed graphical display.

Virtually all commercial discrete simulation software packages allow the modeller to set up visual interactive simulations, although it can be rather time-consuming to do so. Some software can also be linked with graphics post-processors. In these cases, the simulation runs with no graphical output: instead, the simulation outputs values to a file as it runs. This file is then read later by the graphics post-processor, which produces an animated display of the simulation. Clearly it is not feasible to interact with a post-processed display, but it does allow a user to stop the run, to re-wind it as if it were a video-recording or even to fast-forward to interesting aspects. An example of a graphics post-processor is Proof Animation (Henricksen, 1996), provided by Wolverine Corporation, originally developed for use with GPSS-H, but able to be linked to other simulation languages.

8.1.3   Interaction

Computer users interact with their computers in several different ways. The devices they may use include keyboards, light pens, mice, touch screens and sensitive pads, which all allow the user to present information to the program for its operation. The devices may be used to interrupt and interact with a program which is running or may be used to establish parameters for a particular run.

Users of interpreted languages such as VISUAL BASIC are familiar with the rather loose interaction provided in that language. In VISUAL BASIC, users are commonly allowed to interrupt a running program by a key press or mouse click. This stops the program and allows the user to check on the values of variables and to restart or abort the run. Such loose interaction is what makes interpreted systems such as VISUAL BASIC attractive for program development. The programmer need not wait until the run is complete before assessing whether it is successful.

A rather more tightly defined form of interaction is useful for simulation purposes. As the user watches the progress of the simulation on a graphics screen (or even a text screen) it may become obvious that performance could be improved by a small change to one of the variables. For example, in a simulation of a warehouse it might become clear from the screen that too many vehicles are waiting to be unloaded outside the building. It might be thought that adding an extra fork truck could have a dramatic effect on this queue of waiting trucks. With an interactive simulation of such a warehouse, the user might be permitted to interrupt the running program and add an extra fork truck. Continuing the simulation with the new truck would show the effect of the addition. Interrupting the running program, modifying the appropriate variables and restarting the simulation from its previous state, is equivalent to using the program in a gaming mode. Thus the user may quickly home in on suitable operating policies by dynamically interacting with the program.

This type of interactive gaming with a discrete simulation program was suggested by Greenberger & Jones (1968) and became popular through the work of Hurrion (1976), who suggested the addition of animated graphics. Commercial simulation packages virtually all allow sensible interaction, following the trail set by See-Why (described by Fiddy *et al.*, 1981).

8.2 PRINCIPLES OF GRAPHICAL DISPLAY FOR DISCRETE SIMULATION

This Section reviews some of the basic ideas that may be employed in providing graphical output from a discrete event simulation. It is possible to labour for a long time to produce graphical displays which are almost works of art. At the other extreme, it is simple to produce moving images by using the extended character sets provided by a language such as Pascal on IBM PCs. For simulation purposes, a work of art is rarely the objective—neither is the simplest possible display. Any graphical display should be carefully designed so as to convey the required information in as clear a way as possible. The design should be one which quickly conveys information in a way which the user of the system can understand. It should never be an afterthought, grafted on because graphical display seemed a good idea.

8.2.1 Iconic displays

Perhaps the most obvious way to display the simulation graphically is to use a set of icons to represent the entities. The resulting display forms a mimic diagram which gives some schematic representation of the system being simulated. The effect is like watching a video of the system as the simulation proceeds. For example, in a simulation of a warehouse, the display might aim to show a floor plan of the building on which are seen the trucks and pallet loads moving about and the cranes moving to storage locations. A small picture of a truck might be used to represent a truck in the simulation and, as the truck changes state, the truck icon is seen to move around the screen in some appropriate way. The idea of an iconic display is that the screen should resemble the simulated system in some recognisable way. A simple iconic display, produced by the Witness simulation system (available from Lanner Systems) is shown in Figure 8.1.

Iconic displays are often used in the simulation of Flexible Manufacturing Systems (FMS). In these systems, automatic guided vehicles are used to load parts for machining onto large and expensive manufacturing cells. The cells themselves are automatically fed with the correct tools for the job, and the machining instruction is completely under computer control. The resulting FMS is very

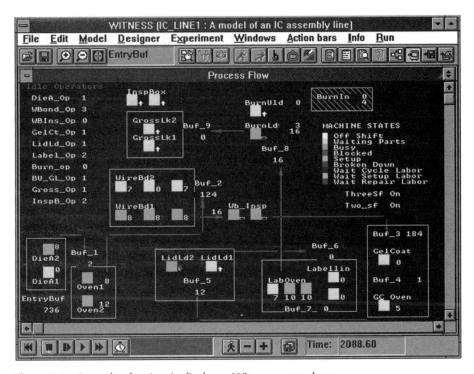

Figure 8.1   Example of an iconic display: a Witness screen dump

expensive, but is intended to allow the manufacturer to produce high-precision components in small batches with a short lead-time. Because such systems are capital-intensive, it is crucial that they are used effectively—thus, they need to be carefully planned. Not surprisingly, therefore, simulation has become an important part of the design of an FMS (Hurrion, 1986).

An iconic display of an FMS allows the designer to check whether the system will achieve its planned level of performance. Usually the display will show the various components of the system—such as cells, guided vehicles, tool delivery systems, etc. These are displayed using icons which resemble the components and show how the components interact to make the FMS work, or otherwise. In this way it is easy to spot whether priority rules are being observed and whether any interference problems are being handled correctly.

8.2.2   Designing an iconic display

In designing an iconic display there are several considerations to be borne in mind:

(1)   *Choice of entities.*   It is not necessary to display all the entities of the simulation. Too much complexity may make the display hard to understand and difficult to follow. The final display should only show those entities which are of concern to the user and important for experimentation. This

suggests that the programmer may require a different display from the user, for the programmer may wish to check on all the entities at some time or another. For the user, the display and the simulation are identical, but things are much more complicated for the analyst.

(2) *Choice of icons.*   Ideally the icons should be easily recognisable by the intended user of the simulation, this being the point of using an iconic display. However, this simple rule is not always easy to follow, especially when there are several similar entities to be displayed. The resolution of the graphic device will be another constraint to be borne in mind when designing appropriate icons. How the icons are constructed and stored will depend on the computer, the terminal and whatever graphics software is available. Graphic images can be heavy users of memory, but this is increasingly less of a constraint in most computers.

(3) *Displaying states.*   The icons are used to show how and when the various entities are changing state in the simulation. Thus, these state changes need to be displayed in some sensible manner. This is not always straightforward, especially in complicated systems—as the designers of analogue displays have found when attempting to plan monitoring and control stations for process control equipment. The screen designer should use the colour, scale, orientation and position of the icon on the screen to represent state changes. All can be effectively used to display the system state in an easily understand-able way.

Obviously, users of text-only systems are rather limited in what they can achieve: however, such screens do have their value when carefully used. In such cases, text symbols must be used as icons in the display.

8.2.3   Logical displays

A logical display is not intended to mimic the appearance of the system being simulated, but instead focuses directly on the logical interactions of the system. Consider, for example, a food manufacturing plant in which the raw materials are mixed, cooked, shaped, cooled and packed. Simulations can be useful in designing such plant, particularly where the various plant sections are known to be unreliable and therefore require in-process buffer stocks. Rather than attempting to develop icons which resemble the plant, it can be entirely satisfactory to use on-screen block diagrams which show the state of the plant sections. A simple logical block display from such a simulation is shown in Figure 8.2.

These block diagrams need not resemble the analogue displays used to control and manage the physical plant, but need only show how the total plant behaves as a system when particular events occur during the simulation. For example, the display of Figure 8.2 could at some stage show the plant oscillating if particular plant sections are going on- and off-line due to failures. The plant sections need only to be shown as named rectangles or other shapes in order to achieve this effect. Various colours and types of line may then be employed to show the different states. Changes in colour and line type show the interaction of the various state changes.

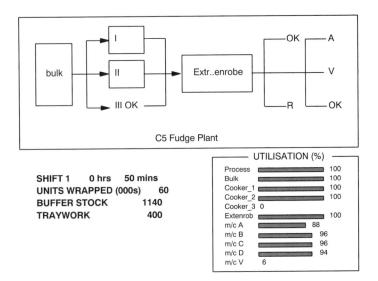

Figure 8.2   Example of a logical display

For this type of display, there is no need for the blocks themselves to correspond directly with the entities whose behaviour is driving the simulation model. That is, the blocks need not represent entities, unlike with iconic diagrams, but may represent more aggregate system components. For example, a single aggregate block might be used to represent the state of all the early processes on a production line, the later processes being shown in detail.

Users of systems which permit only text display may easily produce block diagram display as long as they have full cursor control. Obviously, the ability to draw proper lines and to fill areas with colour will lead to a more attractive display.

8.2.4   Chart displays

This third type of display is seen in its purest form in simulations of financial and economic systems. The chart display takes the form of histograms, line graphs and bar charts which show the performance of the model as measured by specified variables. For example, the display might show the order backlog and cumulative profit when simulating an inventory system. A simple chart display is shown in Figure 8.3.

Whereas an iconic display directly attempts to mimic the physical appearance of the system and a logical display concentrates on discrete system state, a chart display focuses on continuous system performance. As before, the aim is to produce a display which is meaningful to the user of the simulation model, i.e. a display which allows the user to monitor the performance of the model easily as it runs.

Some attempt at chart displays can be made even if only text display is available,

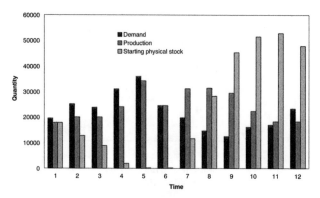

Figure 8.3   Example of a chart display

so long as full cursor control is possible. As with logical block diagram displays, the effect is likely to be more pleasing with proper line drawing, filling and colour.

8.2.5   Combined displays

There is no particular reason why the three types of display cannot be combined in a particular simulation. This combination could be on the same screen image—i.e. part of the screen might be iconic or logical, and the other part may show small charts. Alternatively, some computers and graphics terminals allow the user access to more than one screen image. A different screen could be used to display each of the iconic, logical and text displays and the user could be permitted to switch screens as required while the program runs.

Some graphic devices allow the programmer to overlay the several screens if required. This can be messy, but can also produce the same sort of pleasing effect as using overlay transparencies on an overhead projector in a lecture. A further possibility, permitted by most GUI-based operating systems, is to allow the user to display several windows simultaneously.

8.3   VISUAL INTERACTIVE MODELLING

In many cases, it is not necessary to write a computer program in order to develop a discrete event simulation: instead, a visual interactive modelling system (VIMS) may be used. Many such VIMS have appeared since the early 1990s and current examples include Witness (Thomson, 1996), MedModel (Carroll, 1996), ProModel (Benson, 1996), AutoMod (Rohrer, 1996), Taylor II (King, 1996) and Micro Saint (Micro Analysis and Design, 1992). As Chapter 14 also makes clear, there are VIMS for system dynamics modelling, of which Stella/iThink (High Performance Systems, 1994) is perhaps the best known. The basic idea of all VIMS is that the model is developed in a visual interactive mode as well as running the simulation in such a mode. The development of VIMS rested on the availability of GUI-based operating systems, which are now commonplace even on very cheap computers. These allow models to be represented graphically rather than as text.

8.3.1 Types of VIMS network

The usual way in which a VIMS model is developed is to begin with a blank background screen and then to place icons on the screen to represent the major components of the system. These icons are then linked together by drawing lines on the screen to form a type of network which captures the logical interactions between the entities of the system. Broadly speaking, there are two approaches to this screen painting:

(1) *Machine-based networks* in which each icon represents a machine, or entity or group of entities and the links show the path that some kind of passive object follows through the system. Hence, in a manufacturing example, a part might first go to an inspection centre, then to a machining centre, then to a paint booth and then to final inspection. Each of these machines would be represented by an icon on the screen, and the path of the part would be shown by a line (possibly directed, with arrow heads) from machine to machine. A simple example of this is shown in Figure 8.1, taken from a Witness simulation model.

(2) *Task-based networks* in which each entity represents a task and this task may involve one or more entities, or one or more units of system resource. Hence the tasks are linked logically to show how they are dependent. Figure 8.4 shows a task-based network used when producing a Micro Saint model of Joe's exhaust parlour, which will be introduced in the next section.

Machine-based networks are best suited to situations in which objects follow complex processes (sequences of activities) and in which machines may need to perform more than a single task. On the other hand, task-based networks are best suited to systems in which routing may be relatively simple but for which tasks may require the co-operation of several machines. Either approach is suitable for Joe's exhaust parlour.

8.3.2 Joe's exhaust parlour

Joe owns and runs an exhaust replacement business on an industrial estate. This exhaust parlour provides a service to private motorists who are concerned about the state of their car exhaust systems. Joe has run the business successfully for a number of years but is concerned at the competition from a national franchise which has opened up nearby. He knows that most potential customers will visit his parlour as well as that of the national competitor and he also ensures that his prices are competitive. Given this, he believes that the keys to winning an order are surroundings which are clean and business-like, but not too plush; and also in keeping a customer waiting for the shortest possible time.

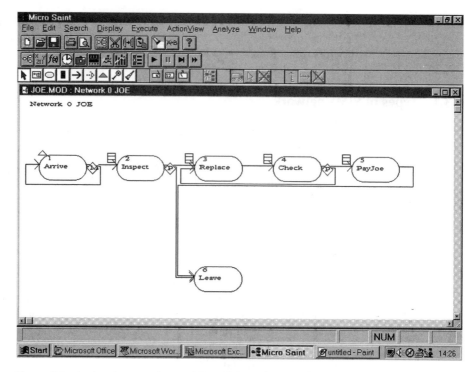

Figure 8.4 Joe's exhaust parlour: a Micro Saint task network

Joe's parlour is open from 9.00 am to 7.00 pm and he and his fitters work throughout that period if there is work to be done. Meals and rest breaks are taken whenever the activity is slack. The mode of operation is as follows:

Motorists arrive unannounced and wait for Joe himself to inspect their car's exhaust system. To do this, the car is driven by Joe onto any free hydraulic ramp so that the car's exhaust system may be checked from below. Joe then advises the customer on the necessary work and 70% of customers elect to stay at Joe's parlour to have the work done. The other 30% go off elsewhere.

Those drivers who choose to have the work done at Joe's sit in the lounge from which they can watch one of Joe's fitters work on their car on the ramp. When the fitter is finished, Joe inspects the work and, if it is satisfactory, he prints out the bill for the driver, who then pays and leaves. If Joe decides that the work is not satisfactory (which seems to happen to 10% of the jobs) then the fitter must rework the job—and this may take as long as the original work. Rework, too, is inspected in the same way as the original job.

Joe would like some advice from you. He needs to know how many fitters and ramps he should employ in the parlour. He is very secretive about his finances and will not give you this information, preferring to carry out a financial analysis himself after you have advised him about fitters and ramps. Ideally, he would like to keep his customers waiting for rather less than 10 minutes before he inspects their vehicle after their arrival; he would also like to ensure that customers spend less than 60 minutes in total at the parlour.

8.3.3   Using Micro Saint to model Joe's exhaust parlour

The easiest way to understand the basics of a VIMS such as Micro Saint is to use an example, and thus this section will use Joe's Exhaust Parlour, as introduced above. A Micro Saint task network for Joe is shown in Figure 8.4. This network was very quick to draw using the built-in functions of Micro Saint. It contains six tasks; *Arrive*, *Inspect*, *Replace*, *Check*, *PayJoe* and *Leave*. Each task is shown on the network as a named icon, and Micro Saint uses a rounded rectangle for that purpose. The tasks are linked by arrows that show the flow of the tasks for the main simulation objects—drivers/cars in this case. Thus, to use a task network of this type it is necessary to think in terms of the main objects that flow through the system. In essence, everything else is treated as a resource. Figure 8.4 shows the following linkages between tasks:

- *Inspect* follows *Arrive*: that is, the drivers/cars are inspected after they have arrived.
- *Replace* follows both *Inspect* and *Check*: that is, the drivers/cars may enter the replace task either from initial inspection or after the quality control check.
- *Check* follows *Replace*: that is, the work done is always QC-checked after replacement.
- *PayJoe* follows *Check*: that is, the customer only pays after completion of a QC Check.
- *Leave* follows both *PayJoe* and *Inspect*: those who pay leave, but so do those who decide not to have the work done at Joe's.

The Micro Saint network diagram has other features that are also shown in Figure 8.4. Immediately after each of the *Arrive*, *Inspect* and *Check* task icons are diamond-shaped icons that are decision nodes at the end of the task. This example has two types of decision in use, indicated by the letter *P* (for probabilistic) in the diamond after *Inspect* and *Check* and by the letter *M* (for multiple) in the diamond after *Arrive*. Probabilistic decisions are, perhaps, the simplest to understand as they split the entity flow (drivers/cars in this case) into several flows. In the case of the probabilistic node after *Inspect*, 30% of the drivers/cars will go direct to the *Leave* task and 70% will go direct to the *Replace* task. Similarly, 10% of the entities will be routed back to *Replace* after *Check* and the other 90% will go to the *Leave* task. To set these parameters (the probabilities for each route) Micro Saint provides a screen form (in standard Microsoft Windows format) in which the user may enter the appropriate values.

The multiple node may be less clear in concept. The effect of a multiple node is to replicate entities, with equal numbers of entities going down each of the outgoing paths from the nodes. This allows the end of one task to permit the start of more than one following task. In the case of the multiple node that follows the *Arrive* task, the effect is to turn the *Arrive* task into what Micro Saint terms a 'spinner' task. A 'spinner' task occurs when the multiple node is used to pass entities back into the task as well as forward to another task. The effect of this is to cause *Arrive*(*n* + 1) to start immediately after the end of *Arrive*(*n*). That is, it causes the inter-arrival operation of entity *n* + 1 to start as soon as the inter-arrival operation of entity *n* ends. This provides a useful, if slightly confusing, way of modelling arrival tasks that generate new entities into the system at regular or irregular intervals. Thus, the main use of 'spinners' (tasks that feed back on themselves) is as entity generators.

As well as tasks and decision nodes, Figure 8.4 also shows a number of vertical rectangles, each with two horizontal lines, by the start of each task icon. These are queue icons that are used to indicate that a queue exists before the relevant tasks. Thus, for example, there is a queue before *Check*, which means that drivers/cars join this queue at the end of their *Replace* task. Thus, to start a *Check* task, the Micro Saint system checks to see if any entities are in the queue. Were there no queue before *Check*, then the next *Replace* task could not begin until the prior driver/car *Check* task had started because the prior driver/car would still be blocking the next *Repair*.

As with all elements of a Micro Saint task network, there are Microsoft Windows-based forms on which the user may provide data to parameterise the elements of the system. These cover aspects such as task durations (which may be samples from probability distributions, or might be constants), details of decision nodes and limits on queue sizes. Sensible default values are provided. The idea of a VIMS is that the user should develop the simulation model by pointing and clicking so as to draw the network using the appropriate icons, linkages and forms. In this way, a basic model can be developed without any computer programming— familiarity with the GUI (Microsoft Windows in this case) is all that is needed. However, to be really useful, a simulation VIMS must allow the user some way to express the logic of the events that govern the behaviour of the entities and their state changes. This logic may be rather complicated.

8.3.4   Task logic in Micro Saint

Each VIMS allows the user to express this logic in different ways. Those that are machine-based will inevitably look somewhat different from those that are task-based. Micro Saint is task-based and it thus allows the user to define the logic of those tasks. Specifically, the user may define the following for each task:

- *Release conditions.*   These are used to specify the conditions under which a task may begin. Thus, for *Inspect*, these would be that Joe is free and that at least one ramp is available. Micro Saint will automatically check that there is a driver/car in the queue, as the queue is linked by the system itself to the correct task.
- *Beginning effect.*   This defines the logic of what happens when the task starts. In the case of *Inspect*, this would be that Joe is no longer free and that there is one less ramp available.
- *Ending effect.*   This defines what happens at the end of the task. In the case of *Inspect*, this would be that Joe is now free again. As with incoming queue logic,

Micro Saint links the probabilistic node after *Inspect* to this task and automatically deposits the driver/car into this node. From there they will proceed either to the *Check* queue or to *Leave*.

- *Launch effect.* This is a bit more subtle and permits the user to carry out tasks after the task duration has been computed, which is done automatically by the Micro Saint control program. This might, for example, allow action to be taken if the task duration would take the task completion time to beyond the end of the working day.

Thus, Micro Saint and other simulation VIMS allow the user to specify the detailed event logic of the system. One problem with these VIMS is that each one seems to use its own programming language for this purpose. In the case of Micro Saint, the language uses a syntax that is rather like a cross between the C and Pascal general purpose programming languages. It might be better if the vendors of these systems could co-operate to define a language standard or adopt an existing syntax (such as C). However, this form of co-operation seems unlikely.

8.3.5   Running a Micro Saint model

As well as providing an easy way to develop a model on-screen, a VIMS such as Micro Saint supports parsimonious modelling. When using a VIMS there is no need to develop a complete model before running it to see how it behaves. In the case of Joe's Exhaust Parlour it would be possible to place just two tasks on-screen (e.g. *Arrive* and *Inspect*) to provide some parameters for these tasks and then to run the model. Once this all-too-simple model runs OK, then other tasks can be added. Similarly, the existence of default logic in the VIMS means that almost 'empty' tasks can be added and the simulation may be run with these in place. The 'proper' logic may then be added, a step at a time, until the model reaches the required level of detail. This step-wise development is crucial and is an entirely normal part of simulation model development. It is unlikely that the precise specification of the model can be known in advance for most simulations.

The second aspect of a VIMS is that it provides an interactive environment within which the model may be run. This means that the simulation can be carried out like a video game with interactive experimentation. As the simulation is run, the screen can be arranged to provide a display that shows the main features of this system being simulated. In some systems, these features can appear in multiple on-screen windows. Thus, the user can watch the model run and might observe, for example, that queues build up very quickly and are not dissipated. This suggests a shortage of system resources of some kind and the display may make it clear where this bottle-neck is occurring. Thus, the user may interrupt the running simulation, may add extra resources and may then re-start the simulation or may continue the run, but with extra resources. In this way the user will use the visual interactive features of the VIMS to navigate towards an acceptable system design.

Micro Saint allows the user to watch a number of different windows as the simulation proceeds. Examples include the following:

- *The network diagram* as drawn on-screen to develop the model, so as to allow the user to check the task logic as the simulation runs. This also gives some idea of the build-up of queues.

- *The variable catalog.* All variables defined by the user are accessible and a selection can be displayed in a window as the simulation runs. This might include queue lengths, for example.

- *Action view.* This is an iconic representation of the model in which objects may be drawn to resemble the physical system. Thus icons may be developed for Joe, the fitters, ramps and cars. Cars may be shown arriving, waiting for service, moving onto and from ramps and the fitters and Joe may be seen attending to them. This can be useful for demonstrating the simulation to a client and convincing them of its acceptability.

- *The event queue.* This is the technical heart of the Micro Saint control program and it shows the calendar onto which events are entered and from which they are executed at the correct simulation time. This can be very useful for debugging a model.

Thus, like other VIMS, Micro Saint provides visual tools for model development, for debugging, for client presentations and for model refinement. In addition there are analysis tools for the analysis of the results of simulation runs, and the simulation output can also be exported in common formats to be read by spreadsheets and statistical analysis packages.

EXERCISES

1. Develop a bit-mapped iconic representation of the harassed booking clerk program developed in Chapter 7.

2. Modify the harassed booking clerk program of Chapter 7 so as to allow the user to interrupt the program while it is running and, at that stage, to see preliminary results. Allow the user to re-start the program.

3. Investigate how the built-in controls of programming languages such as VISUAL BASIC and Java may be used to support visual interactive simulation.

4. Using a VIMS, develop a simulation of the T junction described in exercise 6 of Chapter 4.

5. Using a VIMS, develop a simulation of the Morecambe Bay Hovercraft Company described in exercise 4 of Chapter 5.

6. Using a VIMS, develop a simulation of the accident and emergency department described in exercise 7 of Chapter 4.

REFERENCES

Benson, D. (1996)   Simulation modeling and optimisation using ProModel. *Proceedings of the 1996 Winter Simulation Conference*, Coronada, CA, December. The Society for Computer Simulation, San Diego, CA.

Carroll, D. F. (1996)   MedModel—healthcare simulation software. *Proceedings of the 1996*

Winter Simulation Conference, Coronada, CA, December. The Society for Computer Simulation, San Diego, CA.

Fiddy, E., Bright, J. G. & Hurrion, R. D. (1981)   See-Why: interactive simulation on the screen. *Proc. Inst. Mech. Eng.*, **C293**/81, 167–172.

Greenberger, M. & Jones, M (1968)   On-line, incremental simulation. In J. N. Buxton (ed.) *Simulation Programming Languages*. North-Holland, Amsterdam.

Henriksen, J. O. (1996)   The power of Proof animation. *Proceedings of the 1996 Winter Simulation Conference*, Coronada, CA, December. The Society for Computer Simulation, San Diego, CA.

High Performance Systems (1994)   *Stella II Technical Documentation*. High Performance Systems Inc, Hanover, NH.

Hurrion, R. (1976)   The Design, Use and Requirements of an Interactive Visual Computer Simulation Language to Explore Production Planning Problems. PhD thesis, University of London.

Hurrion, R. (ed.) (1986)   *Simulation. Applications in Manufacturing*. IFS Publications, Bedford, UK.

King, C. B. (1996)   Taylor II manufacturing system software. *Proceedings of the 1996 Winter Simulation Conference*, Coronada, CA, December. The Society for Computer Simulation, San Diego, CA.

Micro Analysis & Design (1992)   *Getting Started with Micro Saint for Windows*. Micro Analysis & Design Simulation Software Inc., Boulder, CA.

Rohrer, M. W. (1996)   Automod tutorial. *Proceedings of the 1996 Winter Simulation Conference*, Coronada, CA, December 1996. The Society for Computer Simulation, San Diego, CA.

Thomson, W. B. (1996)   An introduction to the Witness visual interactive simulator and OLEII automation. *Proceedings of the 1996 Winter Simulation Conference*, Coronada, CA, December. The Society for Computer Simulation, San Diego, CA.

Selecting Discrete Simulation Software

9.1 GENERAL PRINCIPLES

In an ideal world it would be possible to produce a list of all available options for implementing a simulation on a computer. Other authors (e.g. Mathewson, 1989; Banks and Carson, 1985; Kiviat, 1969) have attempted full or partial surveys at various times. Such a list might be made to resemble those found in consumer magazines in which each option is given a relative score which tells the reader which is the 'best buy'. However, trying to do this for computer simulation is unlikely to be profitable for a number of reasons. First, the products available on the market are constantly changing. Completely new products appear and existing software is updated as enhancements are made and bugs are corrected. Thus any attempt at a proper survey would be out of date before this book is printed. Instead, this chapter and the next indicate the trends that have driven simulation software since the early days, and it places products and options in product families and categories.

The second reason why a full survey is pointless is that most computer users are idiosyncratic in their choice of software. Most programmers develop their own preferences for particular languages and can become very evangelistic in their zeal. Thus, FORTRAN programmers are apt to scorn Pascal users as 'quiche eaters' and T shirts are available with the slogan 'real programmers do it in C'. Similarly, there are arguments that rage over object orientation, functional programming, symbolic programming and the rest. Hence, this chapter can only take a general view, though the preferences of the author are bound to come through.

Finally, some software options are better suited to particular applications than others. Perhaps this could be covered by specifying 'best buys' in each category. However, if this is attempted, some software vendor somewhere is bound to feel aggrieved. Hence, this chapter spells out some of the general principles that ought to be borne in mind when selecting simulation software. Particular packages and systems will be mentioned but the coverage will be neither complete nor uniform. The idea is to permit readers to construct their own lists of 'best buys' based on their own needs and the resources available to them.

Perhaps the best place to look for extensive information about a wide range of discrete simulation software is the Proceedings of the Winter Simulation Conference. This annual conference, held in the USA, includes a stream of sessions under the heading 'Modelware', at which the software vendors present information about their products. The *Proceedings of the 1996 Winter Simulation Conference* (Charnes *et al.*, 1996), for example, includes almost 30 papers that describe such sessions. The INFORMS magazine, *OR/MS Today*, also produces occasional surveys of simulation software.

9.2   COMPUTER PROGRAMMING

9.2.1   Logical machines

Digital computers are machines which can obey certain logical instructions, often from a small set of such instructions. Despite such small in-built instruction sets, three features of digital computers make them extremely powerful. First, these simple instructions may be combined to form a higher level of richer and more powerful instructions. Thus, if necessary, repetitive addition can be used to emulate multiplication. Second, these combinations can themselves be stored within the computer and thus the machine may be instructed, say, to multiply. Provided that a multiply program exists within the computer, then this can be obeyed by setting off the required sequence of repeated additions. In this way, digital computers may be programmed in a hierarchical mode, each instruction drawing on several others further down the hierarchy. Third, modern computers can execute these instructions extremely quickly.

For discrete simulation, a further feature of digital computers is attractive. This is that the computer is a logical machine. Thus, the instructions given to the machine need not be concerned with calculation as such, but might be directed towards the completion of certain tasks. Thus, in a different area of work, computers are commonly used to control machines—even domestic appliances such as washing machines. In these cases, the computer keeps track of the state of some system or other and is ordered to take particular action depending on that state. Most of the previous chapters have shown how the behaviour of a system can be modelled as a set of logical actions which lead to particular states. A simulation programming language must, amongst other things, allow the easy expression of this system logic and the resulting states.

Figure 9.1 shows the ways in which people have programmed digital computers. It is not concerned with the design methods that they use, but with the nature of the programming languages that are employed.

9.2.2   Machine code and assembler

At their most basic level, most digital computers operate with a form of binary arithmetic and thus their basic instructions can be given as a sequence of zeros and ones. Often a hexadecimal or octal format is used to express the binary instructions because these are more convenient to read and write than binary.

The individual instructions are normally rather limited in scope and are not very

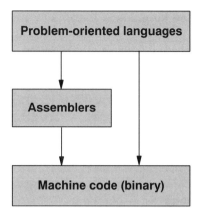

Figure 9.1   Programming languages

powerful. Thus, an apparently simple operation may require a long sequence of instructions in machine code. For example, the simple task of adding two numbers and storing the result requires a long sequence of instructions about retrieving the numbers, moving them about, accumulating a result and then storing that result somewhere else. Nowadays it is very rare for a computer simulation program to be written wholly in machine code. Doing so simply takes too long, is too skilled a task, and can be very frustrating because the process is too error-prone. Some programmers still favour small sections of machine code in their programs when they require specific control of the computer which is prohibited in a higher-level language.

Most computers also have assembly languages in which the instructions are written as alphanumeric mnemonics, these being chosen by the language designer so as to make them more memorable than hexadecimal or binary strings. Assembly language instructions are usually much more powerful than those of the machine code. Each assembly language instruction typically instructs the machine to obey a sequence of machine code instructions. Whereas a sequence of binary instructions may be directly converted into the electrical pulses which operate the computer, some form of translator is needed for the assembly language program. The translator—known as an *assembler*—is a machine code program which reads the assembly language program and produces a stream of machine code which the machine can obey. Thus, assembly language programs are usually thought of as being at a higher level than machine code.

Few discrete simulation programs are nowadays written wholly in assembly language because such programming, although easier than working in machine code, is still very tedious and error-prone. Assembly language programs, though, unlike most higher level programs, do allow the programmer direct access to features of the machine which may sometimes be convenient. This is especially the case when a small portion of a program may need to run extremely quickly because it is frequently accessed as the program is executed. Experienced programmers may sometimes, therefore, include fragments of assembly code in other programs so as to achieve particularly arcane effects.

9.2.3 Problem-oriented languages: compilers and interpreters

Rather than having to think about a program in terms of the computer's capabilities, it is much more convenient to think about the problem itself. Indeed for many tasks, the ideal program is one which is a description of a task, known to be within the capability of the computer, which the computer works out how best to execute. In many areas this is still a pipe-dream and so people fall back on *problem-oriented languages*.

These languages have a syntax which is well suited to their problem domain. Well-known examples are:

- COBOL: which is suited to business data processing in which there is much file handling.
- FORTRAN: which is suited to the solution of many numerical problems in mathematics.
- C: which is useful for virtually all types of programming, although it has a syntax that many people find obscure.
- Java: which is also a general-purpose language, but one which has found particular use on the World Wide Web.

Because their syntax is well suited to particular problem domains, programs written in problem-oriented languages are much easier to read (and write) than those written in lower-level languages. That is, problem-oriented languages are more *expressive*. Typically each statement of, say, FORTRAN implies a sequence of basic machine instructions. Thus, these higher-level problem-oriented languages are usually *powerful* as well as expressive. The computer itself can no more understand programs in problem-oriented languages than it can directly obey those which require an assembler. Thus, another type of translator is required, known this time as a *compiler* or an *interpreter*.

A *compiler* is a program which takes the statements expressed in the problem-oriented language—known as the *source code*—and translates these into the *object* (or *executable*) *code*. This is a basic machine language program which, given some help by its operating system, the computer is able to execute. Compilation is the process of translating the source program into the object program. For some languages, the final executable program may consist of several compiled units or files which are then *linked* into a final executable file. The compilation may be unsuccessful for a host of reasons, usually because of some coding error in the source program. A single error will lead to an unsuccessful compilation. Once the compilation is successful, however, the resulting object program may be stored on as an executable file which may be run many times with no need for re-compilation.

Rather than attempting to translate the entire source code at one sweep, another possibility is to use an *interpreter*. These take the source code one line at a time (or as small groups of lines) and translate this into machine code or some intermediate form. This small section of machine code is then directly executed by the computer. Thus, an interpreter differs from a compiler in two ways. First, no object program results from the translation and thus the source code must be re-interpreted each time the program is to be run. For example, the following Section of a BASIC program would be translated each time the loop is executed:

```
100     Sum = 0
110     For Loop = 1 to 100
120         Sum = Sum + 1
130             Print "Sum = "; Sum
140     Next Loop
```

whereas the following similar segment in Pascal would be translated only once, no matter how many times it is executed:

```
Sum := 0;
For Loop := 1 to 100 do
Begin
    Sum := Sum + 1;
    Writeln('Sum =', Sum);
End;
```

Interpreted languages usually sit within an environment which provides a source program editor and controls the program execution as well as its translation. The most common examples of such interpreted language environments are the many versions of BASIC and SmallTalk.

Why use an interpreter? Unlike a compiler, the interpreter does not need a complete and syntactically correct source program. It will accept a part program and run it until the first error is found. Used sensibly, this can encourage a step-wise approach to program development, for there is no need to attempt a fully working program at one go. A further advantage is that a programmer may halt an interpreted program during a run; at this time the values of variables may be examined and then the program may be allowed to continue its execution. In some ways, this step-wise approach is ideal for computer simulation programming, for it is all too tempting to try to develop a perfect program in one go. It is best to resist this temptation and proceed gradually, making sure each module works before proceeding to the next. However, used wrongly, interpreters can lead to very sloppy and undisciplined programs. Such programs just grow and grow, with patches made here, there and everywhere to deal with particular problems. Hence any step-wise approach needs to be disciplined and, above all, planned.

APL is an example of a programming language which is always interpreted; BASIC is language which is usually interpreted but for which compilers are available; FORTRAN, Pascal and C are languages which are always compiled. Interpreted programs usually run slower than those which are compiled. This is simply because of the need to re-interpret each line each time it needs to be executed. A further reason for this disparity of speeds is that compiler writers have spent many years developing highly efficient compilers for languages such as FORTRAN.

One obvious way to gain the best of both worlds is to have a language for which both interpreters and compilers are available. It is possible to use an interpreter to develop programs and then to compile and produce permanent object code. Another way is to use a translation system which may be regarded as halfway between a compiler and an interpreter. Examples of this approach include the

VISUAL BASIC systems of Microsoft, in which the source code is translated into a shortened (tokenised) form which is then interpreted. This has the advantage of producing an interpreted program that runs rather faster than would normally be the case. Java, too, is usually implemented as a semi-interpreted program in which the code that is run is aimed at an imaginary *Java virtual machine*. The output from this virtual machine is translated in whatever form is needed by the computer being used.

The other way is to provide an environment which allows the programmers to work with a compiled language as if it were interpreted. Thus, there are source code debuggers for languages such as C and Pascal which allow the user to run a program one line at a time while simultaneously watching its variables change their values in windows on-screen. Widely used systems such as those provided by Borland and Microsoft provide this source debugging in their standard language software. Third-party debuggers are also available for common languages and computers.

9.3   INSIDE DISCRETE SIMULATION SOFTWARE

There are many different ways in which discrete simulation software may be provided and later sections of this chapter will describe these. It is important to realise that, like an iceberg, much of a discrete simulation software package is hidden below the surface. Chapter 5 discussed the three-phase approach and Section 6.1 discussed the three-part structure of much discrete simulation software. Chapter 6 showed how approaches other than three-phase also have the same three-part structure that is illustrated in Figure 6.1. This shows an executive (or control program), the model logic and some general tools.

When simulation software is purchased, the software developer will provide the executive and also most of the general tools. It is the task of the modeller or analyst to capture and describe the system logic in whatever form the software package may require. Chapter 7 developed a simple three-phase simulation executive in Pascal and showed how it could be used to develop discrete simulation models. The executive was very simple and not especially efficient, especially for large simulations. Davey and Vaucher (1980) provide a thorough discussion of some of the ways in which better sorting methods may be used to develop more efficient executives. Anecdotal evidence suggests that some commercial discrete simulation software developers have ignored some of the lessons pointed out by Davey and Vaucher and that, therefore, some software runs rather slower than it might. Schriber and Brunner (1996) discuss some of these issues in relation to SIMAN, ProModel and GPSS/H.

As stated above, there are many different ways in which the modeller may be required, by the software in use, to develop and describe the model logic. The two extremes are as follows:

(1)   The user may need to develop a proper computer program. This might be in a general-purpose language such as Pascal, C or Java; or it might be in a simulation language such as SIMSCRIPT or MODSIM.

(2)   The user may be able to employ a GUI-based visual interactive modelling system (VIMS) of the type introduced in Chapter 8. This allows the logic to be developed by selecting icons from an on-screen palette, thus building the model by pointing and clicking with a mouse. Examples of this approach are Micro Saint and Witness.

9.4   APPRAISING SIMULATION SOFTWARE: SOME PRINCIPLES

There are many ways of providing the facilities and features listed in Section 9.3, but is there any single best way of doing so? This chapter takes the view that there is no single best way, although there are certainly rather poor ways of doing so. A range of factors is important when appraising discrete simulation software and the balance of importance will vary between these from case to case. What are these factors?

9.4.1   The type of application

The type of application is likely to play a major part of determining the features of the software to be used to write a simulation model and run a simulation. It is not unusual for software vendors to claim that their product will cope with any type of application. It may be true that the designers of a product intended it to be truly general-purpose but it is unlikely that they have achieved this end. Because any software design involves a set of compromises, there are always horses for courses. For example, some software packages are designed for the simulation of manufacturing systems. Thus they come with pre-defined objects such as parts, machines, conveyors, guided vehicles, etc. They may also include smart ways of simulating common operating rules such as Just-In-Time and, therefore, these packages are much better suited to manufacturing applications than, say, to simulating an airport.

However, it would be a mistake to imagine that they are always well-suited to all types of manufacturing. For example, most such systems assume that parts flow through a network of machines and change their states according to the operations performed at the machines. They then occupy set states as they await in-process stores for their next operation. This is fine for discrete parts manufacturing of the type found in, say, the automotive industry, but is not well-suited to continuous manufacture as in process industries.

Of course, these caveats do not mean that such dedicated packages cannot be used for applications outside their main application domain. However, it does mean that the analyst may need to think rather creatively about how to implement the actual system within the set of options provided by the software package. At one extreme this means no more than accepting that, say in a clinic, a doctor treating patients may be modelled as if he/she was a machine processing part. At the other extreme, the analyst may find that the system simply gets in the way of proper modelling as so many ways have to be found of getting around its restrictions.

If the application being considered is entirely novel then the analyst may have no option but to write a program from scratch, either in a general-purpose language or in a simulation language. Probably any system can be simulated in this way, but it may not be sensible to do so. This type of bespoke software creation is expensive and, even with good programmers, can be very time-consuming. But routine simulations may be best done by using a VIMS.

9.4.2   The expectations for end-use

It is also important to consider the anticipated end-use of the simulation. Is it solely for the use of the analyst who has developed the model, or will it be handed over to a client who may run the simulation unaided? In the former case, it may be less important that the simulation runs neatly and attractively—that it produces results may be enough. If the software is to be run by a client, however, then ease of run and graceful, friendly operation are crucial. In either case it is also important to know whether this simulation will be run just a few times or whether it might be expected to be run many times over a lengthy time period.

Some simulation software packages require a run-time system to be present whenever a model is created or a simulation is run. This is especially true of VIMS but may also be true of programming systems that have their own dedicated development and run-time environments. There may be further complications if the software package is protected by a hardware dongle which must be present before the package can be used. What such restrictions mean is that the organisa-tion must purchase separate packages for each parallel application. If only one simulation is in use at any one time, then this is no problem—but this is rarely the case. Some software vendors provide run-time systems at a lower price than the full development and run-time systems. This allows the organisation to purchase, say, one development system and the number of run-time systems needed for its applications.

9.4.3   Knowledge, computing policy and user support

Few organisations are keen to see a wide range of different computer packages appearing unannounced on their computers. This is true, and for very good reason, however clever the software. All software products need to be supported by someone within an organisation and, possibly, by the vendor. Thus some consistency and standardisation is desirable when planning software purchases. There is obviously the risk that over-bureaucratic standardisation may lead to the continued use of out-dated and unsuitable software. Equally, though, a free-for-all can become a nightmare when things start to go wrong. Thus, software needs to be chosen in the light of an organisation's software policy and bearing in mind the ability of the software vendor to offer extended support.

It would be pleasant to imagine that all simulation software packages are backed up by proper and continued support. Consideration of their market will reveal why this is not, and cannot, be so. Discrete simulation software occupies a niche in the market for software and thus sales volumes are, in total, relatively low. Thus, there may not be enough business for a large number of substantial suppliers and only the latter are able to offer proper support if this is required. Much simulation software is developed and sold by small companies who can only offer limited support. For a one-off and never-to-be repeated simulation exercise this may not matter, but to some organisations it is very important.

9.4.4   Price

Needless to say this is very important. Simulation software can be obtained very cheaply for a few dollars or the purchaser may need to budget tens of thousands of dollars. There is no guarantee that the most expensive products are any cleverer or have a wider application range than the cheaper ones. However, purchase price is only one element in the cost of using simulation software. If a more expensive product can dramatically reduce the time to develop and implement a valid simulation then it may well be worth paying the high price. Of course it can be difficult to assess in advance whether this will be the case, but most vendors of high-priced software should be able to demonstrate the virtues of their product—if they are asked to do so.

In considering cost, the organisation must also bear in mind the support provided by the vendor. This is expensive to provide and thus can be a major element in a purchase price. Not all companies need this expensive support.

9.5   TYPES OF DISCRETE SIMULATION SOFTWARE

There are many different ways in which discrete simulation software can be classified. Some authors (e.g. Kreutzer, 1986; Mathewson, 1989) attempt to develop family trees which show how one product has spawned many others, the later generations being, in general, more powerful than their predecessors. As mentioned at the start of this Chapter, the *Proceedings of the Winter Simulation Conference* and occasional copies of *OR/MS Today* provide up-to-date surveys. But no survey can possibly be complete, for new packages are constantly appearing and so any survey will quickly be out of date. Hence, this section focuses on the ways in which current software is used and offers a classification based on that mode of use. The following list summarises the main approaches that will be discussed in the rest of this chapter:

- Programming approaches in general purpose languages.
- Programming approaches in simulation languages.
- Block-structured systems.
- Visual interactive modelling systems (VIMS).

With the exception of VIMS, most of these approaches have been in use for over 30 years in one form or another. Different generations of familiar products appear from time to time, the idea being to take advantage of changes that have occurred in the general world of computing. Thus, for example, one long-standing simulation programming language is SIMSCRIPT II.5 (CACI, 1985; Russell, 1987). This language began its life on mainframe computers which, although very expensive, were low-powered and very inflexible compared with what is now available. As mini-computers such as the DEC Vax series appeared, so a version of SIMSCRIPT was made available. Similarly, the arrival of UNIX, MS-DOS, Microsoft Windows, X-Windows and OS/2 have led to versions of the same language being used across a wide range of operating systems. In addition, as graphical devices are now commonplace and cheap, established languages such as SIMSCRIPT now include graphical libraries that permit animations of simulations as they proceed.

Thus, many established systems have been developed, tested and debugged over many years. This means that any detailed comments made in this chapter may be out of date in a few years' time. Therefore, such detail will be kept to a minimum, the main aim being to show the principal features of different products and different approaches.

9.6 PROGRAMMING APPROACHES IN GENERAL-PURPOSE LANGUAGES

In the early days of computer simulation in the late 1950s, writing in some general-purpose language was the only option open to the would-be simulator. The languages available have increased and improved since those early days and so it is no longer necessary to write in a version of machine code or assembler. Many simulations are still written in the common computer languages such as FORTRAN, C or Pascal. Given the availability of simulation programming languages, block-structured systems and VIMS, why should this be?

One reason is cost. Some organisations and many academics are unable to pay the prices asked for commercially available simulation software. As should be clear from Chapters 5–7, it is actually not very difficult to write a simulation system from scratch—given reasonable fluency in a programming language. Many people prefer to write programs in a language which they (and their colleagues) understand well and whose compiler is thought to be bug-free.

The second reason is that this approach allows simulation programs which are highly specific, which can be tuned to run extremely fast and which might link into other software which may have very detailed requirements. Thus, bespoke software can be written to suit strange applications which cannot be modelled properly by simulation software packages.

However, anyone taking this approach should beware of a number of disadvantages. The first is the time and cost of developing the software. Writing bespoke software is always time-consuming and, assuming that programmers have to be paid, can be very expensive. It may not be worth paying the price of extended development just for a slightly faster program. It may also not be worth paying this price for a marginally more detailed model. As in all simulation applications, the analyst must ask whether the effort to be expended will be worthwhile.

The second snag is that detailed and developed programming skills are needed. Although a proficient programmer in C or C++ would not find the kernel of a simulation package a difficult challenge, not all organisations have such people available.

Nevertheless, it is still the case that many simulations are written in general-purpose languages and in such cases the analyst should at least choose a language with data structures and syntax well suited to simulation. FORTRAN lovers will not wish to read this, but their favourite suffers from many disadvantages in this regard. Specifically, until recently, it had no mixed data types (such as the records of Pascal and structs of C & C++), it still does not support built-in pointer types for dynamic variables, and it has a limited set of operators.

9.6.1 Pre-written libraries

Anyone who has attempted to write several discrete simulation programs soon realises that the same tasks make up large parts of most such programs. As discussed in Section 9.3, these tasks include the time advance, event scheduling and sampling. Most general-purpose programming languages allow a program to be decomposed into sub-routines (FORTRAN), procedures and functions (Pascal), and functions (C, C++). Some allow a final executable program to be composed by linking together independently compiled files (C, C++) or units (Turbo Pascal). Both of these features lend themselves to the re-use of program code by storing it in a library. It is possible that object-oriented approaches may increase the safety and desirability of such libraries.

To use a library of simulation routines, the analyst must write the skeleton of the program in the host language (FORTRAN, C or whatever). This skeleton consists of the logic and other features which are specific to the application. To use a library properly means that the analyst must be a fluent programmer in that language. The user's program then uses the routines of the library to carry out the general simulation tasks. Note that this is slightly complicated by the fact that the executive calls the application logic blocks (activities, events and processes) and not the other way round.

Pre-written libraries appeared quite early in the history of discrete simulation, as they offered an obvious way to reduce the development time for simulation software. Examples were SIMON (Hills, 1965) which, in its original version, was a set of Algol procedures and which later appeared in a FORTRAN version. The GASP family of products (Pritsker, 1974) is written in FORTRAN. SIMON adopted a three-phase structure and GASP followed a strict event-based approach. A later version of GASP, GASP IV (Pritsker, 1974) also included routines for numerical integration so as to allow the development of programs for mixed/discrete simulation. More recent FORTRAN libraries were those offered as See-Why (Fiddy *et al.*, 1981) and FORSSIGHT, which added routines that enable visual interactive simulation. Thus, these later packages supported animated displays and safe interaction. Neither See-Why nor FORSSIGHT is now in much use.

In addition, it is of course possible for any individual or organisation to develop a simulation library. Indeed, the Pascal routines described in Chapter 7 could be used to form the basis of a (rather limited) Pascal library, as could the other routines that are available on the same World Wide Web page. Individuals or organisations who develop such libraries for their own purposes are likely to add routines which perform tasks that are specific to their own needs. This approach has much to commend it, as long as the library is efficiently written and properly tested and debugged. Documentation is also important.

Some computer operating systems allow programs to be developed from a mixed set of source languages. In these cases, the constraint is that data files and machine function calls have to be consistent. If permitted, such multi-language programming means that the analyst writing a simulation program can write in a language known to him/her rather than the language of the library. A further possibility presented by many operating systems is to write a set of independent applets (mini-applications) which each perform distinct tasks and whose inter-communication is strictly defined. Thus, these applets then form a functional library, whose source language is irrelevant as long as the correct conventions are obeyed.

Hence, it should be clear that the attractions of pre-written libraries are that they permit bespoke programming (in the same way as writing from scratch) but offer some time saving over the do-it-yourself option outlined in Section 9.2. However, they still force the analyst to program in a language which may not be well suited to discrete simulation. Thus, program development may still be a long, drawn-out process.

A further problem which should not be overlooked is that many analysts find that using other people's program code is very difficult. There are two reasons for this. The first is that considerable expertise is often needed if an analyst is to feel confident in using other people's programs. The second reason is that a full library needs extensive documentation which can outface even a dedicated programmer. Thus, a training course is probably essential if the analyst is to get the best from a library. This is especially true when it comes to understanding the error messages which can be produced when a program goes wrong. This usually happens in a way which the analyst believes to be impossible!

9.7 PROGRAMMING APPROACHES IN SIMULATION LANGUAGES

As mentioned earlier, a digital computer is a logical machine which will obey instructions that are sent to it. The language in which those instructions are coded must be one which the machine can obey—this being achieved by a process of translation. In addition, the language should be one which is well-suited to the tasks which the machine is being told to carry out. Problem-oriented languages have a syntax which is well suited to the tasks being implemented on the computer. It is clear that conventional, general-purpose languages do not have a simulation-oriented syntax—hence the development of simulation programming languages.

Many such languages have been developed since the early 1960s and the most popular have passed through a series of revisions as they have been adapted to suit particular computers or as extra facilities have been added. Probably the most widely used languages over that period have been the SIMSCRIPT, SIMULA and ECSL families and, latterly, MODSIM. This section considers the common features of simulation programming languages and investigates two popular language families; SIMSCRIPT and MODSIM. Rather than give extensive illustrations of both languages, SIMSCRIPT will be used to illustrate the general ideas, with the harassed booking clerk (see Section 3.3.2) as the example.

9.7.1 Common features of simulation languages

These simulation programming languages have a number of common features as discussed below:

(1) *A hidden executive.* The system developers have written executives to perform the sequencing and scheduling tasks which underlie any discrete event simulation. In the case of SIMULA the executive is based on the process interaction approach. The SIMSCRIPT family was originally event-based but is usually presented as process-based nowadays. ECSL embodies a quasi-three-phase approach in which those Bs which mark the end of active states are implemented in the activity body by using the AFTER keyword.

(2) *A well-suited syntax.* The syntax of these languages is designed to ease the process of simulation modelling. Indeed, as the system developers have provided the executive, the task of the analyst/programmer is to express the application logic in the syntax of the chosen language. Implicit in the syntax is a set of data structures which support those tasks that are common in discrete simulations. Hence, the SIMSCRIPT family allows a form of set membership which can be used to represent system state as entities move from set to set.

Thus, the syntax of simulation languages, seen in the context of discrete simulation modelling, is both powerful and expressive. It is *powerful* in that one line of program written in these languages might be equivalent to dozens of lines coded in general-purpose languages such as FORTRAN. All the evidence about programming errors is that the number of mistakes is related to the number of lines in the program. Thus, a more powerful language is likely to lead to more rapid program development. The languages are also *expressive* in that, as discussed above, their syntax is well-suited to simulation tasks and to the application being simulated. In simpler terms, expressive languages are easier to read and, once again, this cuts down the risk of errors.

(3) *Variable tracing and data collection.* A simulation program is a set of operations which are conducted sequentially on data that defines the application. Thus, that data must be stored and controlled by the simulation system itself. Hence, simulation programming languages allow the analyst to trace the values taken by any variable through time. Such tracing is useful for debugging but is also valuable for analysis purposes, for example for collecting time series of relevant response variables.

(4) *Experimentation support.* Most simulation languages also provide a control shell within which the simulation program may be run to carry out experiments. Indeed, for this reason, many systems are interpreted rather than fully compiled. Thus, the control shells allow the same model to be run against different data sets or with different random numbers for alternative

sampling (see Chapter 12). Similarly, there may be some support for data collection for the analysis of the results of the simulations.

9.7.2 SIMSCRIPT

The languages of the SIMSCRIPT family have been in use since the early 1960s and are now available on a wide range of computers, from PCs to main-frames and under most common operating systems. The originators of SIMSCRIPT were Markowitz and his colleagues at the RAND Corporation in the USA (Markowitz *et al.*, 1963). They began the task of specifying and implementing SIMSCRIPT as a way of allowing non-specialists to write simulation programs. To contemporary users, SIMSCRIPT looks as complicated as any other programming language, but it must be remembered that, in the early 1960s, the first versions of FORTRAN were also just emerging.

As originally conceived, SIMSCRIPT was a pre-processor for an early version of FORTRAN. Thus, the analyst was to use the syntax of SIMSCRIPT to code the model and then the SIMSCRIPT translator would generate FORTRAN code. The idea was that the syntax of SIMSCRIPT was both more powerful and more expressive than that of FORTRAN and thus it should ease the tasks of simulation modelling and programming. To run the simulation program, the generated FORTRAN program would need to be compiled and could be run away from the SIMSCRIPT system itself.

The FORTRAN pre-processor version of SIMSCRIPT was replaced by later versions which ran within their own environment and did not need a FORTRAN compiler. The most widely used version of the system is SIMSCRIPT II.5 (CACI, 1985), which allows two alternative modelling approaches, event-based and process-based. The SIMSCRIPT II.5 literature encourages the user to take a process-based view where possible. Thus, the basic application logic is built up as a series of process blocks which define the chronological sequence of activities in which each entity class may engage.

PC users who wish to run SIMSCRIPT may do so in SIMLAB, a simulation environment marketed by CACI (CACI, 1987). SIMLAB provides a complete environment in which SIMSCRIPT II.5 programs may be developed, debugged, tested and run. It includes an editor and a debugger as well as a run-time environment. As with most software, PC SIMSCRIPT II.5 allows the programmer to add animated graphics to show the state of a simulation as it runs, and this can be a great boon in experimentation as well as in convincing a client that a model has some face validity.

The best way to appreciate the power of SIMSCRIPT II.5 is to consider an example such as that of the harassed booking clerk, introduced in Chapter 4. This has two classes of customer (personal customers and phone callers) who are served by one or more booking clerks. Using the terminology favoured by Law and Larmey (1984), this means that a SIMSCRIPT II.5 program to simulate this system could represent these as:

● Two process entities: personal customers and phone callers.

- A single resource: the clerk(s) available to serve these two classes of process entity as the simulation proceeds.

In SIMSCRIPT terms, processes stem from entities and require resources if they are to be executed.

Any simulation program written in SIMSCRIPT II.5 must have a certain minimal structure, which can be enhanced for particular applications. This is that the program must include a *preamble* followed by a *main* segment. The *preamble* defines the variables, parameters, processes and events which make up the model. The *main* segment defines the sequence in which the computation will take place. In its syntax, SIMSCRIPT II.5 has some similarities with the various versions of FORTRAN and experts in that language will, therefore, feel more at home than C or Pascal programmers.

The preamble and main segment of the harassed booking clerk model are shown in Figure 9.2. Starting with the *preamble*, the lines of the program are as follows:

- *processes include...* This line defines the processes which will make up the simulation model and in which the entities engage. In this case there are four such processes. Two generate new instances of personal customer and phone caller (Arrive and Call) and the other two follow these two entities from the time that they are deposited in their respective queues awaiting service.

```
PREAMBLE        ''HBC - Simscript Harassed Booking Clerk

    processes include ARRIVE, CALL, PERSCUST, PHONECALL and SHUT

    resources include CLERK

    define NUM.CLERKS as an integer variable
    define MEAN.INTERARRIVAL.TIME, MEAN.CALL.TIME, MEAN.SERVE.TIME,
        MEAN.TALK.TIME, DELAY.IN.QUEUE, DELAY.IN.WAIT and
        RUN.DURATION as real variables

    define .MINUTES to mean units

    tally MEAN.DELAY.QUEUE as the mean and NUM.CUSTS as the number
        of DELAY.IN.QUEUE

    tally MEAN.DELAY.WAIT as the mean and NUM.CALLS as the number
        of DELAY.IN.WAIT

end ''PREAMBLE


main
    call READ.DATA
    call INITIALISE

    start SIMULATION

    call REPORT
end ''main
```

Figure 9.2   SIMSCRIPT II.5 preamble and main section: harassed booking clerk

- *define...*   These three lines are used to define the important variables of the simulation. Several are defined as floating point (real) and NUM.CLERKS is defined as integer. The time units of the simulation are defined as MINUTES.
- *tally...*   These two statements define data to be collected as the simulation proceeds. New personal customers and new calls are placed in the two queues, QUEUE and WAIT respectively as they arrive. The SIMSCRIPT II.5 system recognises that it must collect tally data based on the entities moving to and from the two queues.

There are other SIMSCRIPT II.5 commands which could be incorporated in a preamble, but the example of Figure 9.2 shows some of the common ones.

The *main* segment is also shown in Figure 9.2. This shows that the program calls a routine known as READ.DATA, which sets up the parameters of the simulation. The READ.DATA routine is shown in Figure 9.3 and is reasonably self-explanatory. The main segment then calls the INITIALISE routine shown in Figure 9.4 and then starts the simulation, after which it calls the REPORT routine.

The short INITIALISE routine is shown in Figure 9.4. The first two lines establish that there is only a single class of CLERK entities and that the available clerks (these are resources) is initially set to be NUM.CLERKS—the number of clerks in the simulation. The next three lines tell the SIMSCRIPT II.5 system to

```
routine READ.DATA
    print 3 lines thus

HARASSED BOOKING CLERK: SIMSCRIPT II.5 MODEL
---------------------------------------------
    skip 1 line
    print 1 line thus
"Number of clerks: "
    read NUM.CLERKS
    print 1 line thus
"Simulation duration .."
    read RUN.DURATION
    print 1 line thus
"Personal customers: mean inter-arrival time, mean service time"
    read MEAN.INTERARRIVAL.TIME and MEAN.SERVE.TIME
    print 1 line thus
"Phone calls: mean inter-arrival time, mean service time"
    read MEAN.CALL.TIME and MEAN.TALK.TIME
    print 10 lines with NUM.CLERKS, MEAN.INTERARRIVAL.TIME,
            MEAN.CALL.TIME, MEAN.SERVE.TIME, MEAN.TALK.TIME
            and RUN.DURATION thus
No. of clerks: **

All times are exponentially distributed, mean values are ..
    Personal customer inter-arrival: ***.*
    Phone call inter-arrival:        ***.*
    Personal service:                ***.*
    Phone conversation:              ***.*

Duration: ****.* minutes.

end ''READ.DATA
```

Figure 9.3   SIMSCRIPT II.5 read data section: harassed booking clerk

```
routine INITIALISE
    create every CLERK(1)
    let u.CLERK(1) = NUM.CLERKS
    activate an ARRIVE now
    activate a CALL now
    activate a SHUT in RUN.DURATION .MINUTES
end ''INITIALISE
```

Figure 9.4   SIMSCRIPT II.5 initialise section: harassed booking clerk

enter process notices on its list of processes at time zero. They will be activated in the order in which they are mentioned here. Thus, the arrival of the first personal customer and the first phone call are set up to happen immediately (NOW). Also, the booking office is set to close at the end of the simulation (after RUN.DURATION).

Figure 9.5 shows the five processes which make up the simulation model. These are as follows:

- *ARRIVE*.   This causes new personal customers to be added to the simulation at intervals determined by a negative exponential distribution with a mean value of MEAN.INTERARRIVAL.TIME. As the customers are injected into the simulation, this activates their *PERSCUST* process.
- *PERSCUST*.   This is activated as soon as a new customer is injected into the system and, at this time, the ARRIVAL.TIME variable for this entity is set equal to TIME.V (the simulation clock of SIMSCRIPT). In order to proceed in its process, the entity needs a CLERK, hence it requests 1 of the first (and only) class of CLERK. The process is then suspended until such a CLERK is available. When the service can proceed, the DELAY.IN.QUEUE can be computed from the time elapsed since the process was activated (ARRIVAL.TIME) and the current simulation clock time (TIME.V). The service time is computed from a sample from a negative exponential distribution with mean equal to MEAN.SERVICE.TIME. The process is once again suspended until this time has elapsed, at which point the CLERK is freed.
- *CALL* and *PHONECALL*.   These are the equivalent processes for phone calls.
- *SHUT*.   This process is used to close the simulation cleanly after a time equivalent to RUN.DURATION has elapsed. Thus, this was set up in INITIAL-ISE to occur after RUN.DURATION minutes. It interrupts any active *ARRIVE* or *CALL* processes and thus prevents any more personal customers and phone calls from being injected into the system when it is activated.

One final routine, REPORT completes the model and is shown in Figure 9.6. As should be clear it merely produces a report which summarises the results of the simulation.

Of course there is much more to SIMSCRIPT II.5 than could be presented in a short example of this type. Indeed, one of the problems with SIMSCRIPT is that it has a complicated syntax which may cause some confusion. One example is the *WITH* keyword which can be used in several ways in a SIMSCRIPT II.5 program. These problems apart, SIMSCRIPT II.5 provides a powerful way of developing bespoke simulation programs.

```
process ARRIVE
    while TIME.V < RUN.DURATION do
        wait exponential.f(MEAN.INTERARRIVAL.TIME, 1) .MINUTES
        activate a PERSCUST now
    loop
end '' ARRIVE

process PERSCUST
    define ARRIVAL.TIME as a real variable
    let ARRIVAL.TIME = TIME.V
    request 1 CLERK(1)
    let DELAY.IN.QUEUE = TIME.V - ARRIVAL.TIME
    work exponential.f(MEAN.SERVE.TIME, 2) .MINUTES
    relinquish 1 CLERK(1)
end ''PERSCUST


process CALL
    while TIME.V < RUN.DURATION do
        wait exponential.f(MEAN.INTERARRIVAL.TIME, 2) .MINUTES
        activate a PHONECALL now
    loop
end '' ARRIVE

process PHONECALL
    define ARRIVAL.TIME as a real variable
    let ARRIVAL.TIME = TIME.V
    request 1 CLERK(1)
    let DELAY.IN.WAIT = TIME.V - ARRIVAL.TIME
    work exponential.f(MEAN.TALK.TIME, 2) .MINUTES
    relinquish 1 CLERK(1)
end ''PHONECALL

process SHUT
    interrupt ARRIVE
    interrupt CALL
end ''SHUT
```

Figure 9.5   SIMSCRIPT II.5 processes: harassed booking clerk

```
routine REPORT
    print 2 lines with RUN.DURATION thus

HBC run over at ****.*
    skip 2 lines

    print 2 lines thus
                    Num served        Mean wait time
----------------------------------------------------
    print 1 line with NUM.CUSTS and MEAN.DELAY.QUEUE thus
Personal customers      ***             ***.*
    print 1 line with NUM.CALLS and MEAN.DELAY.WAIT thus
Phone calls             ***             ***.*
end ''REPORT
```

Figure 9.6   SIMSCRIPT II.5 report section: harassed booking clerk

9.7.3 MODSIM

The current version of MODSIM is MODSIM III and it is also sold by CACI. Mullarney (1996), its main developer, gives a good introduction to its features. MODSIM III is object-oriented, an approach that has its roots in SIMULA. A number of papers discuss how object-oriented ideas may be used in discrete simulation (e.g. Pidd, 1995; Joines and Roberts, 1996). It is generally agreed that an object-oriented approach has the following features:

1. *Class mechanisms*

In a strictly object-oriented view, all program variables are objects which are members of classes that are either pre-defined or are defined within the program being developed. C++ permits object orientation and a 16-bit integer variable is, in C++, a member of the class *int*, and this class is usually provided by the language itself. As a class member, a variable not only has a type but also has defined operations, e.g. the use of the +, − and / operators for an *int*. Object-oriented programming languages allow the programmer to define new classes which use other classes which are either built into the language or have been defined earlier in the program.

This ability to define a new class in terms of one or more earlier classes is known as *inheritance* and helps avoid the need to re-invent the wheel, because it means that libraries of pre-defined classes can be used as the basis for new classes. For example, a discrete simulation program might include a class of general entities, which might be known as the *GEntity* class. Thus, for a simulation of a road network it might be sensible to define vehicles as a descendent class of *GEntity* and this new class, *Vehicle*, therefore inherits the defined fields of the *GEntity* class. In addition, the *Vehicle* class is a specialisation of the *GEntity* class and, if we need to know the current location of the vehicle, we might add extra fields to represent (x, y) co-ordinates and the current speed of the vehicle.

A class definition will also normally include member functions which will be used to change the values of these variables and to examine them.

2. *Encapsulated entities*

A second feature of an object-oriented approach is that the class definitions and declarations are self-contained modules of code, i.e. they are (relatively) independent. Thus, a class definition consists of a segment of computer program which has two parts, data structures and operations on that data. The data structures, sometimes known as data members, define the internal data of that class. Any variable which is defined to be a member of a class is considered to be an *object* which has access to its own internal data: other variables cannot directly access this data unless explicitly permitted. How, then, is this private data to be manipulated or examined? To do this, the programmer must make use of the member functions of the class which define the operations that are permitted on an object which belongs to the class.

In a way, this is a straightforward extension of the record concept of Pascal and the struct of C. The difference is that, whereas Pascal records and C structs contain only data, a class definition also defines ALL of the ways in which that data can be manipulated and examined. Thus, data and methods are not normally global within a program but are only local to a particular class.

To understand the implications of this for discrete simulation, consider that one way of developing a discrete simulation would be to define similar entities to be objects which are members of the same class. The definition of this class in object-oriented terms includes:

- *Data members.* These represent the internal state of the entity, for example the time at which it is next due to change state.
- *Methods or member functions.* Used to modify the internal state of the object or to report on its internal state. In a discrete simulation, this will include the activities, events and processes.

Because none of the data fields of the entity may be altered except by calling the methods which are defined for that object, then this means that many types of accidental damage to the internal state of an entity are impossible. To use the member functions, they are called with a general syntax of the following type:

ClassName.MemberFunction()

that is, the calling reference specifies the class of the object to which the call is sent. In object-oriented parlance, this is known as message-passing, since it is analogous to passing a request to a person to ask them to do something. This approach means that the same message may be passed to objects from different classes and the different objects may interpret the same message in different ways.

3.   Polymorphism

It was mentioned earlier that object-oriented languages such as C++ permit different classes to contain functions which have the same name. Thus, the definitions of two classes, for example *CommercialVehicle* and *Car* might both define their own versions of a function called *Repair()*. To use these functions, the programmer must ensure that the object name is given with the function name when it is called. Thus, if *VolvoTruck* is a member of the *CommercialVehicle* class and *Rover* is a member of the *Car* class the function call:

VolvoTruck.Repair()

will cause the *CommercialVehicle* version of *Repair()* to be executed on the *VolvoTruck* object, whereas the call:

Rover.Repair()

will lead to the *Car* version of *Repair()* being executed on the *Rover* object.

This permanent linking of the function call to the class type of object is known as *static binding*, so-called because the function is linked to the class type of an object, which is known when the program is compiled and which cannot therefore be re-defined dynamically as the program runs. Static binding is useful because it means that only functions which are members of the class definition may be used with that class—this prevents unintentional changes to the data of the class. It is also useful in a more straightforward way because it allows the re-use of meaningful function names within the same program.

To be more useful, most object-oriented languages also allow *dynamic* or *run-time binding*. This allows the programmer to write a program in which it is not necessary to specify the precise type of an object at compilation. For example, a simulation programmer may develop a traffic simulator but will not know how many vehicles will be active, or what their mix is likely to be in any particular experiment.

If the two classes *CommercialVehicle* and *Car* are both descendent classes of *Vehicle*, then dynamic binding may be possible if a prototype function for (say) *Repair()* is defined in the *Vehicle* class. This dynamic binding, also known as function overloading, avoids the need to have cascading if/then/else statements in the program to cover all possible contingencies.

Instead, dynamic binding may be used if all of the vehicles are all defined as dynamic objects (in the case of C++, this mean using pointers) belonging to classes which all descend from the *Vehicle* base class. Thus, if *ThisVehicle* is an instance of some class that descends from the *Vehicle* class, it is possible to write something like *ThisVehicle –> Repair()*.

If *ThisVehicle* has been defined as a dynamic member of the *Vehicle* class or to one of its descendent classes, this line tells the compiler to execute whatever function called *Repair()* is defined in the definition of that descendent class of *Vehicle*. The compiler does not need to know which type of vehicle will be invoked at run-time. When the program runs, it maintains information about the correct class of each vehicle which has been created and should execute the correct version of *Repair()* for *ThisVehicle* if it belongs to a class which descends from *Vehicle*. This makes it much easier for another programmer to add a new type of vehicle: the programmer merely defines a new class which is a novel descendent of *Vehicle* and which has its own version of *Repair()*.

This polymorphism has two direct benefits. First, it makes the use of extendible class libraries possible because there is no need to tinker with an existing class to define a new one. Second, it makes program enhancement much safer, because only the class definitions and declarations are updated and not the detailed program code.

MODSIM III

MODSIM III uses these object oriented ideas in its syntax for discrete simulation. As with SIMSCRIPT II.5, the simulation objects must be defined and this is done in a *Definition* block which specifies the classes of the simulation. Thus, Mullarney (1996) gives the following example:

```
Aircraft = OBJECT;
  BestCruise : INTEGER;
  InFlight :BOOLEAN;
  ASK METHOD SetCruise(IN Speed: INTEGER);
  TELL METHOD Fly(IN Distance: INTEGER);
END OBJECT;
```

This defines a class (confusingly known as an Object in MODSIM III) with two data fields and two member functions. The first member function is known as an *Ask Method*: this is a function which asks the object to return a value specifying its current speed. The second member function is known as a *Tell Method*, and this is a function that instructs the object to do something during which simulated time will elapse.

Once the MODSIM III classes have been defined, their actual operation is specified in an *Implementation* block. Continuing with the same example from Mullarney (1996), this might include the following:

```
OBJECT AircraftObj;

    ASK METHOD SetCruise(IN Speed : INTEGER);
    BEGIN
    BestCruise := Speed;
    END METHOD;

    TELL METHOD Fly(IN Distance : INTEGER);
    BEGIN
        InFlight := TRUE;
        WAIT DURATION Distance/BestCruise;
        END WAIT;
        InFlight := FALSE;
        OUTPUT('Arrived safely at', SimTime);
    END METHOD;

END OBJECT;
```

It should be clear from this that MODSIM III assumes a process interaction approach (see Chapter 6). Thus, a *Tell Method* allows the process template for the *Aircraft* object's *Fly* method to be specified. If classes that descend from *Aircraft* were to be defined, for example *Jumbo* or *TurboProp*, then they would inherit the *Aircraft* definition which could be modified to suit their performance characteristics. In this way, the in-built object library of MODSIM III can be extended to suit particular types of application. As with most similar software, MODSIM III comes with its own support and development environment for compilation, debugging and object management.

9.8   BLOCK-STRUCTURED SYSTEMS

To develop a simulation program using a general-purpose language or a simulation language requires the modeller to be a competent computer programmer. Because of this, a number of block-structured systems (described as flow diagram systems in the Third Edition of this book) have been developed. The original idea of these systems, the first of which appeared in the early 1960s, was to enable non-programmers to develop discrete simulations. This was done by defining a set of flow-charting symbols which relate to discrete simulation. The modeller would then develop a flow diagram on paper to represent the system which was to be modelled. In the early days, each such symbol had an associated punched card on which parameters (e.g. the number of entities) would be punched. The 'program' was a deck of these cards that were fed into the computer. The two earliest such systems were GPSS (developed in a co-operative effort by IBM and Bell Laboratories) and HOCUS (originally developed by Robin Hills, 1971). GPSS used its own special flow diagram symbols and HOCUS used simple activity cycle diagrams. A later block diagram system was SIMAN, developed by Dennis Pegden. This Section will discuss GPSS and SIMAN.

9.8.1   GPSS

The original idea of GPSS (General Purpose System Simulator) was to produce a system for simulating telecommunications networks, with the proviso that GPSS would be simple enough to use by engineers who were not expert computer programmers. That this design goal was sensible is seen by the fact the versions of GPSS are still in use 30 years after its appearance on the market. GPSS has spawned a family of products based on its ideas, and a good description of the GPSS approach is to be found in Greenberg (1972), Gordon (1969) and Schriber (1974).

GPSS does not use the concept of activity cycle diagrams. Instead, the user needs to envisage a simulation as consisting of transactions which flow around a network. These transactions are equivalent to entities and the nodes of the network are equivalent to points at which the progress of the entities may be delayed in their life cycles. Note that, as would be expected from its origins, the terminology of GPSS is rooted in the telecommunications world of the early 1960s.

Although GPSS is classified here as a block-structured system, according to Greenberg (1972) there is rarely any need to actually draw the GPSS diagram. Instead, GPSS is often described as a simulation language—but this is something of a misnomer. What is commonly referred to as a GPSS program is in fact a sequence of commands, each of which corresponds to a block type which can be shown via a GPSS template. Hence, a perusal of a GPSS program shows blocks such as GENERATE, SEIZE, ADVANCE, etc. and with each of these blocks is a set of numerical attributes which define how a block is to be used.

Rather than using the conventional terminology of entities, activities, events and processes, GPSS uses the following:

- *Transactions.*   These are the temporary entities of the system which are created and may be destroyed as the simulation proceeds. These transactions move through the various blocks which are permitted in GPSS. A generate block is used to create a transaction and a terminate block ends its life. The sequence of blocks make up the processes of these temporary entities.
- *Facilities.*These are permanent entities of the system which may be used to represent the resources needed by the transactions at the nodes of the network. These can be regarded as countable resources.

GPSS uses other terminology as well, but the above is all that is needed to gain a basic understanding of its operation.

As with all such systems, the best way to gain some understanding of GPSS is to consider a simple example and one such is shown in Figure 9.7. This is a GPSS listing of a single-server queuing system which has exponential service and inter-arrival times. This queue type is known as M/M/1 to queuing theorists. The example shown in Figure 9.7 was produced using a PC version of GPSS. To make things easier to follow, the example is shown with line numbers. The listing shows the following:

- *Lines 1–11*: these set up the variables and functions which are needed to model this simple system in GPSS. Note that this version of GPSS has no built-in negative exponential function and that this had to be provided as a histogram as shown in lines 7–11. Lines 2–6 tell the GPSS system that SERVER is entity number 2 (a FACILITY), LINE is entity number 1 (a QUEUE), SYST is entity number 3 (a QUEUE) and that EXPON is the defined function.
- *Lines 12–14*: these define three tables for data collection as the simulation proceeds. Thus, Table 1 is a histogram of times spent by customers queuing in the system. This histogram will have 50 cells, the cell interval will be 4 and the maximum of the first cell will be 1. Histograms are also defined for the time within the system and the imaginary system queue length.

```
GPSSR/PC  V2.1D  26-APR-1989   9:25      PAGE 1
   mm1.LST=mm1.gps

LINE BLOCK

1         *       M/M/1 QUEUE MEAN ARRIVAL TIME=20, MEAN SERVICE TIME =16
2                 RMULT      ,31415
3         SERVER  EQU        2,F
4         LINE    EQU        1,Q        SYMBOLS EQUATED TO
5         SYST    EQU        3,Q        NUMERICAL VALUES
6         EXPON   EQU        1
7         EXPON   FUNCTION   RN$2,C24
8         0,0/.1,.104/.2,.222/.3,.355/.4,.509/.5,.69/.6,.915/.7,1.2
9         .75,1.38/.8,1.6/.84,1.83/.88,2.12/.9,2.3/.92,2.52/.94,2.81
10        .95,2.99/.96,3.2/.97,3.5/.98,3.9/.99,4.6/.995,5.3/.998,6.2
11        .999,7/.9998,8
12        1       QTABLE     1,1,4,50   TIMES SPENT IN QUEUE
13        2       TABLE      Q$3,1,1,50 NUMBER IN SYSTEM
14        3       QTABLE     3,4,4,50   TIMES SPENT IN SYSTEM
15                SIMULATE              RUN SIMULATION
16    1           GENERATE   20,FN$EXPON CUSTOMER ENTERS SYSTEM
17    2           QUEUE      SYST       COLLECTS STATS FOR SYSTEM
18    3           QUEUE      LINE       COLLECTS STATS FOR QUEUE
19    4           SEIZE      SERVER     CUSTOMER GETS SERVER
20    5           DEPART     LINE       FINISH STATS OF QUEUE TIME
21    6           ADVANCE    16,FN$EXPON SERVICE TIME
22    7           RELEASE    SERVER     CUSTOMER LEAVES SERVER
23    8           DEPART     SYST       FINISH STATS OF SYSTEM TIME
24    9           TABULATE   2          COUNT SYSTEM QUEUE
25    10          TERMINATE  1          CUSTOMER DESTROYED
26                START      100,NP     WARM-UP RUN WITH NO PRINT
27                RESET                 ;CLEAR STATISTICS
28                START      999        RUN FOR 1000 TERMINATIONS
29                END
```

Figure 9.7 GPSS program: M/M/1 queue

- *Lines 15–25*: these are the simulation itself.
  - ◇ 16: Generates customers at random intervals sampled from the negative exponential function with mean of 20.
  - ◇ 17: Notes the time that the customer enters the system (an imaginary queue).
  - ◇ 18: Notes the time that the customer enters the queue for the server—as in line 17, this is the creation time of the customer.
  - ◇ 19: When the customer is at the head of the queue, it seizes the server.
  - ◇ 20: At this same time it departs the queue, which allows the GPSS system to compute its time in the queue.
  - ◇ 21: This line computes the service time from the negative exponential function with a mean of 16. The server and customer stay together for that time.
  - ◇ 22: The server is released.
  - ◇ 23: The customer departs the imaginary system queue. This allows the GPSS system to compute the time that the customer has spent within the entire queuing system.
  - ◇ 24: The GPSS system adds the current imaginary system queue length to its histogram.
  - ◇ 25: The customer is now of no interest and so its record is destroyed.
- *Lines 26–29* control the running of the simulation.

Figure 9.7 and the discussion above should make it clear that GPSS employs a version of the process-based approach which is described in Chapter 6. Thus, the analyst must produce a chronological sequence of operations which are modelled as the blocks through which the entity must pass. In the M/M/1 queue, the customers are created as transactions and two 'physical' queues are updated. The first is the customers waiting to be served (queue 1) and the second is the customers waiting to enter the system (queue 3). These queues are held in FIFO order and customers leave queue 1 to be linked to the server until the service is complete. When the service is complete, the customer record in the system queue (queue 3) is removed, the server is freed and the customer is destroyed.

It should be clear that the GPSS approach provides a fast and powerful way to develop certain types of simulation model. It is ideal for certain types of queuing network in which there is relatively limited interaction between classes of transaction. If the system being simulated does contain complicated interactions, e.g. those in which there are operations which involve several classes of entity and for which the operation may be interrupted by exogenous events, then GPSS may not offer the best way forward. Gordon (1979, p. 23) makes it clear that such complex interactions can cause problems for some versions of GPSS. Thus, the main virtue of GPSS is its appealing simplicity, but this simplicity comes at a price—a loss of flexibility for some types of application.

As was mentioned earlier, there are many versions of GPSS available on the market and it would be almost impossible to give a complete list that would be regarded as accurate for more than a short time. Versions exist for most mainframes, super-minis such as the DEC Vaxes, PCs and MacIntosh platforms, and perhaps the version most commonly used nowadays is GPSS/H, from Wolverine

Software (Crain, 1996). Another version which runs on PCs and MacIntosh systems is Micro-GPSS (Stahl, 1990), which extends the scope of a reduced number of the block types of basic GPSS to bring it closer to a programming language. Whether it makes much sense to use a textual modelling approach with a graphical platform such as a MacIntosh is another issue altogether.

9.8.2   SIMAN/ARENA

SIMAN, developed by Dennis Pegden, is sold by Systems Modeling Corporation and, nowadays, SIMAN is marketed as a fundamental part of the ARENA package (Markovitch and Profovich, 1996). An introduction to SIMAN is given in Pegden *et al.* (1990) and the current version of SIMAN is known as SIMAN V. A thorough discussion of its major features is given in Banks *et al.* (1995) and, like the GPSS family, SIMAN is a block-structured language. Thus, a SIMAN program is actually a listing of blocks which have parameters associated with them. For example, the customer process in a queuing system might be represented in something like the sequence of block commands shown in Table 9.1.

If the above were a proper simulation program to be represented by the sequence of block commands, then each would have attributes associated with it, e.g. the QUEUE block can have three attributes (known as operands) associated with it. These are as follows:

- *Queue ID.*   An identifier for the queue. This may an integer or a text expression.
- *Capacity.*   An integer expression that indicates the maximum size of the queue or a logical expression that specifies the conditions under which it is regarded as full.
- *Balk label.*   A label used to identify the block that will specify the action to be taken if an entity balks when there are capacity problems.

Hence, if a customer were to join a queue *WaitingLine*, with a capacity of 5, then the block command would be written as:

QUEUE, WaitingLine, 5;

Only the Queue ID operand is mandatory.

Thus, the basic face presented by SIMAN has close affinities by that presented in

Table 9.1

SIMAN Block	Meaning
CREATE	Create a new customer instance (this implies a time interval)
QUEUE	Place the customer in the queue where it might have to wait
SEIZE	When at the head of the queue, seize the server
DELAY	Hold onto the server until the service is complete
RELEASE	Release the server back into an idle state
DISPOSE	Lose interest in the customer and destroy its record

GPSS. It does, however, include a great many special purpose blocks that are used to model common elements of manufacturing systems such as conveyors.

SIMAN models consist of two files, known as frames:

(1)   The MODEL FRAME: this is the simulation program that describes the logical interaction of the entities that make up the simulation. As should be clear from the simple example above, SIMAN is process-oriented (see Chapter 6).

(2)   The EXPERIMENTAL FRAME: this file is used to control the simulation run, using an appropriate model frame. The experimental frame provides data that is used by the simulation, defines experimental parameters and generates the output of the simulation.

Thus, SIMAN is more than just a simulation programming language, for the ability to control simulation experiments is a fundamental part of its design and this is explains much of its popularity. When a SIMAN simulation program is compiled, the compiler translates both the model and experimental frames and links these to provide executable files.

Early versions of SIMAN came with a separate program, known as CINEMA, which was used to generate animated graphical output. Thus, SIMAN could be used as visual interactive simulation language (see Chapter 8). It is now available with the ARENA environment, which makes it possible to use SIMAN as part of a VIMS. As with other VIMS, the user interacts with ARENA by pointing and clicking within a graphical user interface. In effect, icons are selected to represent the blocks, and fill-in forms are used to parameterise these. Thus, ARENA may be used to support the development of the model and experimental frames and it also supports animated graphical output. ARENA comes with different templates that are designed to support modelling in particular application areas, such as manufacturing or business process re-engineering.

9.9   VISUAL INTERACTIVE MODELLING SYSTEMS (VIMS)

The use of visual interactive modelling systems has been covered in some depth in Chapter 8 and so only a brief review is needed here. Some writers, notably Law and Kelton (1991) refer to these as *simulators*. Most VIMS are aimed at particular application areas such as manufacturing or business process re-engineering. As described in Section 8.3, VIMS rely on the existence of computer operating systems that present a graphical user interface (GUI) such as Microsoft Windows. Examples of VIMS suited to manufacturing include AutoMod (Rohrer, 1996), ProModel (Benson, 1996), Taylor II (King, 1996) and Witness (Thomson, 1996). Systems suited to business process re-engineering include SIMPROCESS (Binun, 1996) and Extend+BPR (Krahl, 1996). A variation on the same theme, but for applications in healthcare systems, is MedModel (Carroll, 1996). Chapter 8 used Micro Saint (Micro Analysis and Design, 1992) as its exemplar for VIMS since, unlike most others, it is not specifically designed for a particular application area.

Models are created using a point-and-click approach with a mouse to select pre-defined simulation objects and place them on-screen. In a manufacturing application, the icons most commonly represent machines and workstations, between which parts flow as they are manufactured. In a business process application, the icons might represent people, computers or other processing stations between which paperwork and messages pass. The paths taken by the parts, paperwork or messages are created on-screen by drawing lines that link the workstation icons together into a logical network. In most such software, the user may click on any icon and open a window which provides fill-in forms by which the object in question may be parameterised, e.g. this may be used to specify the size and speed of a machine. Also, similar fill-in forms are used to specify complicated event logic which cannot be shown directly on the diagram, usually via some form of macro language.

Hence, most of these VIMS employ a network as their underlying generic model. Thus, entities are assumed to flow through a network from node to node. At the nodes they may be delayed as they engage in activity with whatever entities and resources are placed on the nodes. The entities placed at the nodes may also have their own private lives. For example, in a manufacturing application, they may be machines which occasionally fail or are maintained from time to time. Their underlying generic model is a general-purpose simulation program that takes information from the diagram and from the fill-in forms, checks it for consistency and then runs a simulation if all appears to be in order. In most cases, the user must be satisfied with the pre-defined objects provided by the system developer of the VIMS as it is rarely possible to extend these in any useful way. Hence, although VIMS are quick and easy to use, they do have their limitations.

9.10   WHICH TO CHOOSE? HORSES FOR COURSES

9.10.1   VIMS

As should be clear from the brief description of Micro Saint in Chapter 8 and the comments in the previous section, VIMS are simple to use and do not require the user to be fully conversant with the internal operation of a simulation model. This greatly expands the number of people who are able to gain the undoubted benefits of simulation. However, there are a couple of drawbacks which must be stated.

The first is that it is currently impossible to use these systems for very detailed work within large simulations. For such special applications there is little escape from bespoke programming in either a simulation language or a general-purpose language. VIMS are growing more powerful but just may not be suitable for some applications. As an analogy, consider the chore of painting a house which has whitewashed walls and many small Georgian windows. The best way to paint the walls is to use a large roller or a paint spray. However, if these are used on the windows, they tend to obscure the view! For the detailed work on the windows, it is best to use a fine brush—it takes time, but is the only way to produce a good result. VIMS are, in their present states, best thought of as the paint rollers. They offer splendid tools for relatively standard applications. Sometimes, however, bespoke programming is needed.

The second drawback might sound like intellectual snobbery. It is sometimes rather harder to interpret the results of a simulation than to build the model with a

VIMS. This is because many simulations are highly stochastic and their results need careful analysis by people who are reasonably well-trained in statistics. One day there may be AI systems which act as intelligent statistical advisors, but these are not yet on the market. If they existed, they would at least reduce the possibility for horrendous mistakes. But the solution to this problem is not to stop using these systems, it is to educate their users.

9.10.2   Simulation languages

The advantages of simulation programming languages are that they employ a syntax which is both powerful and expressive and that, therefore, they can greatly reduce the time taken to develop a working computer simulation. They make programming a simulation model simpler and more accessible.

Their disadvantages also need to be considered, however. First, the organisation needs to acquire the special software needed to develop, translate and run the simulation programs. As is always the case in commercial software, some of the products available are cheap but others are rather expensive. The issue of continued support is also important for many organisations and this is seen in two considerations. First, it is important that the whole expertise does not rest in the brain of a single employee—a passing bus or the attraction of a long visit to the Pacific may remove that expertise. Second, the organisation needs to be sure that the software vendor can offer long-term support and training.

REFERENCES

Banks, J., Burnette, B., Kozloski, H. & Rose, J. (1995)   *Introduction to SIMAN V and CINEMA V.* Wiley, New York.

Banks, J. & Carson, J. S. (1985)   Process-interaction simulation languages. *Simulation,* **44**(5), 225–236 (May).

Benson, D. (1996)   Simulation modeling and optimisation usingProModel. *Proceedings of the 1996 Winter Simulation Conference,* Coronada, CA, December. The Society for Computer Simulation, San Diego, CA.

Binun, M. (1996)   Business process modelling with SIMPROCESS. *Proceedings of the 1996 Winter Simulation Conference,* Coronada, CA, December. The Society for Computer Simulation, San Diego, CA.

CACI (1985)   *The SIMSCRIPT II.5 Reference Handbook.* CACI, La Jolla, CA.

CACI (1987)   *PC SIMSCRIPT II.5. Introduction and User's Manual,* CACI, La Jolla, CA.

Carroll, D. F. (1996)   MedModel—healthcare simulation software. *Proceedings of the 1996 Winter Simulation Conference,* Coronada, CA, December. The Society for Computer Simulation, San Diego, CA.

Crain, R. C. (1996)   Simulation using GPSS/H. *Proceedings of the 1996 Winter Simulation Conference, Coronada, CA, December.* The Society for Computer Simulation, San Diego, CA.

Charnes, J. M, Morrice, D. M., Brunner, D. T. & Swain, J. J. (1996)   *WSC96: Proceedings of the 1996 Winter Simulation Conference,* Coronada, CA, December. The Society for Computer Simulation, San Diego, CA.

Davey, D. & Vaucher, J. G. (1980)   Self-optimised partitioned sequencing sets for discrete event simulation. *INFOR,* **18**, 41–61.

Fiddy, E., Bright, J. G. & Hurrion, R. D. (1981)   See-Why: interactive simulation on the screen. *Proc. Inst. Mech. Eng.,* C293/81, 167–72.

Gordon, G. (1979)   The design of the GPSS language. In N. R. Adam & A. Dogramaci (eds) *Current Issues in Computer Simulation*. Academic Press, New York.

Gordon, G. (1969)   *System Simulation*. Prentice-Hall, NJ.

Greenberg, S. (1972)   *GPSS Primer*. Wiley, New York.

Hills, P. R. (1971)   *HOCUS*. P-E Group, Egham, Surrey.

Hills, P. R. (1965)   SIMON—a simulation language in Algol. In S. M. Hollingdale (ed.) *Simulation in Operational Research*. English Universities Press, London.

Joines, J. A. & Roberts, S. D. (1996)   Design of object-oriented simulations in C++. *Proceedings of the 1996 Winter Simulation Conference*, Coronada, CA, December. The Society for Computer Simulation, San Diego, CA.

Law, A. M. & Kelton, W. D. (1991)   *Simulation Modeling and Analysis*. McGraw-Hill, New York.

Law, A. M. & Larmey, C. S. (1984)   Introduction to Simulation Using SIMSCRIPT II.5. CACI, La Jolla, CA.

King, C. B. (1996)   Taylor II manufacturing system software. *Proceedings of the 1996 Winter Simulation Conference*, Coronada, CA, December. The Society for Computer Simulation, San Diego, CA.

Kiviat, P. J. (1969)   *Digital Computer Simulation: Computer Programming Languages*. RM-5883-PR, The RAND Corporation, Santa Monica, CA.

Krahl, D. (1996)   Modeling with Extend. In *Proceedings of the 1996 Winter Simulation Conference*, Coronada, CA, December. The Society for Computer Simulation, San Diego, CA.

Kreutzer, W. (1986)   *System Simulation: Programming Languages and Styles*. Addison-Wesley, Sydney.

Markovitch, N. A. & Profozich, D. M. (1996)   ARENA software tutorial. In *Proceedings of the 1996 Winter Simulation Conference*, Coronada, CA, December. The Society for Computer Simulation, San Diego, CA.

Markowitz, H. M., Hansher, B. & Karr, H. W. (1963) *SIMSCRIPT: A Simulation Programming Language*. RAND Corporation RM-3310-pr 1962. Prentice-Hall, Englewood Cliffs, NJ.

Mathewson, S. C. (1989)   The implementation of simulation languages. In M. Pidd (ed.) *Computer Modelling for Discrete Simulation*. Wiley, Chichester.

Micro Analysis & Design (1992)   *Getting Started with Micro Saint for Windows*. Micro Analysis & Design Simulation Software Inc., Boulder, CA.

Mullarney, A. (1996)   MODSIM III—a tutorial. *Proceedings of the 1996 Winter Simulation Conference*, Coronada, CA, December. The Society for Computer Simulation, San Diego, CA.

Pegden, C. D., Shannon, R. E. & Sadowski, R. P. (1990)   *Introduction to Simulation Using SIMAN*. McGraw-Hill, New York.

Pidd, M. (1995)   Object orientation, discrete simulation and the three-phase approach. *J. Opl Res. Soc.*, **46**, 362–374.

Pritsker, A. A. B. (1974)   *The GASP IV Simulation Language*. Wiley, London.

Rohrer, M. W. (1996)   Automod tutorial. *Proceedings of the 1996 Winter Simulation Conference*, Coronada, CA, December. The Society for Computer Simulation, San Diego, CA.

Russell, E. C. (1987)   *SIMSCRIPT II.5 Programming Language*. CACI, La Jolla, CA.

Schriber, T. & Brunner, D. (1996)   Inside simulation software: how it works and why it matters. *Proceedings of the 1996 Winter Simulation Conference*, Coronada, CA, December. The Society for Computer Simulation, San Diego, CA.

Schriber, T. (1974)   *Simulation Using GPSS*. Wiley-Interscience, New York.

Stahl, I. (1990)   *Introduction to Simulation with GPSS on the PC, MacIntosh and VAX*. Prentice-Hall, NY, New York.

Thomson, W. B. (1996)   An introduction to the Witness visual interactive simulator and OLEII automation. *Proceedings of the 1996 Winter Simulation Conference*, Coronada, CA, December. The Society for Computer Simulation, San Diego, CA.

10

Model Testing and Validation

In some sense or other, management scientists strive to be scientific in their work, although what this can mean will vary somewhat between individuals and may depend on the work they are doing. One important aspect of this scientific ideal is the notion that models should be thoroughly tested or validated before use. The idea is that the management scientist should ensure that the model is wholly adequate and appropriate for the task for which it is intended. Simple though this notion of validation may sound, in practice it can be very difficult to validate a simulation model properly.

This chapter considers the problems of validating the types of simulation model commonly used in management science. It shows why this is sometimes difficult and suggests approaches to validation that are practically useful and which are also based on a sound theoretical framework. It focuses on the issues that arise when simulations are performed as part of management science projects, rather than on those that arise in very large-scale simulation projects such as those found in the defence sector. For a thorough discussion of the issues that arise in the latter, see Balci (1994), Sargent (1982) or Miser and Quade (1988).

10.1 THE IMPORTANCE OF VALIDATION

10.1.1 The difficulty of validation

Why is validation of a simulation model so important? There are two fundamental reasons. First, from a practical standpoint, the simulation model is usually being developed with a view to taking some action in a human activity system. Sometimes the model is of a system that already exists but some new insight into its operation is required. For example, manufacturing facilities are increasingly automated and may run at high speed but with little in the way of in-process stocks. It is not unusual for such systems to perform somewhat below the efficiency specified at the design stage. Simulations are often used to understand why this should be so.

On other occasions, the target system exists but the aim of the simulation is to demonstrate that some new mode of operation would be preferable. To take the automated plant example again, having understood why the plant is not performing well, the next stage is to find some way of operating it so as to bring its performances up to the specification. That is, the model can be used for experimentation. This is somewhat more difficult from a validation point of view, because the suggestion may be that the plant is operated in wholly novel ways. There is thus no existing 'real' system with which to compare the results of the simulation experiments.

A third case occurs when the model is of a system which does not yet exist but where possible new designs are being considered. To continue with the automated plant example, the designer usually has several possible plant configurations to consider and must select the one which best meets whatever performance and cost criteria have been agreed. An obvious way to do this is to try to simulate the options and then to compare the results of the various simulations. As with the second case above, the validation problem occurs because there is no 'real' system with which to compare the model.

As well as these practical considerations, there is an important theoretical point to be weighed. The simulation model is, in some sense, a set of beliefs and assumptions about how a system should behave or is intended to behave. The model incorporates rules which are believed to govern the behaviour of the elements and objects of the system. If learning and progress are to occur, then it is important that these beliefs and assumptions be tested in some way or other. Organisations whose beliefs and assumptions are closest to 'reality' are likely to be in a good position to achieve their goals.

10.1.2   The 'real' world, the model and observation

While this is not intended to be a philosophy text, it is important to consider what is meant when we think of comparing a model with what is so often called the 'real' world. Only by understanding this concept of the 'real' world can the difficulty of validation be appreciated.

The easiest concept of all is the model: after all, this is the creation of the modeller or analyst and is intended to be a representation of some system or other. The model may be entirely external and concrete, say as a scale model of a building. On the other hand, it may exist solely within the mind of the modeller as a set of ill-defined concepts and beliefs and may thus be termed a mental model. Between these two extremes of implicit, mental models and explicit, concrete models are various other possibilities, including the models usually associated with computer simulation in management science. The main characteristic of such models is that they are the creations of an individual or a group of people. To be cruel, there is therefore no excuse for the modeller not understanding the model which he/she has created.

What then of the 'real' world? To avoid too many problems, this discussion assumes that some form of reality exists external to an observer. It assumes too that it is possible for two or more independent observers to experience that external reality, even though their descriptions of that same reality may differ. That is, for present purposes it will be assumed that the external reality and the observations of it can exist quite separately. This is an important point, for what is often meant by the 'real' world is some set of observations made by one or more people. If the notion of validation implies a comparison between a model and the 'real' world, this usually implies a comparison between two sets of observations. One set comes from the model, which should be intimately known by its creator, and the other set comes to the observer from the 'real' world. The notion of validity rests very heavily on these observations.

10.1.3   The hypothetico-deductive approach

Popper (1959) argues that scientific method is best seen as theory-driven rather than being driven by independent observation. In this regard, his main argument is that scientific observation is always biased (not necessarily in a sinister way) by pre-existing theory and is therefore not wholly disinterested. Thus, the role of scientific experimentation is the provision of observations which are relevant to particular hypotheses and theories. After all, the experiments are devised to test the theories in some way or other. Popper's main argument is that scientific work depends on the generation of hypotheses from which deductions can be made. These deductions can be tested by properly designed experiments that aim to show whether or not the deductions, and therefore the hypotheses, are correct. More precisely, the experiments may produce observations which support the hypotheses or which refute it.

In another work, Popper (1965) takes this idea slightly further by arguing that conjectures, hypotheses and theories can never by proved in an absolute sense but can only be refuted. That is, all knowledge is in some sense conjectural. A common way of explaining this is to think of the following conjecture:

All swans are white.

Experimentation to test this conjecture is simple enough and involves straightfor-ward observation of all swans—if that were possible. In practice, the experimenter would have to settle for a finite sample of swans and see whether their colour supported the hypothesis. But this creates a problem. Even if all the swans in the sample were white, this does not rule out the possibility that somewhere else there might be a black, blue, green, red or yellow swan. Thus, the experiment could never demonstrate that the conjecture is wholly true. The most decisive experi-mental result of all is one which refutes the conjecture and which leads on to other conjectures.

In Popper's view, therefore, a scientific theory is a conjecture about the 'real' world which may be tested by some form of experimentation. The experimentation may support the theory or may, decisively, refute the theory by demonstrating that it is false. What are popularly referred to as scientific 'laws' are no more than theories which have not been refuted—usually within very specific assumptions (e.g. Newton's laws of motion). That is, they are found to be valid for certain specific purposes.

10.1.4   Validation and comparison

With what can a simulation model be compared for validation? Ideally, it would be compared directly with the system that it will simulate—but, as shown above, this is not always straightforward. This is because the comparison is between two sets of observations, one of the model and one of the 'real' system. Thus, at best, the modeller can be satisfied that the observations of the model display identical characteristics to the observations from the 'real' system. More likely, the two sets are not identical but are similar enough for the purpose in hand. However, it is always possible that some other observations could be made of both systems (model and 'real') in which there is massive disagreement between the two. Thus, in Popperian terms, a valid model is one which is unrefuted within some specific assumptions.

Now this means that models for simulation purposes cannot be shown to be true or valid in any absolute sense. There always remains the possibility of making observations of the model or the 'real' system which are in conflict. What can be said is that a model is valid for some particular purpose, that is, under certain specific assumptions. Validation, then, is to be seen against the intended use of the model and not in an absolute sense.

10.1.5   Experimental frames

Chapter 3 briefly introduced the idea of experimental frames as suggested by Zeigler (1976). This idea is defined by Zeigler in terms of set theory, but the basic idea is quite simple. This is that, when considering the question of the validity of a model, this can only be done against the backdrop of this experimental frame which defines the use to which the model will be put. The same term is used by the developers of the simulation language SIMAN (see Chapter 9), although the meaning is rather different in that context.

Zeigler (1976) is careful to distinguish between the following, which are shown in Figure 10.1.

- *The real system.*   This is defined as the source of observable data. Even if we do not understand the real system, we can still observe its behaviour. The observable data consist of a set of input : output relations which need not be simple.
- *An experimental frame.*   This is defined as the limited set of circumstances under which the real system is to be observed or experimented with.
- *The base model.*   This is defined as some hypothetical model which would account for all of the input : output behaviour of the real system. This may not exist in any tangible form and must be imagined if there is no real system in existence—such as when a new system is being developed from scratch.
- *A lumped model.*   This is defined as an explicit and simplified version of the base model and is the one which will be used in management science.
- *A computer program.*   In which the lumped model is implemented and which is intended to generate the input:output relations of the lumped model.

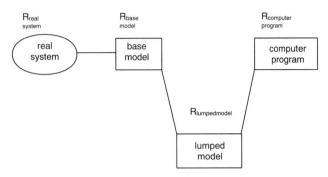

Figure 10.1   Zeigler on modelling

Thus, the idea is that, when faced with the need to develop a model of some complex system, we begin with a base model which we have in mind as we try to build the lumped (or conceptual) model which may then be implemented in a computer program. The intention is that the models should be used in relation to the purposes defined by the experimental frame.

Zeigler (1984) develops a notation system, based on set theory, which allows the convenient expression of some useful ideas. In this chapter we will just use one of these ideas, that of an input:output relation. This embodies the idea of a reference system (Zeigler's real system) as a form of black box that can be observed and from which we can relate inputs to outputs. This is known as the input:output relation of the real system. Zeigler points out that we wish to know the true input:output relation of this system but that in fact we can only observe it at some point of time t (of which there may be many). Ideally, the input:output relation of the model should be the same as that of the computer program and the same as that of the real system.

Program verification and model validation

In Zeigler's terms, *verification* is a process by which we try to assure ourselves that the lumped model is properly realised in the computer program. In one sense this is straightforward, since the lumped model is, by definition, fully specified and the computer program exists in a tangible form. *Validation* is a process whereby we assess the degree to which the lumped model input:output relations map onto those of the real system. This implies the existence of the experimental frame. At its simplest, therefore, Zeigler sees validation and verification as *black box* in approach—see Section 10.2.

This distinction between program verification and model validation is very important in the development of large-scale simulation models that are implemented via proper computer programming and which may be used repeatedly over a long time period. In these terms, verification focuses on the computer program(s) that are supposed to embody the lumped or conceptual model. This implies that the lumped model needs to be unambiguously stated if verification is to be properly done. Hence, for these large-scale exercises, model documentation that is separate from program documentation is absolutely crucial. Verification itself proceeds by a series of formal tests on the simulation program and its components to see if it properly embodies the lumped model.

The first such tests focus on the program code itself and are based on 'walk-throughs' in which the program code is examined line-by-line, preferably by third parties. The use of programming languages that are expressive (see Chapter 9) is a great help in this regard. The second set of tests take program modules and subject them to test inputs to see if the output is as expected. The third group take the entire simulation program and also checks its input:output relations.

As frequently pointed out in this book, many management science simulations make use of visual interactive modelling systems (VIMS) and there is no separate program code as such. In addition, the conceptual model may not exist separately from its VIMS realisation. This is because the model and its realisation may have been developed in a stepwise manner through time. In such cases, the distinction between verification and validation is artificial and can be abandoned.

10.1.6   The importance of process and other aspects

Balci (1994) points out that computer simulation studies are cyclic, in that models are refined gradually and thus simple models become more complex as time progresses. This fits well with the principle of parsimony espoused in Chapter 4. In a proper sense, therefore, assessment and validation are activities which should continue throughout a simulation project. The same should be true of any quantitative modelling in management science that follows the principle of parsimony. Therefore it would be wrong to focus all the assessment and validation effort at the end of a modelling project. Instead it should be a fully fledged part of all stages of the modelling work, part indeed of a critical approach. Balci (*op cit*) suggests tests and assessments that can be made at each point of the simulation modelling cycle. He suggests that many of these could be built into simulation support environments.

Also writing about computer simulation, Robinson (1996) points out that, 'Three terms are often used in the context of simulation model and simulation study assessment: validity, credibility and acceptability'. He quotes Schruben (1980) as arguing that '*credibility* is reflected in the willingness of persons to base decisions on the information obtained from the model'. This is clearly as much a feature of the trust that the model user or client places in the analyst or group building the model as it is in the credibility of the model itself. Acceptability is usually a reference to the entire study, which includes the model and is also clearly a reflection of the relationship between the modeller(s) and the user or client.

10.2   BLACK BOX VALIDATION

As was introduced in Section 1.5.1, it is useful to consider two approaches to the validation of simulation models. As with all such simple typologies, there is bound to be some overlap between the two, but there are also important differences between black box validation and white box validation.

10.2.1   Black box validation: a model's predictive power

As the name suggests, the basic assumption here is that both the model and the 'real' system are black boxes. That is, that the inner workings of both are unknown but that it is possible to observe their results. Thus, the intention is to analyse the function of both so as to decide whether their functioning is sufficiently similar. Notice that this basic assumption of black box validation is quite false, for the modeller actually has little or no excuse for not understanding the detailed working of the model. Despite this, there is still something to be gained from this approach.

The practical strategy of black box validation is simple enough. The behaviour of the 'real' system is observed under specified conditions and the model is then run under conditions which are as close as possible to these. If the model is valid in a black box sense, then the observations of the model should be indistinguishable from those of the 'real' system.

10.2.2   How valid?

If the two sets of observations are to be compared, then some comparison methodology must exist so as to inform that comparison. Most commonly, the comparison is performed using the methods of statistical inference—details of which can be found in most texts on statistics (see, e.g. Wonnacott and Wonnacott, 1982). The notion here is that the observations may be used to test some specific hypothesis, the credibility of the test being expressed as a probability value. For example, the modeller may wish to know whether there is a statistically significant chance of a difference between the mean values of some observations of the model and of others from the 'real' system. This chance is usually expressed as an acceptable probability of error, the idea being that there is a less than $x\%$ chance that the hypothesis is wrongly accepted or rejected.

It should be noted here that the same caveats about classical statistics mentioned later in Section 12.1 also apply here. That is, if the observations of the model or of the 'real' system form a series in which each value is in some way dependent on one or more previous observations (i.e. there is autocorrelation in the series), then the methods of classical hypothesis testing must be used with great care. Most classical hypothesis tests assume that the observations are independent (uncorrelated) and care must be taken to ensure that this is the case. Chapter 12 gives more details.

10.2.3   Validation errors

Statisticians usually distinguish between two types of possible error in hypothesis testing. These are known as Type I and Type II errors and can be applied to black box model validation as follows:

- *Type I errors.* In classical hypothesis testing, these occur when a correct hypothesis is wrongly rejected. In modelling, a Type I error occurs when a valid model is wrongly rejected. Why should this happen? It occurs because of the nature of statistical inference in which there is a finite probability that an error may occur. That is, the tests are designed to achieve a certain percentage reliability. Most users of such tests unthinkingly plump for significance values of 95% or 99%. That is, they allow a 5% or 1% chance that an error may occur. In general, the smaller the acceptable chance of error then the larger must be the samples to test the hypothesis.
- *Type II errors.* These occur when a hypothesis which is actually false is accepted as true by the user of a hypothesis test. Thus, in simulation modelling, such an error occurs when an invalid model is taken to be valid. As with Type I errors, errors of Type II are inevitable from time to time—how often depends on the confidence levels set for the test.

As well as these two error types, it is as well to accept that a much more severe type of error is possible both in hypothesis testing and in model validation. This is usually known as a Type Zero error.

Type Zero errors occur when the modeller/tester simply asks the wrong questions altogether. The result is a model which does totally the wrong thing, possibly in a highly sophisticated and rapid manner. This is probably the most important mistake to avoid in any validation of a simulation model. Expressing it in other terms, it happens when the model is found to be utterly and wholly valid on statistical grounds but turns out to be useless in practice because it addresses the wrong issues. Less severely, a model may include unnecessary detail which leads, due to shortage of time, to a loss of important detail elsewhere in the model.

10.2.4   Testing model components

A black box approach can be applied to the parts of a model as well as to the whole creation. If the model represents a system which does not yet exist then such partial validation is one of the few options open to the would-be validation. In most such simulations, various of the subsystems of the proposed 'real' system do already exist and their performance can be compared with their simulated counterparts. The problem is that there is no guarantee that the whole model is valid just because most of the parts have been tested.

10.3   WHITE BOX VALIDATION

10.3.1   Detailed internal structure

In some ways 'white box' is an unfortunate name, for the assumption is that the model and 'real' system are transparent rather than white. That is, the assumption is that the internal structures of both are well understood. Clearly, this should be the case for the simulation model, so long as the modeller is in tune with his/her own creation. For the 'real' system, this can never be wholly true but can be true enough for useful comparison to occur. White box validation most usefully takes place while the model is being constructed rather than after the event, and is usually applied to the model components in turn. As far as possible, it is also applied to the interaction of the model components.

Whereas the stress in black box validation is on the predictive power of the model as captured in hypothesis tests, the emphasis in white box validation is on the detailed internal workings of the model. In particular, such validation will need to focus on at least the following aspects.

10.3.2   Input distributions

In a discrete event simulation much of the model behaviour depends on the statistical distributions which are chosen to model the objects of the system. The distributions are used to model uncertain or indeterminate behaviour—such as the varying intervals between successive arrivals at a queuing system. They are appropriate when the process which produces this behaviour cannot be understood in any deterministic sense. Most commonly they are used to represent the varying time taken to complete some activity within the simulation.

Selecting the appropriate distribution is sometimes rather difficult and two guidelines may be followed. The first is rather obvious, and that is to select a distribution which behaves in the same way as the object being modelled. Usually, this behaviour of the 'real' object is understood from a statistical analysis of a sample of observations. Thus, the analyst may calculate the mean, variance and higher moments of the distribution. The idea is to specify some distribution for the model with the same values for the mean, variance and other moments. The usual way to do this is to compare a theoretical distribution with the sample data using a goodness-of-fit test, as described in most statistics textbooks. Ideally, the distribution will be a perfect fit to the data sample.

This sounds simple enough, but in practice it is almost unknown for any distribution to be a perfect fit over the sampled data. This is not because of incompetent sampling, but is expected from the theory of sampling. The result is that there may be several candidate distributions for the part of the model under scrutiny. None will fit perfectly and several may have their own distinct advantages. Which should be chosen?

To avoid this difficulty, the modeller should follow the second guideline. This is to bear in mind the assumptions which underlie the behaviour of the object in the 'real' system and the assumptions of the distribution. Ideally these should be well suited to one another in at least the following ways:

(1)   *Discrete or continuous variables.* Some distributions (e.g. the negative exponential and Normal distributions) are continuous (i.e. the variable may take any of the infinite set of values in the specified range). Others (e.g. the binomial and Poisson distributions) are discrete (i.e. the variable may only

take integer values within the specified range). It should therefore be obvious that the selected distribution should be continuous or discrete, depending on the variable being modelled.

(2)   *Infinite or finite range.*   Some distributions (for example, the Normal distribution) actually assume that the variable is distributed from negative infinity to positive infinity. Others (e.g. the negative exponential) assume that the value may range from zero to positive infinity. A third group, such as the uniform distribution, may be specified over a finite range. The modeller must ensure that the distribution selected has a range appropriate to the values taken by the variable.

(3)   *The process producing the values.*   All analytical distributions have underlying assumptions which specify how the distributed values arise. For example, the Poisson, negative exponential and Gamma distributions assume there is an underlying Poisson process. Put simply, if a source of entirely random occurrences is imagined, then it is a Poisson process if:

- The number of occurrences in any non-overlapping time intervals is entirely independent;
- The distribution of the number of occurrences in any interval depends only on the length of that interval;
- In any very small time interval there is a negligible chance of more than one occurrence.

For a more mathematical statement of these assumptions see any mathematical statistics text, such as Meyer (1970). Other distributions have their own assumptions, which need to be understood. Thus, it is important for simulation modellers to have a good grounding in statistics in order to appreciate the limitations of any of the distributions which they might select for a particular model.

10.3.3   Static logic

Most simulations include some static logic which governs the behaviour of the objects of the system. In a discrete simulation these are rules of the type of:

If (conditions) then (actions)

For example, a rule might specify that a machine cannot be started unless its tools are set, the operative is available, a job is waiting for completion and the material supply exists. These rules are intended to mimic those which govern the objects of the 'real' system. In a continuous simulation they are more likely to be rules which govern the behaviour of the system in extreme conditions, such as when a variable reaches a critical value. Rules of this latter type are obviously also present in discrete simulations. If this static logic is wrong then the model cannot correctly mimic the behaviour of the 'real' system and thus it is of some importance to subject them to detailed scrutiny. It is better that this is done before the model is fully programmed, although sometimes such logic errors only become obvious when a programmed model is in use.

The key to checking for such errors is to use the knowledge of all the people involved in the study and not just that of the modeller. Most commonly, the client of the study and the users of the results will know more about the system than the modeller. It is therefore crucial to tap this knowledge in some way or other. The problem is the technical jargon which surrounds most computing studies. There are two approaches to this problem and ideally they will be used together.

The first is to use non-technical methods of expressing the model logic. Hence, before the model is built the modeller could use natural-language descriptions of the logic or could rely on simple flow diagrams such as activity cycle diagrams (see Chapter 4). The idea is to allow the clients and users to participate in the validation and to use their knowledge. If possible, the users could participate in the construction of such diagrams or verbal descriptions during a joint session.

The second approach is to find some rapid way of prototyping the model into a working program which employs animated graphics to show the model state. Chapter 8 gives details of doing the latter for discrete simulation. Systems such as Stella (see Chapter 14) for system dynamics are a useful way of rapidly developing models on-screen and then running them immediately. For discrete systems, VIMS such as Witness (Thomson, 1996) allow the modeller to set up prototypes quickly from an activity cycle diagram and then to run the resulting model. These systems allow participation in validation by the rapid revision and re-running of models.

10.3.4 Dynamic logic

If a simulation were simply concerned with the static logic of the objects of the system then it would be quite unnecessary. Why simulate what is already fully understood? A simulation is used to mimic the dynamic behaviour of system and not just of its individual components. Thus it is important to be able to validate the dynamic performance of the model as it runs—or, at the very least, during a run.

Perhaps the best way of doing this is to make sure that animated displays are an integral part of the simulation program. Thus, important variables and the system state can be monitored as the program runs and this can make it relatively easy to spot errors in the dynamic logic of the model. As with the static logic, it is sensible to make use of the knowledge of the clients and possible users of the simulated system by making the dynamic display as easy to understand as possible.

Before the availability of cheap graphical systems and interactive operating systems, this was a tedious task which involved sifting through piles of printout. Fortunately, this is rarely necessary nowadays. The key, then, is the dynamic display of crucial features of the system state as the program runs on the computer. As described in Chapter 8, if the system state is represented by carefully chosen icons, tables and graphs it is easily possible to monitor the progress of the system as the model runs. It is also possible to interact directly with the running program; then it may be possible to force the simulation into extreme conditions as a further test of its validity.

10.4   TYPE ZERO ERRORS

Section 10.2.3 introduced the concept of Type Zero, I and II errors, the latter pair being well known to statisticians. Type Zero errors arise from an inadequate attempt at problem structuring and are as liable to occur in simulation modelling as in any other management science activity. Throughout this book runs an assumption that simulation models evolve over time and are extremely unlikely to be correct on a first attempt. Hence, earlier Chapters lay great stress on modelling and programming practices which lead to modular programs which are relatively easy to modify. Accepting that the first attempts to build a particular model are likely to end in, at best, partial success is the starting point for avoiding serious Type Zero errors.

10.4.1   Over-elaboration

One common mistake in simulation modelling is to make the model too elaborate in an attempt to capture as much realism as possible. This occurs because a simulation approach offers a relatively low level of abstraction, compared, say, to mathematical models. Thus, it is possible to develop very detailed simulation models which mimic very closely the fine interaction of the objects of the 'real' system. This is not always a good thing.

For example, consider a simulation of an arrivals terminal of an international airport. As passengers disembark from the aircraft, they must pass through customs, immigration and (sometimes) an agricultural checkpoint. Meanwhile, their baggage should be unloaded from the aircraft hold and routed to the correct carousel for the passengers to collect it. When designing a new arrival area, one consideration is that passengers should not be subject to unnecessary delay. As in a factory, the key to this is the sizing and speed of operation of the sequence of processes through which the passengers pass. An important feature of this is the size of baggage carousels—thus, baggage-handling systems have been the subject of several simulation studies. It is very tempting, partly because this is encouraged by some of the commercial simulation software, to try to track each individual item of baggage and each passenger through the system. In most cases, this is quite unnecessary as all that matters is whether congestion occurs at certain points within the system and not whether particular (simulated) bags or customers are involved. This avoids having to build an elaborate and slow-running simulation model which addresses the wrong issues.

10.4.2   Over-simplification

On the other hand, it is all too easy to over-simplify and the result may be a model which has insufficient detail to handle the full complexity of the simulated system. In the case of a handling system for specialised cargo, it may be crucially important to know how long it takes to process particular types of object. In such cases, it may be necessary to track the individual lives of each item as objects of the simulation model.

10.4.3   Steering a sensible course

There are two keys to avoiding over-simplification and over-elaboration. The first is to ascertain, as soon as possible, the intended use of the model. If detailed results are needed then a detailed model may be required—at a cost. The second is to adopt an explicit and evolutionary approach to model and program development. If the model starts simply, it can probably be elaborated gradually as the need arises. It is better to get a skeleton, but simple, model working than to have an over-elaborate disaster that no one understands.

REFERENCES

Balci, O. (1994)   *Validation, verification and testing techniques throughout the life cycle of a simulation study.* In O. Balci (ed.) *Annals of Operations Research*, Vol 23: *Simulation and Modeling.* J. C. Balzer, Basel.

Meyer, P. L. (1970)   *Introductory Probability and Statistical Applications* (2nd edn). Addison-Wesley, Reading, MA.

Miser, H. J. & Quade, E. S. (1988)   *Validation.* In H. J. Miser & E. S. Quade (eds) *Handbook of Systems Analysis: Craft Issues and Procedural Choices.* Wiley, Chichester.

Popper, K. R. (1959)   *The Logic of Scientific Discoveries.* Hutchinson, London.

Popper, K. R. (1965)   *Conjectures and Refutations.* Routledge, London.

Robinson, S. W. (1996)   Service quality management in the process of delivering a simulation study. Paper presented to the 14th Triennial Conference of the International Federation of OR Societies, July 8–12, Vancouver, BC.

Sargent, R. G. (1982)   Verification and validation of simulation models. In F. E. Cellier (ed.) *Progress in Modelling and Simulation.* Academic Press, London.

Schruben, L. W. (1980)   Establishing the credibility of simulations. *Simulation*, **34**(3), 101–105.

Thomson, W. B. (1996)   An introduction to the Witness visual interactive simulator and OLEII automation. *Proceedings of the 1996 Winter Simulation Conference*, Coronada, CA, December. The Society for Computer Simulation, San Diego, CA.

Wonnacott, J. R. & Wonnacott, R. H. (1982)   *STATISTICS, Discovering Its Power.* Wiley, New York.

Zeigler, B. P. (1976)   *Theory of Modelling and Simulation.* Wiley, New York.

Zeigler, B. P. (1984)   *Multi-faceted Modelling and Discrete Event Simulation.* Academic Press, New York.

11

Sampling Methods

11.1 BASIC IDEAS

It should be clear from the previous chapters that many discrete event simulations include elements that are random or stochastic. For example, in the harassed booking clerk problem we do not know how long a service will take, all that we know is that the service times follow a probability distribution. In the Micro Saint model of Joe's Exhaust Parlour in Chapter 8, a proportion of the car owners decide not to have their car exhausts replaced, although we do not know which ones. Such instances are common in virtually all discrete event simulations and therefore many systematic approaches have been developed to aid this sampling.

It is important to realise that the modeller must decide whether to model something within a system by a sampling procedure. It is a moot point, philosophically, whether the real world contains any randomness, for some would argue that probabilities are simply statements about our uncertain state of knowledge rather than descriptions of what is actually there. For example, consider a production process of the type often used to produce large quantities of chocolate bars. These are typically deposited on a moving conveyor that carries them through a cooling tunnel and into wrapping and packing machines. The conveyors might be a metre or two across and, were the equipment all to be working properly, each row of chocolate bars would be identical and evenly spread across the conveyor with no gaps. However, in reality there are often gaps in the rows of chocolate bars and it is not unusual to see something like Figure 11.1 when viewing these conveyors. The gaps appear for many reasons, all of which could be determined if necessary. However, it may be perfectly acceptable to model the appearance of gaps as if it were a random process if all we wish to know is the number of chocolate bars to be wrapped. In such a case, a probability distribution could be used to represent this statistic, rather than bothering to determine the cause of each and every gap.

On other occasions, it might (paradoxically) be acceptable to model something that appears to be probabilistic as if it were deterministic. For example, although the time taken for a product to appear in a warehouse after ordering it from the manufacturer may be known to vary slightly by a day or two, it may be acceptable to use the average delay when looking at the monthly operations of the warehouse and its distribution systems. The important point is to ensure that the decision of whether or not to include probability distributions is taken sensibly in the light of the variation seen in the system. All models are approximations, and the aim, as discussed in Chapter 10, is to develop a model that is appropriate for its intended purpose.

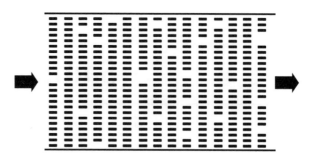

Figure 11.1   Stochastic or deterministic variation?

11.1.1   General principles of random sampling

Random sampling is used within a discrete simulation so as to produce from a probability distribution a set of samples that have two important properties. Firstly, the samples that are produced should have the same distribution as the probability distribution from which they are taken. That is, the distribution of the samples should be in the same proportions as the distributions from which they come. In statistical terms, the sample moments (the mean, the variance, etc.) should be the same as the population moments (the mean, the variance, etc.), as shown in Figure 11.2. In fact, this will never be the case, since an infinite sample size would be needed to guarantee this. Instead, the sample moments should be adequate estimates of those from the population. Thus, the first aim in random sampling is to produce a set of samples that are representative of the distribution from which they come.

The second aim in random sampling is to ensure that when a set of samples is placed in the sequence in which it is produced, there is no unintended pattern in that sequence. That is, *random* samples are required, otherwise probability theory

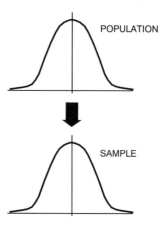

Figure 11.2   Representative samples

does not apply and it is crucial, when analysing simulation output (see Chapter 12) that this theory should apply.

11.1.2 Top-hat sampling

Chapter 2 introduced the basic ideas of sampling from histograms in the disk failure example of Section 2.3.2. The approach used in Chapter 2 is often known as 'top-hat sampling' and it illustrates the basic principles of most random sampling algorithms. The example was based upon the histogram shown here in Figure 11.3, and the sampling method relied upon the conversion of the histogram into the cumulative form that is also shown in Figure 11.3. Samples were taken from the probability distribution by using the vertical axis of the distribution (which runs from 0 to 1) and using a random number (distributed from 00 to 99) to select a point on that axis. Thus, a value of 45 points to a life of 4 days in Figure 11.3.

The approach is called 'top-hat sampling' because it could be conducted as follows:

(1) Take 100 counters (use poker chips or tiddly-winks) and number them in the same proportion as the life distribution of the disks. Hence, 5% should be marked with the number 1, 15% with the number 2, 20% with the number 30, 30% with the number 4, 20% with the number 5 and 10% with the number 6.

(2) Place all 100 counters in a hat, preferably a top-hat, and shake it so that the counters are randomly distributed in the top-hat.

(3) Without looking into the hat, place a hand inside and select, at random, a counter and write down the number that is written on it.

(4) Replace the counter in the hat, shake the hat and repeat the sampling until enough samples have been produced.

This procedure is an example of sampling with replacement. The hope is that, if enough samples are taken, the sample histogram will be the same shape and at the

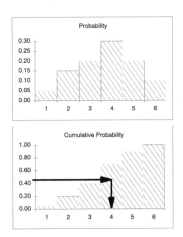

Figure 11.3 Top-hat sampling

same position as the histogram in Figure 11.3. The unseen selection of randomly distributed counters should guarantee that the samples occur in a random sequence.

As employed in a discrete event simulation, top-hat sampling does not rely on a top-hat and counters. Instead, the method relies on random numbers. The random numbers are usually distributed on the interval 0 to 1 (but excluding the value 1 itself), which is usually written down as (0, 1). They are converted into the correct distribution by using a look-up table. In the example of Chapter 2, for which the histogram is shown in Figure 11.3, the table might be as follows, if the random numbers are accurate to two decimal places. The random numbers correspond to the edges of the steps that occur on the cumulative histogram of Figure 11.3. Hence, for each random number, the look-up table can be examined to find the life of the disk unit to which it corresponds:

Life	Random numbers
1	0.00–0.04
2	0.05–0.19
3	0.20–0.39
4	0.40–0.69
5	0.70–0.89
6	0.90–0.99

11.1.3 The fundamental random sampling process

In principle, the random sampling algorithms used in discrete event simulations are based on the same two stage process that underlies top-hat sampling, which is as follows:

(1) Produce one or more random numbers.
(2) Convert these random numbers into samples from the required distribution, either by using a look-up table or by employing a suitable algorithm.

The rest of this chapter will describe the main features of random numbers as used in discrete simulation and will show some of the common algorithms used as stage two of the process.

11.1.4 Use of pre-written libraries of algorithms

In many cases, it is not necessary to write code to implement these algorithms, since there are libraries of these routines available from a number of sources, written in common programming languages such as C, C++, Pascal and FORTRAN. Examples include the NAG libraries, widely used in the UK and the ISML libraries widely used in the USA. In addition, there are sites on the Internet that include code which can be downloaded for random number generation and for generation of samples from probability distributions. A suitable search engine should find the appropriate sites.

11.2   RANDOM NUMBER GENERATION

So far, the question 'What is meant by random?' has been carefully ignored, but it is important to understand that term. An obvious point is that it is not sensible to speak of any single number as 'random'. There is no such thing as a single random number. Generally, what is meant by randomness is that the process which produces the number is not deterministic, that is, we cannot be sure what number will be produced next. In this sense, the idea of 'randomness' is a confession of ignorance that relates to the process producing the numbers and not to the numbers themselves. Consequently, early random number generators were produced by physical processes that were believed to be inherently random in this way.

11.2.1   Truly random numbers

Streams of numbers that have been produced by a process that is believed to be random are usually described as 'truly random numbers'. One example might be the spinning of a roulette wheel. This is rather a slow method of producing random numbers, yet some people find these devices to be of compelling interest. Another example might be the throw of six-sided dice, with which the same group of people also seem to be fascinated.

A discrete event simulation usually needs long streams of random numbers and this precludes the use of these manual devices for practical purposes. It is possible to devise truly random generators that are much faster by using electronic and radio-active devices. Most machines that draw lottery numbers around the world are of this type, because the truly random nature of their operation is very important and no suggestion of favouritism in their selection of numbers can be allowed. These fast physical devices rely on particle emission theories such as those from radio-active sources. In these, the number of particles emitted in a short time period is known to be random. Hence, something like a Geiger counter can be used to count these particles in each unit time interval and these can be converted into random numbers on the unit interval. Tocher (1963) describes several such generators that are of historical interest. However, these truly random devices are not used in discrete event simulation for reasons other than their unfortunate effect on transistors and on humans.

11.2.2   Pseudo-random numbers

A discrete event simulation can be regarded as a complex sampling experiment. As the simulation proceeds, samples are taken from various distributions and are combined to produce the behaviour of the model. That is, many of the conditions within the simulation are determined by the results of the random samples and their combination. The random samples themselves are determined by the random numbers used to produce them. If a simulation is being used to compare various ways of operating a system, it is clearly important to ensure that each policy is examined under the same conditions. These conditions are at least partially determined by the samples taken, which are themselves determined by the random numbers used. Hence, to control a simulation and to ensure fair comparisons, it may be important to ensure that the same random numbers are used for each policy alternative. For this reason, it is important that the stream of random numbers be reproducible.

An obvious way round this problem would be to use a truly random device to generate a stream of random numbers and then to store these numbers in some way or other. They could then be used several times, once for each policy option. Random number tables, as found in most books of statistical tables, are examples of numbers treated in this way. One such random number table was produced by the RAND Corporation (RAND Corporation, 1955) and consists of a million random digits. In principle, such a sequence could be stored on a disk file and then read into a computer simulation as the numbers are needed. If computer memory were unlimited, they could be read from RAM instead.

However, there are other ways to proceed, once it is realised that even truly random numbers cannot really be random once they have been written down. How can they be random if we know what is coming next by looking at the list or table in which they are stored? Once held in this way, the list is determined and the sequence is deterministic. This suggests another approach, the use of methods that are deterministic, but which produce streams of numbers that look as if they are random. These pseudo-random numbers are produced by generators that are based on well-understood mathematics. The streams of numbers that they produce pass the same tests as those passed by truly-random numbers, if we were to pretend that we have no idea how the pseudo-random numbers were produced. That is, they are good enough to fool an observer who is ignorant of the method by which they are generated.

11.2.3   Congruential generators

Although many methods have been used over the years to produce pseudo-random numbers, the consensus for some time has been that congruential generators are satisfactory for most discrete event simulations in management science. It should be noted, though, that L'Ecuyer (1994) points out that other approaches should be used if very long streams of random numbers are required. They were first proposed by Lehmer (1951) and they have the following general form:

$$X_{i+1} = aX_i + c \pmod{m} \qquad \text{for } i = 0, 1, 2, \ldots, n$$

Where:

- $\{X_i\}$ is a stream of random integers on the interval $(0, m-1)$;
- c and m are constants, where a is known as the multiplier, c as the increment (or additive constant) and m as the modulus;
- X_0, the initial value of the stream, is known as the seed, and $\pmod{m}$ means divide the right hand side by m and use the remainder as the result.

As a trivial example, suppose that $a = 3$, $c = 0$, $m = 5$ and $X_0 = 4$. This gives a generator of the form: $X_{i+1} = 3 X_i \pmod 5$. Hence, its operation is as follows:

i	X_i	$3X_i$
0	4	12
1	2	6
2	1	3
3	3	9
4	4	12
5	2	6

This simple example illustrates two important points about these generators: first, that their maximum value is $m - 1$; second, that they are cyclic or periodic. That is, once a value recurs, then the generator will repeat itself. In the above example, $X_4 = X_0$, $X_5 = X_1$, and in general, $X_{i+4} = X_i$ for all values of i.

These congruential generators produce integers on the range $(0, m - 1)$ and this integer series is converted to values on the range $(0, 1)$ by dividing the integers by m. That is:

$$\{U_i\} = \{X_i/m\} \quad \text{for} \quad i = 0, 1, 2, \dots n$$

where $\{U_i\}$ is on the range $(0, 1)$ and X_i is on the range $(0, m - 1)$.

When referring to 'random numbers' in the rest of this chapter, this term will mean that they are uniformly distributed on $(0, 1)$, unless stated otherwise.

11.2.4   General requirements for these generators

It is clear, from the simple example above, that the selection of the values given to the parameters a, c and m is crucial in determining whether the random number generator will be of any practical use. In general, we wish to ensure that the generator has a number of features:

(1)   The numbers produced should be uniformly distributed over the interval $(0,1)$. That is, all values within the this range should occur with equal frequency.

(2)   The numbers produced should be independent of one another. That is, any particular value cannot be predicted from the remainder of the sequence. In statistical terms, this means that the sequence of values ($\{X_i\}$ and $\{U_i\}$) should have no serial correlation. This means that all values should be equally likely to occur anywhere in the sequence, as should all pairs of values, triples and n-tuples.

(3)   The cycle length (or period) should be as long as possible. The maximum period for a congruential generator is m, as the values may range from 0 to $m - 1$. Some generators do not have a full period, since some values are missed. The larger the value of m, the larger the maximum period of the generator. Whether the generator will have a full period will depend on the values chosen for the parameters.

(4)   Since many discrete simulations require a large number of random numbers, the arithmetic needs to be fast so as to ensure efficiency at run-time.

Number theory provides the key to the selection of values for the parameters so as to meet these four requirements. For a useful survey of this theory and its application see Knuth (1981). Fishman (1978) and Ripley (1987) also provide good coverage of the same issues.

11.2.5   Multiplicative congruential generators

These are simpler than the general form, as they have the increment c set to zero. Their recurrence relation is therefore as follows for their underlying integer sequence:

$$X_{i+1} = aX_i \,(\text{mod } m) \qquad i = 0, 1, 2, ..., \text{n}$$

The maximum period for a multiplicative generator is $m - 1$, since the integer sequence must exclude the value 0. To ensure a full period within this range, the integer seed (X_0) and the modulus (m) must be relatively prime. That is, their only common divisor must be 1. Perhaps the simplest way to ensure that this condition is met is to use a large prime number for the modulus. One commonly used generator that has good statistical properties and a maximum period of $m - 1$ uses the following values:

$$a = 16,807 \quad \text{and} \quad m = 2^{31} - 1 = 2,147,483,647$$

this value of m being the largest integer if 32-bit arithmetic is used. This generator is very simple to program using integer arithmetic in any computer that permits 32-bit long integers.

Fishman (1978) suggests that the same value of $m = 2^{31} - 1$ can be used with a multiplier of $a = 630,360,016$ and that the generator will behave well. Kleijnen and van Groenendaal (1992) add the values of 397,204,094 and 950,706,376 to this list. Hence, with 32-bit integer arithmetic, the following values are held to be the basis of reasonable multiplicative congruential generators:

m	2,147,483,647			
a	16,807	630,360,016	397,204,094	950,706,376

However, it should be noted that unless m is a prime number, which is the case with the value 3,147,483,647, then the generator should always be given an odd number as its seed. For a larger list of possible values for a, with $m = 2^{31} - 1$, see Fishman and Moore (1986).

With personal computers it is straightforward to program the prime modulus generator described above, being sure to use long integer (32-bit) arithmetic. If only 16-bit arithmetic is available, then some programming languages (e.g. Turbo Pascal and Borland C) allow integer overflow. What this means is that, with integer arithmetic, if the result of a computation returns a number that exceeds the maximum integer value $(2^{15} - 1$, or 32,767, for 16-bit arithmetic) its sign is reversed and 32,768 is subtracted from its value. This, of course, only applies if the number is in the range 32,768–65,535. In this way, the period of the generator can be extended from 32,787 to 65,535. As ever, care must be taken to ensure that suitable values are used for a and for X_0.

If faced with the task of programming a multiplicative congruential random number generator in machine code then the arithmetic is much faster if m is put to some power of 2. This is because the division necessary to compute the modulus operation is replaced by a shift m places to the left. This is analogous to division by some power of 10 in decimal arithmetic. For example, if the number 123,456 is divided by 1,000 (that is by 10^3), then the division produces 123.456, i.e. the decimal point has shifted 3 places to the left. This means that 123,456 (mod 10^3) is immediately seen to be 456, i.e. the right hand three digits. The same principle applies in binary arithmetic.

Clearly, if m is made some power of 2 then the seed X_0 must be an odd number to guarantee much from the generator. The selection of a value for a, the multiplier, is also important if m is some power of 2. Knuth (1981) gives proofs for the assertion that, if a computer employs w-bit arithmetic, then suitable values are guaranteed if the following conditions hold:

$m = 2^{w-1}$ where $w \geqslant 5$;
$\quad a \equiv 3$ or 5 (mod 8);
i.e. $a = \pm 3 + 8k$ where k is some positive integer.

This implies, of course, that X_0 is odd, as will be all further values $\{X_i\}$ in the integer sequence. This means that the period will be, at most, $m/4$. Although multiplicative generators using m as some power of 2 may provide good, uniform coverage of their period, there is no guarantee that they will be well-behaved from a statistical point of view.

11.2.6 Improving on simple generators

Multiple recursive generators

A number of ways of improving on simple congruential generators have been suggested and two, both of value, are discussed here. The first, known as multiple recursive generators, use linear combinations of previous values as follows:

$$X_{i-1} = a_1 X_i + a_2 X_{i-1} + \ldots + a_t X_{i-t-1} \text{ (mod } m)$$

Thus, they rely on the storage of a number of previous values generated by the congruential recurrence relationship. As an example:

$$X_{i+1} = (19{,}031 X_i + 9298 X_{i-1}) \text{ (mod } 65{,}536)$$

is a generator with a long period, but whose statistical properties are poor—as will be seen later. A better example:

$$X_{i+1} = (10{,}7374{,}182 X_i + 104104{,}480 X_{i-4}) \bmod (2^{31} - 1)$$

is reported by L'Ecuyer, who claims that it passes virtually all statistical tests applied to pseudo-random number generators and can therefore be whole-heartedly recommended.

The advantage of such combinations is that they produce generators with a long period, but understanding their statistical properties can be very difficult.

Shuffling

A second approach is to use a composite generator and shuffle its output. These can be used with 16-bit generators that have an inherently short period and they work as in the following example. Consider two multiplicative congruential generators, g_1 and g_2:

(1)   Fill a vector **V** with the first k values from g_1, which gives $\mathbf{V} = (V_1, V_2, ..., V_k)$.
(2)   Use g_2 to generate a value i on $U(1, 2, ..., k)$.
(3)   Select the ith value of **V**, and use V_i as the required sample.
(4)   Generate another value from g_1 and use it to replace V_i.

These generators produce behaviour which is statistically very good and which has a very long period. Their only snag is that it is hard to determine seeds that allow sampling to begin at some defined point in the cycle.

11.2.7   Using in-built random number generators

Most programming languages and spreadsheets provide their own in-built random number generators but the manuals are often remarkably coy about the details. If in doubt, the advice is to test the generator using one of methods described in the following sections. There is a further problem with many of these in-built generators and this is that each run of a program may only permit the user to use a single seed. As will become clear in the next chapter, this is often not good enough if we wish to minimise the sampling errors that occur due to short(ish) run lengths.

11.3   TESTING RANDOM NUMBER GENERATORS

It is important to realise that the selection of values for a, c and m when designing a suitable congruential generator is done with the aim of meeting the requirements listed in Section 11.2.4. These refer to independent uniform distribution, to long periods and to fast generation. The current section is concerned with tests that may be applied to the output of a generator to see whether it is statistically well-behaved. As mentioned earlier, randomness is rather a difficult property to define for pseudo-random sequences. Knuth (1981) quotes Lehmer (1951) as saying that a random sequence 'is a vague notion embodying the idea of a sequence in which each term is unpredictable to the uninitiated and whose digits pass a certain number of tests, traditional with statisticians and depending somewhat on the uses to which the sequence is put'. Knuth (*op cit*) tries to make this rather vague statement more precise by specifying the mathematical properties necessary if a sequence is to be considered as random.

The testing of the sequences produced by these generators is mainly concerned with establishing whether they display the statistical properties that would be expected in a sequence produced by a truly random generator. Thus, most of the tests are used to examine a sequence for uniform distribution and for statistical independence. Note, however, that uniformity is guaranteed with a full period generator, which simplifies the task of checking a purpose-designed generator. The literature of random number generation contains many suggested tests and these include variations on most standard non-parametric statistical tests. Generators designed for very specific purposes may need to be tested in very specific ways.

It ought to be true that the generators provided with commercially produced discrete simulation software are known to be good. However, this cannot be guaranteed and, unless published evidence is available, it is as well to remain sceptical about these generators. This means that, when using such software for the first time, it is worth spending some effort in testing the generator or in getting the software vendor to show that the generator is sound.

11.3.1   Scatter plots

Before getting immersed in the conventional statistical tests of random number generators, it can be illuminating to take a different approach by the use of scatter plots. If a series of values $\{U_i\}$ is being examined, then a scatter plot may be displayed on a computer screen with the vertical axis representing U_k and the horizontal axis representing U_{k-n}, where n is the lag or interval between the two values. What is being sought is a random scatter of points around the square, that is there should be no obvious patterns. If obvious patterns are apparent then this suggests that the random number generator which produced the sequence may have its problems. The person most associated with these plots is Ripley (1977) who provides an overall approach to such spatial patterns.

As an illustration, consider the two scatter plots of Figures 11.4 and 11.5. That of Figure 11.4 was produced by a generator which clearly has problems. The generator is a linear combination congruential one of the form:

$$X_{i+1} = 19,031X_i + 9298X_{i-1} \ (\text{mod } 65,536)$$

It was designed to utilise the overflow available for 16-bit integers within Turbo

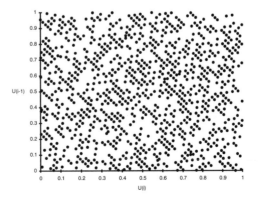

Figure 11.4   Scatter plot: bad generator, $n = 1000$

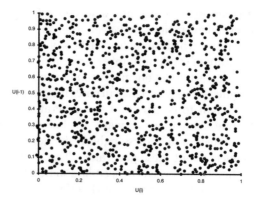

Figure 11.5   Scatter plot: better generator, $n = 1000$

Pascal. The scatter plot shows the first 1000 pairs of consecutive values and the regular lattice is apparent after only a few hundred pairs of values are plotted. The generator also has a short period—indeed, the number of pairs needed before the lattice is complete is a good indicator of the period of the generator.

The next plot, shown in Figure 11.5, is from a rather better generator, this time the simple multiplicative generator with the form:

$$X_{i+1} = 16,807X_i \quad (\mathrm{mod}\ 2^{31} - 1)$$

As with the previous figure, the plot of Figure 11.5 shows the first 1000 pairs of values and, although not perfect, has no obvious lattice structure. Indeed, allowing the generator to run for 30,000 pairs produces a nicely filled square. This generator has a long period as it is based on 32-bit arithmetic.

11.3.2   Auxiliary sequences

The tests that follow can sometimes be applied to the $(0,1)$ series $\{U_i\}$ or must, otherwise, be applied to a sequence of integer values. If the tests are being applied to a purpose-designed generator for which the underlying integer series is accessible, then they may be applied to that sequence $\{X_i\}$. If this sequence is not accessible then the integer tests must be applied to an auxiliary sequence $\{Y_i\}$, which consists of integer values distributed on the interval 0 to $d-1$ obtained by computing $d.\{U_i\}$ and putting $\{Y_i\}$ equal to the integer part of $d.\{U_i\}$.

The following tests assume that those which require integer values are applied to the auxiliary sequence $\{Y_i\}$, but they could be applied to the underlying integer sequence $\{X_i\}$ if that is available.

11.3.3   Frequency tests

These tests aim to check whether the values are uniformly distributed in the sequence. They are not needed if a full period generator is being used. Two basic forms are in use. The first applies a chi-square test to either the auxiliary series $\{Y_i\}$ or to the $(0, 1)$ series $\{U_i\}$.

(1) If the auxiliary series $\{Y_i\}$ is being tested, then for each integer in the period of the generator (which will be 0 to $d-1$) count the number of times that the value occurs in sequence of n values. For the chi-square test, this gives an expected frequency of n/d for each integer. These may be compared with the observed count of these integers on $d-1$ degrees of freedom.

(2) If the series $\{U_i\}$ is being tested, then the usual approach is to divide the range $(0, 1)$ into s equal sub-intervals with the intention of counting the number of values found in each sub-interval. Thus, if a sequence of n values is being examined, their expected frequency will be n/s in each sub-interval if they are uniformly distributed. These may be compared with the observed frequencies on $s-1$ degrees of freedom.

Alternatively, a Kolmogorov–Smirnov test may be applied directly to the series $\{U_i\}$.

11.3.4 Serial test

This, and the other tests that follow, aims to assess whether the values in the sequence are independently distributed. A simple version of this test takes pairs of values from the auxiliary sequence $\{Y_i\}$ and examines the frequency with which they occur by applying a goodness-of-fit test to the observed and expected values.

Assuming a sequence of length $2n$, consider the pairs of values:

$$(Y_0, Y_1), (Y_2, Y_3), (Y_4, Y_5), \ldots, (Y_{2k}, Y_{2k+1}), \ldots$$

There are d^2 such values on the integer interval $(0, d-1)$, and thus a chi-square test with d^2-1 degrees of freedom may be used, the expected frequencies of each pair being $2n/d^2$.

The same idea can be extended to triples and to higher k-tuples, though the value of d that is used to generate the auxiliary sequence must be chosen to avoid small observed frequencies.

11.3.5 Gap test

This is based on a search for the gaps between occurrences of ordered values within a specified range and may be applied directly to the series $\{U_i\}$. Consider a sub-interval (a, b) within the $(0, 1)$ range and any two real numbers r_i and r_{i+k}. If these two numbers occur within the interval (a, b), but the intermediate values of $r_{i+1}, r_{i+2}, \ldots, r_{i+k-1}$ do not, then there is a gap of length k in that interval.

Given that the series $\{U_i\}$ should be uniformly distributed over $(0, 1)$, then the probability that r_j lies within the interval (a, b) is $(b - a)$. Hence, the expected frequencies of each gap can be computed because the probability of a gap of length k is $(b - a)(1 - b - a)^{k-1}$. A chi-square test with $k - 1$ degrees of freedom may be used to compare the observed and expected frequencies.

11.3.6   Other tests

The tests described above should give a reasonable indication of whether a generator is suitable for general purpose use. If a generator is to be used in ways that might test its randomness to the limit, then there are many other tests that can be applied—although it should be noted that, according to Kleijnen and van Groenendaal (1992, p. 25) there can still be no cast-iron guarantee that it is a good generator. Thorough descriptions of these tests are given in Knuth (1981), Fishman (1978), Ripley (1987) and L'Ecuyer (1994). It should be noted that L'Ecuyer (1994) finds fault with virtually all of the generators that are in common use; however, some of these failings may be less important in the type of simulations carried out within management science.

11.4   GENERAL METHODS FOR RANDOM SAMPLING FROM CONTINUOUS DISTRIBUTIONS

Section 11.1.3 pointed out that most random sampling procedures used in discrete simulation rely on the availability of one or more random numbers, which may then be transformed into a sample from the required distribution. This may be done via a look-up table or by the use of some suitable algorithm. This section describes the main general algorithms that have been developed to cope with continuous probability distributions.

11.4.1   Inversion

This method is more or less equivalent to top-hat sampling and may be applied to some continuous probability distributions. It relies on the formal definition of a probability density function, which is as follows.

Consider a continuous random variable X that takes values x, as shown in Figure 11.6:

$$Pr(x < X < x + \delta x) \approx f(x)\delta x \quad 0 \leqslant x \leqslant \infty$$

where $f(x)$ is the probability density function (p.d.f.) of X. The cumulative density function (c.d.f.) of X is as follows:

$$F(x) = \Pr(X \leqslant x) = \int_{-\infty}^{x} f(t)\mathrm{d}t$$

An example of a c.d.f. is shown alongside its p.d.f. in Figure 11.6.

As with top-hat sampling, the vertical axis of the c.d.f. is replaced by U, where U is a uniform random variable distributed on the interval $(0, 1)$—that is, by a random number generator. Thus, any value of U may be transformed into a value of x from the curve $F(x)$. Expressed algebraically:

$$\text{If } U = F(x) = \int_{-\infty}^{x} f(t)\mathrm{d}t$$

$$\text{then } x = G(u) = F^{-1}(u)$$

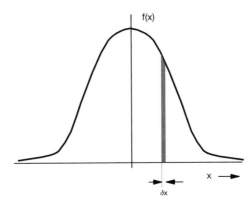

Figure 11.6 Definition of a probability density function

where $G(u)$ is known as in the inverse cumulative function and is employed to transform a value u into a sample x.

Inversion may be used if two conditions hold. The first is that $f(x)$, the p.d.f., is known. The second is that the p.d.f. is tractable so that the inverse cumulative function, $G(x)$, can be formed by integration.

Negative exponential distribution

One of the most common uses of inversion is to take samples from a negative exponential distribution, sometimes known as the exponential distribution. This has the following p.d.f:

$$f(x) = \lambda e^{-\lambda x} \text{ for } 0 \leqslant x \leqslant \infty$$

This distribution is commonly used in queuing systems in which the arrivals are governed by a Poisson process, i.e. the arrivals are independent and random. It has a mean and standard deviation which are both equal to $1/\lambda$. The inversion proceeds as follows:

$$F(x) = \int_0^x \lambda e^{-\lambda t} dt$$
$$= 1 - e^{-\lambda x}$$
$$\therefore u = 1 - e^{-\lambda x}$$
$$\therefore (1 - u) = e^{-\lambda x}$$
$$\text{or } \log_e(1 - u) = -\lambda x$$
$$\therefore x = -\frac{1}{\lambda} \log_e(1 - u)$$

Now, if u is uniformly distributed on $(0, 1)$ then so is $(1 - u)$. Hence the required sample is obtained from:

$$x = -\frac{1}{\lambda} \log_e(u)$$

Uniform distribution

The method of inversion also makes sense of the common-sense method sampling from a uniform distribution such as that shown in Figure 11.7. The common-sense method relies on the realisation that to transform U, a uniform $(0,1)$ variable into one distributed over the interval (a, b), then the value of U must be scaled and shifted. The inversion proceeds as follows:

$$f(x) = \frac{1}{(b-a)}$$

$$\therefore F(x) = \int_a^x \frac{1}{(b-a)} \, dt = \frac{(x-a)}{(b-a)}$$

$$\therefore u = \frac{(x-a)}{(b-a)}$$

$$\therefore x = a + u(b-a)$$

That is, u is scaled by multiplying it by $(b-a)$ and then shifted by a.

11.4.2   Rejection

This approach is suitable for any continuous random variable with a known p.d.f. and a defined range, even if the c.d.f. cannot be formed by direct integration. Conceptually, the method is like throwing darts at a dart board and only counting those that strike certain values—assuming (which is reasonable in the author's case) that the aim is random! It is equivalent to the use of the Monte-Carlo method of numerical integration.

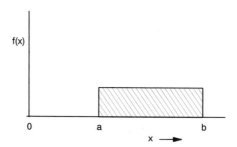

Figure 11.7   A uniform distribution

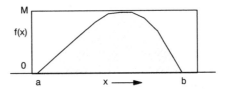

Figure 11.8   Rejection sampling

The basic method works as follows. Consider a random variable X, as shown in Figure 11.8, with known p.d.f. $f(x)$, such that:

$0 \leqslant f(x) \leqslant M$ for $a \leqslant x \leqslant b$
and $f(x) = 0$ elsewhere

Suppose that we have two uniformly distributed random variables, r on the range (a, b) and s on the range $(0, M)$. These may be used to define the co-ordinates of points within the rectangle that encloses the distribution as shown in Figure 11.8. If the co-ordinates lie within the distribution, then the pair of values is accepted and r is returned as the sample of X. Otherwise the pair is rejected and the process is repeated until the point (r, s) lies under the curve of $f(x)$.

The practical use of this procedure works by scaling the c.d.f. $f(x)$ so that its maximum value is 1 and by generating a sample from a uniform distribution on the interval (a, b). Hence the practical procedure is as follows:

(1)   Choose a constant c, so that $c.f(x) \leqslant 1$ for $a \leqslant x \leqslant b$.
(2)   Redefine x so that $x = a + u(b - a)$ where u is uniformly distributed on $(0, 1)$.
(3)   If $u_2 \leqslant c.f(a + u_1(b - 1))$, than accept u_2 and use $x = a + u_1(b - a)$ as the sample, otherwise reject u_2 and repeat the procedure.

It is clear that the closer that the enclosing rectangle fits the distribution, then the more efficient this procedure will be:

The proportion of values rejected is $\dfrac{(b - a) - c}{(b - a)}$.

11.4.3   Composition

This approach, sometimes called decomposition and sometimes called the method of mixtures, relies on a creative realisation that some complicated distributions may be represented by a combination of several simpler ones.

The procedure is illustrated for sampling from a Normal distribution in Section 11.6.3. Composition may be a preferred approach for sampling from negative exponential distributions when a very large number of samples are required. Fishman (1978) gives a composition algorithm for the negative exponential distribution.

11.5 RANDOM SAMPLING ALGORITHMS FOR DISCRETE DISTRIBUTIONS

Not all random variables are continuous, some are discrete—that is, they take only certain integer values. An example would be a Poisson distribution, which represents the number of events per unit time in some random processes. More specifically, if the interval between successive arrivals at a service point follows a negative exponential distribution, then the number of arrivals expected in any unit time (say each hour) should follow a Poisson distribution. General methods for sampling from discrete distributions are similar to those for continuous random variables.

11.5.1 Sampling from histograms

Section 11.1.2 introduced top-hat sampling for histograms and the approach can be formalised to show how samples may be taken from many discrete distributions. A discrete random variable whose p.d.f. may be represented by a histogram can be defined as follows. Consider a discrete random variable X, taking values x_i, such that

$i = 0, 1, 2, .., n$, and
$x_k > x_j$ for all values of x_k and x_j in which $k > j$.

Referring back to Figure 11.3, which shows a histogram and its cumulative form, the task of top-hat sampling can be thought of as a form of search. In the simplest case, the search begins with the first value of X, that is, with x_1. It continues, as if climbing up the stairs formed by the cumulative histogram, until it reaches the correct level. Expressed in pseudo-code, an algorithm might rely on the following data structures:

p[]: a one-dimensional array of real values, to be used a vector that contains the values $\{x_i\}$, for $i = 0, 1, 2, ... n$
x: an integer, which will be the required sample
u: a real variable, which will hold a uniform (0, 1) random number

Thus, the algorithm might be as follows:

```
u: = Rand();           {take a random number}
x: = 0;                {initialise x}
While (p[x] < u) do
    x: = x + 1;        {climb up p[], looking for the correct value}
Return x               {the required sample from the histogram}.
```

This use of repeated trials characterises many algorithms used for random sampling from discrete distributions. Clearly, if the histogram has a large number cells then some more efficient search procedure may be used in the place of this algorithm. An obvious improvement would be to begin the search half-way up the range, rather than at the first value.

11.5.2 Implicit inverse transformation

Section 11.4.1 introduced the idea of inversion sampling from continuous distributions and a similar approach may be used with discrete distributions. The only requirement is that the p.d.f., now expressed as $\Pr(X = x)$ is known: where X is the random variable, and $\{x\}$ is the set of values $(0, 1, 2, ..., n)$ taken by X. By definition:

$$\Pr(X \leqslant x+1) = \Pr(X \leqslant x) + \Pr(X = x + 1)$$
$$\text{and also, } \Pr(X = x + 1) = A_{x+1}.\Pr(X = x)$$

where A_{x+1}, depends on the distribution as well as on the value of x. Its effect, as with the systematic approach to sampling from histograms, is to provide a way of climbing up the c.d.f. in a systematic manner.

The data structures of a general algorithm for implicit inverse transformation could be as follows:

p: a real, to be used to hold the $\Pr(X = x)$
b: a real, to hold the value of the $\Pr(X \leqslant x)$
A[]: a real array to hold the A_{x+1} values
x: an integer, which will be the required sample
u: a real variable, which will hold a uniform $(0, 1)$ random number

Thus, the algorithm might be as follows:

x: = 0;	{initialise the counter}
p: = 0;	{initialise the probability}
b: = p;	(initialise the cumulative probability}
u: = Rand();	{take a random number}
While (u < b) do	{climb up the cumulative}
x: = x + 1;	{increment x}
p: = p*A[x];	{compute the next value of p}
b: = b + p;	{compute the cumulative probability
Return x.	{the required sample from the distribution}

Geometric distribution

As an example of the use of this approach, consider the geometric distribution, which can be thought of as the discrete equivalent of the negative exponential distribution. Imagine a container that contains two types of ball, A and B, in known proportions. Suppose that we wish to find a type A ball but that we cannot see inside the container and must take balls from it until we find one that is type A. The distribution of the number of type B balls that we pick before we find a type A ball, follows the geometric distribution. In general it models the number of failures in some trial before there is a success. Suppose that the proportion of type A balls is p, therefore the proportion of type B balls is $1 - p$.

The geometric p.d.f. is as follows:

$$\Pr(X = x) = p.(1 - p)^x,$$

where $x = 0, 1, 2, \ldots$; p is the probability of success and x is the number of independent trials before a success is recorded.

Hence, $\Pr(X = x + 1) = p.(1 - p)^{x+1}$, which means that $A_{x+1} = (1 - p)$.

Poisson distribution

This approach may also be used to sample from a Poisson distribution for which the p.d.f. is:

$$\Pr(X = x) = \frac{e^{-\lambda}.\lambda^x}{x!}, \qquad x = 0, 1, 2, \ldots$$

where λ is the mean number of occurrences per unit time and x is the actual number of occurrences per unit time. It is obvious that:

$$\Pr(X = x + 1) = \frac{e^{-\lambda}.\lambda^{x+1}}{(x + 1)!} = \frac{e^{-\lambda}.\lambda^x}{x!} \cdot \frac{\lambda}{(x - 1)}$$

$$\therefore A_{x+1} = \frac{\lambda}{(x - 1)}$$

Thus, the implicit inversion algorithm can be simply applied to a Poisson distribution, without even the need to store the values of A_{x+1}, since they can be computed at each step.

11.5.3   Discrete rejection—samples from a Poisson distribution

As with inversion, a discrete version of rejection (see Section 11.4.2) may also be employed in some cases. As an example, consider a Poisson distribution as this provides a second way to sample from this distribution in addition to implicit inverse transformation. In this case, the method relies on the well-known result that, if the number of events per unit time follow a Poisson distribution, then the intervals between those events follow a negative exponential distribution. That is, if a discrete random variable x follows a Poisson distribution:

$$\Pr(X = x) = \frac{e^{-\lambda}.\lambda^x}{x!}, \qquad x = 0, 1, 2, \ldots$$

then the interval between the events, y, follows a negative exponential distribution as:

$$f(u) = \frac{1}{\lambda} . e^{-y/\lambda}$$

The method uses an inversion of $f(y)$ to generate successive exponential deviates

$t_0, t_1, t_2, \ldots$ until:

$$\sum_{i=0}^{x} t_i \leqslant 1 < \sum_{i=0}^{x+1} t_j, \qquad \text{where } x = 0, 1, 2, \ldots$$

That is, compute a succession of exponential deviates, keeping a running sum of their values until that sum exceeds the length of the unit interval with which the Poisson distribution is concerned, at which point the number of deviates (the value x) follows a Poisson distribution with mean λ. If inversion sampling is used for the exponential distribution of y, then the condition can be re-written as:

$$-\frac{1}{\lambda} \log_e(u_i) \leqslant 1 < -\frac{1}{\lambda} \sum_{i=0}^{x+1} \log_e(u_i)$$

$$\text{that is, } -\sum_{i=0}^{x} \log_e(u_i) \leqslant \lambda < -\sum_{i=0}^{x+1} \log_e(u_i)$$

$$\text{which is the same as } \prod_{i=0}^{x+1} u_i < e^{-\lambda} \leqslant \prod_{i=0}^{x} u_i$$

This result allows the following algorithm to be used for sampling from a Poisson distribution. The data structures might be as follows:

M: real, the parameter of the Poisson distribution;
x: integer, the sample from the Poisson distribution;
u: real, random numbers;
b: real, the running product of the uniform variates generated so far.

The algorithm might then be as follows:

```
x: = -1;              {initialise the counter}
b: = 1;               {initialise the running product}
Repeat                {take successive random numbers, compute their
  u: = Rand();         running product and increment x until the product is
  b: = b*u;            less than e^{-M}}
  x: = x + 1;
Until (b < Exp(M));
Return x.
```

There are other, more efficient, algorithms that may be employed for Poisson distributions that have a large mean value, see Fishman (1978) for details.

11.6 SAMPLING FROM THE NORMAL DISTRIBUTION

The Normal distribution merits special attention for two reasons. Firstly it is a distribution that is needed in many simulations and secondly, its p.d.f. is rather awkward. It is usual to work with a standard Normal distribution of z which has a mean of 0 and a variance of 1, for which the p.d.f is as follows:

$$f(z) = \frac{1}{\sqrt{2\pi}} e^{-z^2/s}$$

Which can be converted to a Normal distribution of x, with mean μ and variance of σ^2, by using the conversion formula:

$$x = \frac{z - \mu}{\sigma}.$$

By way of caution, it should be noted that the Normal distribution covers the entire range from plus to minus infinity. Thus, the methods employed may produce extreme values. In fact, in most discrete simulations, the processes that are being represented by Normal distributions are truncated at certain values, specifically at the value zero in many cases, since negative activity durations are most unwelcome! Hence the output from any algorithm employed should be checked and rejected, causing a re-sample, if the value lies outside the required range. Therefore, the methods themselves need to sit inside the protection of a rejection/acceptance shield.

11.6.1   The original Box–Müller method

Although it is impossible to use a full inversion procedure on a Normal distribution, Box and Müller (1958) devised an ingenious partial inversion. The method is exact and it produces two standard Normal deviates from a pair of random numbers. When implementing the algorithm, care should be taken to use both values in each pair, and not to throw half of them away.

The joint distribution function of two independent standard Normal variables x and y is as follows:

$$f(x, y)\delta x . \delta y = \frac{1}{2\pi} . e^{-(x^2 + y^2)/2} . \delta x . \delta y$$

If x and y are regarded as the Cartesian co-ordinates of some point, then these co-ordinates may be transformed into their polar forms:

$$x = r.\cos\theta \quad \text{and} \quad y = r.\sin\theta$$
$$\text{where } r^2 = x^2 + y^2 \quad \text{and} \quad \theta = \tan^{-1}(y/x)$$

and it can be shown that the joint distribution of these polar variables r and θ is as follows:

$$f(r, \theta)\delta r . \delta\theta = \frac{1}{2\pi} . \exp(-r^2/2)r . \delta r . \delta\theta$$

and that this implies that $r^2/2$ and θ are independently distributed, θ with a uniform distribution over $(0, 2\pi)$ and $r^2/2$ with a negative exponential distribution whose mean is 1.

If U_1 and U_2 are uniform random variables on $(0, 1)$, then they can be substituted into the above formulae to give:

$U_1 = \exp(-r^2/2)$, which implies that $r = \sqrt{-2 \log_e U_1}$ and
$U_2 = \theta/2\pi$, which implies that $\theta = 2\pi U_2$

These results can be used to generate a pair of independent standard Normal variates from a pair of random numbers as follows:

$$z_1 = \sqrt{(-2 \log_e U_1 . \cos(2\pi U_2))}$$
$$\text{and } z_2 = \sqrt{(-2 \log_e U_1 . \sin(2\pi U_2))}$$

This result is simple to program and produces exact samples. However, the following polar variation of this method is to be preferred since the computation of trigonometric functions can be very slow.

11.6.2 Box–Müller polar variation

This variation on the original Box–Müller was suggested by Marsaglia and Bray (1964) and it incorporates a rejection procedure. Like the original Box–Müller method, this takes two random numbers and produces a pair of independent standard Normal variates. In this algorithm, the two random numbers, V_1 and V_2 are distributed across $(-1, +1)$ rather than $(0, 1)$ and the sum of their squares, W, is constrained to lie within the interval $(0, 1)$. This is equivalent to considering points within a circle, centred at $(0, 0)$ that has a radius of 1. From this transformation:

$$\sin 2\pi U_2 = \frac{V_1}{\sqrt{(V_1^2 + V_2^2)}} \text{ and } \cos 2\pi U_2 = \frac{V_2}{\sqrt{(V_1^2 + V_2^2)}}$$

Hence, the two standard Normal variates can be computed from:

$$z_1 = V_1 . \sqrt{\frac{-2 \log_e W}{W}} \text{ and } z_2 = V_2 . \sqrt{\frac{-2 \log_e W}{W}}$$

where $V_i = -2.U_i + 1$, if U_i are uniformly distributed across $(0, 1)$ for $i = 1, 2$ and $W = (V_1^2 + V_2^2)$, with $W \leqslant 1$.

Hence, a suitable algorithm might utilise the following data structures:

v1, v2: real, the two random numbers on the interval $(-1, +1)$;
w: the sum of squares;
z1, z2: the two standard Normal variates.

The basic algorithm may therefore be as follows:

```
Repeat
    v1: = 2*Rand() −1;              {compute v1 and v2, form w}
    v2: = 2*Rand() −1;
    w: = v1*v1 + v2*v2;
Until (w ⩽ 1);                      {reject w if too large}
z1: = v1*SQRT(−2*LOG(w)/w)         {form z1 and z2}
z1: = v2*SQRT(−2*LOG(w)/w)
Return z1 and z2.                   (return with standard Normal variates}
```

Fishman (1978) and Atkinson and Pearce (1976) report that the polar variant is about 30% faster than the original method. Hence, for most purposes, this is the algorithm of choice when Normal variates are needed.

11.6.3   Sampling from a Normal distribution by composition

Section 11.4.3 introduced the idea of sampling by composition, in which one distribution is broken down into others that are more convenient to handle. Despite the high quality of the polar Box−Müller method, there are occasions when a composition approach is to be preferred. Essentially these are circumstances where a very large number of normal variates are needed. Under these circumstances, even the polar Box−Müller method may be too slow according to Atkinson and Pearce (*op cit*).

The common algorithm, developed by Marsaglia, MacLaren and Bray (1964) composes a Normal distribution of the four components, shown in Figure 11.9:

(1) A set of rectangles that account for about 86% of the area under a Normal curve;

(2) A set of triangles, that sit on top of the rectangles, and account for a further 11% or so of the area under the Normal curve;

(3) A set of strange shaped residual densities that account for about a further 2% of the area;

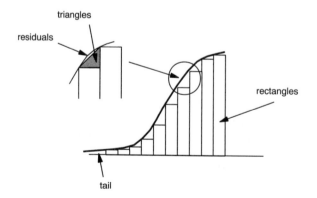

Figure 11.9   Sampling by composition

(4)   A small area of under 0.3% that relates to the extreme tails of the distribution.

As discussed in Section 11.4.3, the method will always need at least two random numbers for each sample. The method produces only positive values and so each variate needs to be given a random sign in order to produce a standard Normal variate. The algorithm works as follows, assuming that all of the random numbers u_i are from the range $(0, 1)$:

Generate u_0;
If $(u_0 \leqslant 0.8638)$ then return $z = (u_1 + u_2 + u_3 - 1.5)$, which samples from the rectangles;
Else if $(u_0 \leqslant 0.9745)$, then return $z = 1.5(u_1 + u_2 - 1)$, which samples from the triangles;
Else if $(u_0 \leqslant 0.99773002039)$, use a rejection method for the residuals;
Else use a modification of the polar Box–Müller method to sample from the tails.

The reason that this method is fast is that, on about 97% of the occasions, it takes fast samples from the rectangles or the triangles.

11.6.4   A poor way to sample from the Normal distribution

By way of a cautionary tale, some people still insist on using an approximate algorithm for generating Normal variates. The method in question relies on the Central Limit Theorem, which states that:

'the sum of n identically and independently distributed random variates is approximately Normally distributed when n is large.'

Hence, the method in question relies on the generation of n random numbers and the computation of their sum, which should have a mean of 0.5 and a variance of $1/12$:

If $n = 12$, then this sum approximates a standard Normal deviate z, where

$$z = \sum_{i=1}^{12} U_i - 6$$

However, this is only an approximation and it has the special defect that it is impossible for $|z|$ to exceed 6, which means that it will not provide a good representation of the tails of a Normal distribution.

In general, this method is to be avoided, since it is neither fast nor accurate.

11.7   DERIVING ONE DISTRIBUTION FROM ANOTHER—LOGNORMAL VARIATES

Sometimes, one distribution may be formed from another and the easiest example of this type to understand is the LogNormal distribution. If a random variable X is distributed Normally with mean μ_X and variance σ_X^2, this is usually represented as:

$$X \sim N(\mu_X, \sigma_X^2)$$

If there is another random variable Y, where $Y = e^X$, then Y is LogNormally distributed with mean μ_Y and variance σ_Y^2. This is usually represented as:

$$Y \sim LN(\mu_Y, \sigma_Y^2).$$

Hence to compute a LogNormal variate, first compute the appropriate underlying Normal variate and then exponentiate the value to get the required sample.

It is important to be sure which mean and variance are being used, as these could be for the LogNormal distribution of Y or for the underlying Normal distribution of X. It can be shown that the following results allow conversion from one to the other:

$$\mu_Y = \exp\left(\mu_X + \frac{\sigma_X^2}{2}\right)$$

and $\sigma_Y^2 = \mu_Y^2 [\exp(\sigma_X^2) - 1]$

Or, if the distribution is expressed the other way, that:

$$\mu_X = \log_e(\mu_Y) - \frac{1}{2} \log_e\left(\frac{\sigma_X^2}{\mu_Y^2} + 1\right)$$

and $\sigma_X^2 = \log_e\left(\dfrac{\sigma_Y^2}{\mu_Y^2} + 1\right)$

11.8   SAMPLING FROM NON-STATIONARY PROCESSES

The sampling methods described so far have all related to stationary distributions, that is to distributions whose parameters are constant through time. This is not always the case in practice, mostly commonly when simulating arrival processes. For example, if the arrivals at a service centre are random then it may be reasonable to simulate them with a Poisson process that allows us to generate the inter-arrival times from a negative exponential distribution (see Section 11.4.1). However, it may be the case that the arrival rate varies through the day, as shown in Figure 11.10. Thus, in Figure 11.10, the arrival rate is at its highest between 08:00 and 10:00 and between 15:00 and 17:00. Hence, the inter-arrival times should be lower in these periods.

There are two ways of handling this problem, only one of which is to be recommended. The wrong way of handling this problem is to divide the day into discrete time periods and to establish an arrival rate (or average inter-arrival time) for each of these periods. Hence, if there were 10 such periods in the day, the arrival rate λ, would take values $\lambda_1, \lambda_2, \lambda_3, ..., \lambda_{10}$. Thus, in this non-recommended method, a different arrival rate (and thus, a different average

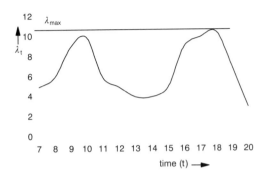

Figure 11.10 Non-stationary arrival rate

inter-arrival time) would be applied, depending on the current clock time in the simulation.

The problem with this approach is that, if a period with a low arrival rate comes just before one with a high arrival rate, the result of the low arrival rate will be a long inter-arrival time. This long inter-arrival time may mean that the next arrival is due quite some time into the period of a high arrival rate. Hence this peri' d of more intense arrivals may begin, in the model, too late, causing an under-estimate of the average arrival rate and a poor estimate of congestion at busy periods. Instead, an approach known as thinning may be used.

11.8.1   Thinning

This approach was suggested by Lewis and Shedler (1979) and it works by rejecting samples in periods of low intensity. The method involves generating the arrivals by a stationary Poisson process that uses the maximum arrival rate, which is shown as λ_{max} on Figure 11.10. This will, of course, generate too many arrivals during most of the day, since it has used the maximum value. In turn, if a negative exponential distribution is being used to generate the time of the next arrival, then the use of $1/\lambda_{max}$ will lead to inter-arrival times that are too short during most periods.

If a graph like that of Figure 11.10 can be produced for the non-stationary process, then, if the simulation clock has reached time t and the simulation needs to generate the interval to the next arrival, thinning works as follows:

(1)   Use a stationary distribution with λ_{max} to generate the time of the next arrival.
(2)   Generate a uniform $(0, 1)$ random number U and use this to reject the sample if $U > \lambda_t/\lambda_{man}$, accepting the sample otherwise. Repeat this step until a value is accepted.

That is, a second random number is used to reject a proportion of the samples at those times when the arrival rate is lower than the maximum. This approach provides good estimates of congestion in non-stationary Poisson processes.

EXERCISES

1. If you have a simulation system available (a language or a VIMS), investigate what control it permits over random number generation. Plot the lagged pairs shown in Figures 11.4 and 11.5 to assess whether the generator is a good one.

2. If you have a simulation system available (a language or a VIMS), apply the serial and gap tests to the random number generator.

3. Using a spreadsheet with which you are familiar, generate 1000 random numbers and plot the lagged pairs as shown in Figures 11.4 and 11.5. If the generator looks a poor one, investigate why this is so.

4. Using a spreadsheet with which you are familiar, apply the serial and gap tests to the random number generator.

5. Using a programming language or a spreadsheet with which you are familiar, program one of the random number generators recommended in this chapter. Plot the lagged pairs as shown in Figures 11.4 and 11.5.

6. Using a programming language or spreadsheet with which you are familiar, write a program to generate negative exponential variates. Collect the results from 1000 variates and use statistical inference to decide whether the sample appears to come from the negative exponential distribution.

7. Using a programming language or spreadsheet with which you are familiar, write a program to generate standard Normal variates using the polar Box–Müller method. Be sure to use both values generated. Collect the results from 1000 variates and use statistical inference to decide whether the sample appears to come from the Normal distribution.

8. Modify your algorithm developed for the standard Normal distribution (exercise 7) so as to generate values with a mean of 10 and variance of 4.

9. Modify the algorithm developed for the non-standard Normal distribution (exercise 8) so as avoid negative values.

10. Modify your algorithm for the negative exponential distribution (exercise 3) so as to enable non-stationary distributions to be simulated.

REFERENCES

Atkinson, A. C. & Pearce, M. C. (1976)   The computer generation of beta, gamma and Normal random variates. *J. R. Stat. Soc. A.*, **139**, 431 ff.

Box, G. E. P. & Müller M. E. (1958)   A note on the generation of Normal deviates. *Ann. Math. Stat.*, **28**, 610–611.

Fishman, G. S. (1978)   *Principles of Discrete Event Digital Simulation.* Wiley-Interscience, New York.

Fishman, G. S. & Moore, L. S. III (1986)   An exhaustive analysis of muliplicative congruential random number generators with modulus $2^{31} - 1$. *SIAM J. Statis. Comp.*, **7**, 24–45.

Kleijnen, J. P. C. & van Groenendaal, W. (1992)   *Simulation: A Statistical Perspective.* Wiley, Chichester.

Knuth, D. E. (1981)   *The Art of Computer Programming* (2nd edn), Vol. 2: *Seminumerical Algorithms.* Addison-Wesley, Reading, MA.

L'Ecuyer, P. (1994) Uniform random number generation. In O. Balci (ed.) *Annals of Operations Research*, Vol. 23: *Simulation and Modeling*. J. C. Balzer, Basel.

Lehmer, D. E. (1951) Mathematical methods in large-scale computing units. *Ann. Comp. Lab. Harvard University*, **26**, 141–146.

Lewis, P. A. W. & Shedler, G. S. (1979) Simulation of non-homogeneous Poisson process by thinning. *Nav. Res. Logist. Quart.*, **26**, 403–413.

Marsaglia, G. & Bray T. D. (1964) A convenient method for generating Normal variables. *SIAM Rev.*, **6**(3), 260–264.

Marsaglia, G., MacLaren, M. D. & Bray, T. D. (1964) A fast procedure for generating Normal deviates on a digital computer. *J. Assoc. Comp. Mach.*, **7**, 4–10.

RAND Corporation (1955) *A Million Random Digits with 100,000 Normal Deviates*. The Free Press, Glencoe, IL.

Ripley, B. D. (1977) Modelling spatial patterns. *J. Roy. Statis. Soc. B.*, **39**(2), 172–212.

Ripley, B. D. (1987) *Stochastic Simulation*. Wiley, New York.

Tocher, K. D. (1963) *The Art of Simulation*. English Universities Press, London.

12

Planning and Analysis of Discrete Simulation Output

12.1 FUNDAMENTAL IDEAS

12.1.1 Simulation as directed experimentation

The usual purpose of a computer simulation is to bring about some improvement in the system being simulated. Hence the output of the simulation should be interpreted with some care, the risk being that wrong decisions will be taken. Assuming that the simulation model is considered valid and that all computer programs used have been verified, further difficulties remain in most discrete event simulations because they commonly include stochastic elements. Figure 12.1 shows that a simulation experiment involves subjecting the model to inputs (or factors) at various levels and interpreting their effects on the output (or responses).

As a simple example, consider again the problem of the harassed booking clerk introduced in Chapter 4. Possible measures of performance might be the average waiting times of personal enquirers and phone calls, or the numbers waiting to be served. Thus, the queue lengths and the waiting times would be the response variables for which estimates need to be found. The inputs whose effects are being investigated are in two groups:

(1) Those parameters which define the configuration of the system: for example, the number of booking clerks or the priority rules for different types of customers.

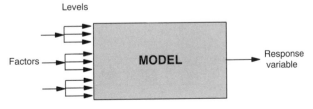

Figure 12.1 Formal simulation experimentation

(2)   The random samples from the various probability distributions, such as those for inter-arrival times. Some of these samples may be exogenous, that is they stem from outside the controlled system: for example, the arrivals come from the world outside. Others may be endogenous, that is, they are a result of the activity within the system.

Suppose that the management of the theatre wishes to investigate the effect of a variety of system configurations: such as one or two clerks, or no priority to personal enquirers. The inputs include stochastic elements: that is, the random samples and simulating the same configuration with different sets of random numbers will produce results that differ, at least slightly. This effect, due to sampling variation, is clearly seen in Figure 12.2. This shows the length of the queue of personal enquirers during two simulations employing different sets of random numbers. Thus, the analyst simulating even such a simple system needs to be sure that different estimates of the average queue length are due to the system configuration and are not just the result of sampling variation.

Generalising from this simple example, it is important to distinguish clearly between the effects of sampling variation and those effects that result from the system configurations, or policies, being examined. Making this distinction and maintaining this separation is one of the key issues in planning a discrete simulation and interpreting its output. This is because the response variables are random variables, whose estimation requires careful statistical analysis. This chapter introduces the basic ideas of this analysis and suggests how the major problems should be faced in practical terms. For a thorough treatment of the main issues in output analysis, see Kleijnnen (1974, 1975, 1987) or Fishman (1973, 1978).

12.1.2   Estimation and comparison

Because the response variables are random variables, simulations are often used to determine the parameters (mean, variance, etc.) of their distributions. For

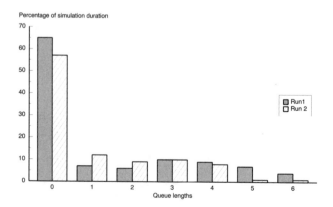

Figure 12.2   An example of sampling variation

example, an airport might be simulated to gain estimates of its capacity under a particular operating condition. Another possible use for a simulation is to compare different policies or configurations, for example, to compare different ways of operating the airport. This too involves the estimation of response variables, but it also requires their comparison and, sometimes, this may be easier than gaining a precise estimate of a single random variable.

Comparison can, of course, be reduced to the problem of estimating a statistic that is some function of the difference between two variables. In such cases, estimating the difference may be easier than giving a precise estimate of either of the single variables. This is because sampling variation may easily lead to bias in estimates of the variables. If some way can be found to ensure that this bias equally affects both variables involved in the comparison, then working with the difference of the two variables will remove the bias. As will be discussed later in Section 12.4, a number of so-called variance reduction techniques have been developed to support the production of better estimates of random variables.

12.1.3   Three important principles

In analysing the output from discrete simulations, three principles need to be borne in mind:

(1)   Most such simulations include a number of sampling processes and these samples are combined to give one or more response variables. Hence it is sensible to regard these simulations as complex sampling experiments. It can sometimes be very difficult to understand the effects of these combinations, and were the effects of these combinations straightforward, then it is unlikely that a simulation approach would be needed at all.

(2)   Because these simulations run through simulated time, many output variables take the form of time series and the observations may, therefore, include significant serial correlation. This means that the observations are not statistically independent. Therefore, care must be taken in any analysis because the presence of this serial correlation means that many classical statistical analyses are inappropriate. There are ways of coping with this problem and these will be discussed later in this chapter.

(3)   Although there are many similarities between simulation output analysis and classical experimental design, there is one important difference. Simulation output is the result of running a *created* model through time and the inner workings of that model can be explored and manipulated. By contrast, much classical experimental design assumes that it is a game against nature. When analysing simulation output it is sensible to take advantage of any knowledge that is available about the inner workings of the model. Many variance reduction techniques (see Section 12.4) make use of this knowledge.

12.2   DEALING WITH TRANSIENT EFFECTS

12.2.1   Terminating and non-terminating systems

Some systems, and therefore some simulations, can be regarded as self-terminating. What this means is that some natural event terminates the operation of the system. As an example, the flight of a missile is expected to terminate when it hits its target, or it hits some other object, or it passes harmlessly into oblivion. Another example would be a one-off task such as an evacuation, which begins with a serious incident and ends with (we hope) a successful evacuation.

By contrast, some systems are not self-terminating in this way, because there is no such natural event that terminates the system's operation. An example might be an air traffic control system in which any day, week or month is just a snapshot in a continuous stream of activity. Most factory and logistics simulations are non-terminating. This does not mean that they are eternal, it merely implies that the simulation provides a moveable window on their activity.

Finally, some systems sit between the two extremes and may be treated one way or other. For example, consider a factory in which work begins at 08.00 and ends, each day, at 17.00. In one sense this is a self-terminating system, since there is a natural event (reaching 17.00) that closes down the operation of the system. However, in another sense, the system is clearly a continuing one, since work will continue at 08.00 the next day. On this next day the model will probably use as its starting work-in-progress that which was left at the end of the previous day. In these cases, the analyst may need to make an arbitrary decision about how the system is to be regarded.

Although there are exceptions to this rule, in general, our interest is as follows:

- In self-terminating systems it is normal to be interested in transient behaviour, for this transience will be what brings the system to its climax. The data which capture this behaviour may be highly correlated and data analysis must take this into account. Many self-terminating systems never achieve a steady state of any kind.
- In non-terminating systems it is common for interest to centre on the long-run or steady-state behaviour of the system and the main concern is with average values and their confidence limits. It is also important to ensure that the transient effects, due to initial bias, are lost before embarking on a steady-state analysis.

In most cases, therefore, the analysis of non-terminating systems focuses on the steady state. This concept is not as obvious as it may seem and any useful definition embodies two linked ideas. The first is that, when a simulation is in a steady state, this is a state of dynamic equilibrium in which the effects of the starting conditions of the simulation have been lost. The second, more formal view, is that a simulation is in a steady state 'if the probability of being in one of its states is governed by a fixed probability function' (Kleijnen, 1974, p. 69). This does not mean that the system does not change state, but rather that the probability of it being in any of its states can be determined. If, for example, a simulation of the harassed booking clerk problem were to be in a steady state, then the length of the queue of personal enquirers waiting for service would vary somewhat and this variation would be predictable, in statistical terms.

When planning simulation experiments and analysing their output, it is crucial that the analyst considers whether the analysis is to focus on the steady state or on the transient effects. For example, if a manufacturing job shop is being simulated, then measurements of the mean waiting time for the jobs are best taken when the simulation has reached a steady state. If, on the other hand, the simulation is of a doctor's consulting room in which the clinic opens with 20 or more patients already waiting, then these starting conditions may be crucial when deciding on, say, an appointments system—which might be the reason for the simulation. That is, in this second case, a major focus of the simulation may be the effect of the initial conditions of the model.

As will become clear later, the response variables are random variables, whose values are therefore determined by probability distributions. Hence, to estimate those distributions requires multiple values for the response variables. This means that the sample size is a crucial aspect of the analysis of discrete simulation output. If the simulation reaches a steady state, then observations made at intervals (e.g. of queue lengths) can be treated as statistically independent. If no such steady state is reached, then a more creative approach is needed.

12.2.2   Achieving steady state

The easiest way of bringing a simulated system into a steady state is to control its starting conditions. For example, suppose that the simulation model is of a commercial airport and that its main purpose is to see the effect of increasing its runways from one to two. A commercial airport is never wholly idle, except on the very first day that it is open. Hence, if a simulation were to begin with no activity in progress, then that starting state would not be typical in any way. If the simulation were, however, started in that null state and then were left to run for some time then, if the simulation model is valid, it should eventually move into steady states that reflect the actual operating conditions of the airport. This, of course, assumes that the real airport operates in some form of steady state. The problem is that, if the main focus is on this steady-state operation, then any observations taken whilst the simulation model moves from its initial null state into a steady state are not relevant for analytical purposes.

In general, when attempting to analyse the steady-state behaviour of a non-terminating system, it is important to ensure that initial bias is lost before collecting data for analysis. Even an analysis of a single run needs to be rid of the early transience if steady-state estimates are required. Also, if policies are being compared, then the same treatment of transience is essential for all policies. Two approaches have been suggested for achieving this end: typical starting conditions and run-in periods (sometimes known as warm-up periods). If, on the other hand, transience is the main interest (as is often the case in self-terminating systems), then these approaches should not be used.

The idea of typical starting conditions is deceptively attractive, but not to be recommended. The basic notion is that the simulation should begin in some state that is believed to be typical of the system when it is operating in 'reality'. Hence, in a simulation of a factory, someone might assume certain initial values for work-in-progress and for machine occupancy at the start of the simulation. There are a number of clear problems with such a proposal:

- We may not know the typical conditions because the system may not actually exist.
- We may not know the typical conditions because we are investigating how the system might operate under novel circumstances.
- We may be comparing policies and we may unwittingly bias our comparison by giving an unfair advantage to one policy rather than the other through the choice of initial conditions.

As a further example of this problem, consider the hypothetical airport simulation mentioned earlier. It would be reasonable to suppose that an airport with three runways would end up, at steady state, coping with more traffic than with just two runways. Hence, it would seem reasonable to start the simulation with the two policy options loaded somewhat differently. If the aim of the simulation is to find whether the third runway is worthwhile, then a simulation started in this way looks dangerously like a self-fulfilling prophecy.

Conway (1963) expressed the problem elegantly as follows:

(1) I wished to compare two systems, A and B.
(2) I anticipated that system A would yield a greater mean value of attribute M than would system B.
(3) I conducted an experiment in which the initial value of attribute M for system A was greater than for system B.
(4) The experimental results demonstrate that the mean value of attribute M for system A is significantly greater than for system B.

12.2.3   Using a run-in period

Using a run-in period takes a little more care, but is much better, as it addresses the problems mentioned above. The idea is that a simulation run should begin with some unrealistic, and effectively null, system condition. The simulation should then be run until it is believed to have achieved some steady-state condition. Data collection for analysis purposes should begin at that point. Most modern software allows the user to specify the time at which data collection is to start—the end of the run-in period.

The practical question to be asked is, 'How long should the run-in period be?'. If it is too long, then time will be wasted (although computer time is an increasingly cheap resource). If it is too short, then transient effects may be included by mistake and the results may, unintentionally, be biased. There is no straightforward technique that will always determine a suitable run-in period, but some general principles are clear.

One way to proceed is to select some suitable variable (or variables) and to treat it (or them) as a response variable(s) about which data may be collected as time series from the start of the simulation. This variable or variables can be displayed on a graph as the simulation proceeds. In most cases, such a graph will indicate when the initial transience is over and, from this, the time for the start of data collection can be determined. For example, if the variable is of queue lengths in the simulation, then if these are still generally increasing, the initial transience may not have been lost—or it implies that there are insufficient service resources in the system to manage the demand from customers. The basic idea is shown in Figure 12.3.

A second approach is to record such variables as time series and to export the values to a spread-sheet or statistical package. As well as allowing graphs of the variables to be quickly and easily displayed, the data series may also be analysed, to see if steady state has indeed been reached. A discussion of the types of analysis that might be performed on such data is given in Law and Kelton (1991).

12.3   DEALING WITH LACK OF INDEPENDENCE

Discrete event simulations involve the unfolding of a system's behaviour through time, in a model that approximates these changes as a sequence of discrete states. Because the progress of the model is a sequence of state changes, then it is highly likely that observations of response variables (such as queue lengths), which are taken as the simulation proceeds, will not be independent. That is, the value at some instant will be a function of its previous value or of previous values. In statistical terms, the time series of the observations will display significant serial correlation. This will be true whether or not the initial bias has been removed from the set of results. How then should the data that comprises the simulation results be analysed? Is it acceptable to make what some cynics describe as 'the declaration of independence'?

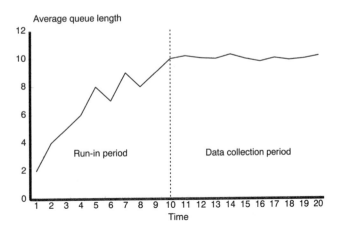

Figure 12.3   Using a run-in period

12.3.1   Simple replication

Perhaps the simplest strategy is to make many independent runs of the simulation, taking just a single reading from each run. In this way multiple replications of the same operating conditions are made. This is achieved by ensuring that different random numbers are used for each replication of the simulation under the same policy. For example, if a random variable X is of interest in the simulation, then running the simulation n times under the same conditions, but with different random numbers, should result in n independent observations of X. If these observations of X are x, then a suitable estimate of the mean value of X might be $(\Sigma x)/n$.

This, of course, implies that the random number streams can be fully controlled, for different random number streams will be needed for each replication of the simulation. In fact, this means that different seeds must be applied to each replication of the simulation since, as discussed in Chapter 11, the random number generators in common use are cyclic (see Figure 12.4) and the random number seed selects the starting point of the generator in its cycle. This in turn implies that the random number generator needs to have a very long period, otherwise the replications will employ sub-sequences from the generator that may overlap in some way or other. If these sub-sequences turn out (by accident) to overlap significantly, then even 'independent' replication will not produce truly independent observations.

If a suitable random number generator is used, which should lead to independent observations of the response variable(s), the variance reduction techniques described in Section 12.4 may be used. If a run-in period is being employed, then this should obviously be used for each and every replication.

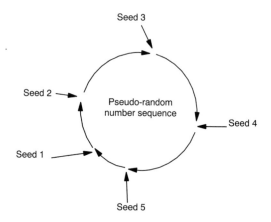

Figure 12.4   A pseudo-random number generation cycle

12.3.2 Batching

Rather than run a simulation many times, each time wasting results during a run-in period, an alternative approach is to make one long run of the simulation and then to divide the results into a sequence of batches. The basic idea is shown in Figure 12.5. The idea is to ensure that observations within one batch are independent of those within any another batch. In a simple queuing simulation, the run might extend to, say, 100,000 customers and these might be broken down into, say, 10 batches, each of 10,000 customers. The hope is that, although customer n is clearly likely to be affected by what happened to customer $(n-1)$, customer n is unlikely to be much affected by what happened to customer $(n-10,000)$. Kleijnen and van Groenendaal (1992) and Kleijnen (1987) suggest tests that might be applied to such batches to see if they are independent, but a few rules of thumb also present themselves for practical application.

The first problem is to decide how long each batch should be. Suppose that a long run is divided into n batches, each of which consists of k observations of some random variable X, taking values $x_1, x_2, ..., x_k$. Each batch should provide a sample from which a single estimate of the parameters of X may be made. Hence, from batch j, the estimate of the mean of X might be:

$$\bar{x} = \frac{1}{k} \sum_{i=1}^{k} x_i$$

The overall estimate of the mean of X would be the grand mean of the n samples, that is:

$$\bar{X} = \frac{1}{nk} \sum_{j=1}^{n} \sum_{i=1}^{k} x_i = \frac{1}{n} \sum_{j=1}^{n} \bar{x}_j$$

and the overall variance would be the sum of the batch variances, if the batches are independent. This is likely to hold if k is made large enough, which also has the advantage that the central limit theorem will apply to the observations in each

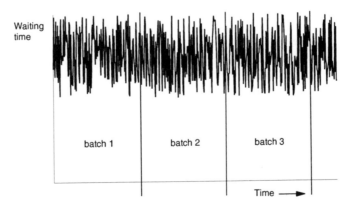

Figure 12.5   Batching of long simulation runs

batch. Similarly, if n is large enough, the central limit theorem will apply across the batches, which means that classical methods of statistical inference can be applied.

Hence, the practical advice is to make k very large (several thousand)—since if there is correlation between the batches, then the method collapses. As with deciding on run-in periods, it may be sensible to plot the batch means that result from the batching, just to make sure that there is no pattern in their sequence. The number of batches n needs to be large enough to apply the central limit theorem with some confidence, which suggests that n needs to be about 30 or higher.

12.3.3   Regenerative methods

Sometimes known as renewal analysis, this approach relies on the fact that some stochastic systems and, therefore, some simulations, return to special states from time to time. These special states are ones which imply that the events prior to their occurrence are independent of those after their occurrence. For some queuing systems, an obvious example is the state in which all servers are free and all waiting lines are empty. When a new customer arrives whilst the system is in this state, an independent cycle of activity is beginning—if the arrivals are governed by a Poisson process. In one sense, this approach resembles the batching method, except that the length of the batches varies and their start and finish is determined by the activity in the model and not by the analyst.

The point at which one cycle ends and the next one starts is usually known as regeneration point. The lengths of the cycles are known as epochs, or as regeneration cycles. As with batching, the intention is that each epoch should be treated as a set of observations that is independent of the previous epoch. In this way, the central limit theorem, and all of the classical statistics that go with it, may be applied to the simulation output.

Kliejnen and van Groenendaal (1992) argue that the use of regenerative methods has a further advantage in that it removes the need for the analyst to determine a run-in period (see Section 12.2.3). This is because the period from the start of the simulation to the first regeneration point is simply one epoch in the series to be analysed.

One practical problem is that true regeneration points may occur very rarely. For example, if the servers in a queuing system are over-worked, that is, the traffic intensity is high, then such a state will occur only rarely. Hence there will be few independent epochs for analysis. One suggestion is that 'nearly renewal' states may be used. An example might be the state when there is just a single customer waiting. This is clearly less likely to generate truly independent epochs, but it may be good enough for many practical purposes.

Fishman (1978) provides a thorough coverage of regenerative methods. It should be noted that this approach, like many aspects of the analysis of simulation output, relies on the privileged position of the analyst. The model is not a black box which is not understood; rather, it is product of human endeavour which the analyst should understand. Regenerative methods are one example of the ways in which this knowledge may be used to support appropriate analysis.

12.4   VARIANCE REDUCTION

There are many techniques in use that claim to help reduce the variance of the output variables. They are needed because the response variables of discrete simulations often display somewhat large variance and this makes the problem of estimation and comparison rather difficult at times. As can be seen from Figure 12.6, the size of the output variance makes a great difference to the confidence that can be placed in any comparison of two or more policies. The top part of Figure 12.6 shows the distribution of the response variables from two policies A and B. Because both response variables have a large variance, then there is a high probability of wrongly concluding that policy A has a higher mean value of X than policy B. The bottom part of Figure 12.6 shows something much more satisfactory. This is because the variances of the response variables are much lower, meaning that a comparison is much more likely to lead to the correct conclusion.

12.4.1   The basic problem—sampling variation

To understand the basic problem, consider a simulation from which someone wishes to estimate the mean value of some random variable X. The common-sense way to do this would be to run n independent replications of the simulation, each time collecting a new value of x. Hence, a suitable estimator for the mean value of X might be the arithmetic mean of the values of x, which could be bounded by some confidence limits. These limits provide upper and lower bounds on a confidence interval in which there is some known probability that the true mean of X lies within the interval. Expressing this is in algebraic terms produces the

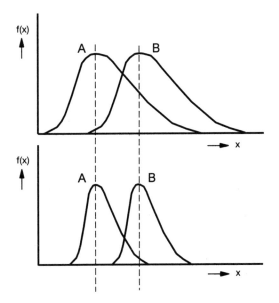

Figure 12.6   The effect of variation on inference

following:

$$\mu = X \pm a_n \frac{s}{\sqrt{n}}$$

where μ is the true mean of X and s is the sample standard deviation. This gives confidence limits on the estimate of the mean value of X. The value taken by the parameter a_n is distribution-dependent as well as dependent on the degree of confidence that we are seeking. As an example of this, consider Figure 12.7. The dotted lines shown are 95% confidence limits from a simple discrete simulation and the solid line is the sample mean. Note that the confidence limits converge as the number of runs (i.e. the sample size) increases. However, the problem is that this convergence is only rapid in the first few samples, thereafter it is slow. This is because the convergence is a function of the square root of the sample size. Thus, in moving from two samples to four the convergence is rapid, but to make an equivalent reduction again will require 16 samples, and so on.

Thus, a sure-fire way to end up with reasonable estimates that have narrow confidence limits is to run a huge number of replications. But this is time-consuming and there are better ways to proceed than this blunderbuss approach. Variance reduction techniques are employed to help this convergence along a little. Kleijnen (1974) lists the following variance reduction techniques:

- Stratified sampling
- Selective sampling
- Control variates
- Importance sampling
- Antithetic variates
- Common random numbers

Of these, only common random numbers, control variates and antithetic sampling are widely used in the types of discrete simulation carried out with management science. Each of these three techniques is discussed below.

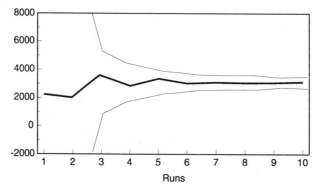

Figure 12.7   Converging confidence limits

12.4.2   Set and sequence effects

It can be quite illuminating to think about the sources of the variation that is seen in simulation output, which stems from the use of random sampling algorithms to develop finite samples in which:

- The moments of the sample distribution may not what they should be (the shape and position may be wrong).
- The sequence in which samples are combined might also make its effect known, even though the individual random numbers are found to be 'properly' random.

This is because random numbers are used (see Section 11.1.3) for two purposes in the standard random sampling algorithms. They are used to select a set of values and also to ensure that this set is presented in a pattern-free, i.e. random, sequence. These two aspects can be captured in two effects (which have been studied by analysis of variance techniques; Saliby, 1980).

- *The set effect.*   These are errors due to the set of values produced by the sampling process. With a finite sample size, we may be unlucky and may end up with a poor, unrepresentative coverage of the distribution. If we use random numbers to select the set of values then these errors are inevitable unless we employ huge sample sizes.
- *The sequence effect.*   This is a bit more subtle and results from the sequence in which the random numbers (and the resulting samples) are produced and combined.

With care, the set effect can be partially controlled, but the sequence effect is more problematic. To illustrate this, consider two sampling processes that are combined within a simulation. Suppose that these are known as X and Y and that both produce integer values; where X is $\{0, 1, 2, ... 9\}$ and Y is $\{0, -1, -2, ... -9\}$. Imagine that we wish to estimate $Z = X.Y$ and that there is some way to ensure that the set effect is eliminated, so that all 10 values for X and Y are included in each 10 samples of each variable. Consider two runs of the simulation and suppose that they produce the results shown in Table 12.1.

In the first case, the estimate of Z is -19.8, and in the second case, the estimate for Z is -22.0. The difference in these estimates for $Z = X.Y$ is purely a result of the short sequences in which the values produced are combined. This effect will occur in all discrete simulations that incorporate random sampling, since all such simulations will have finite sample sizes.

It is important to realise that these errors, whether due to the set or sequence effect, are undesirable. In planning a simulation and analysing its output, the stress is on good estimates and on error-free comparison. Neither is possible if there is much sampling error. It so happens that much of the set effect is reasonably straightforward to control; however, the sequence effect is less straightforward. The following variance reduction techniques are attempts to reduce the sampling error.

Table 12.1 The sequence effect in combining samples

	Run 1			Run 2		
Sample	X	Y	Z = XY	X	Y	Z = XY
1	2	−9	−18	6	−5	−30
2	1	−6	−6	3	0	0
3	3	−5	−15	0	−4	0
4	0	−3	0	9	−8	−72
5	5	−4	−20	7	−7	−49
6	6	−2	−12	4	−6	−24
7	7	−8	−56	2	−1	−2
8	4	0	0	8	−3	−24
9	9	−7	−63	5	−2	−10
10	8	−1	−8	1	−9	−9
Mean	4.50	−4.50	−19.80	4.50	−4.50	−22.00
SE	0.96	0.96	6.97	0.96	0.96	7.44

12.4.3 Common random number streams and synchronisation

This approach, sometimes known as *streaming*, is used when the aim is to compare the effect of different policies on a response variable. In the simplest case, consider a simulation which is used to compare two policies, X and Y, which produce random variates x and y in their output. We wish to estimate $Z = X - Y$.

If the two policies are compared via a set of runs that are statistically independent, then:

$$VAR(Z) = VAR(X) + VAR(Y).$$

However, if we ensure that the sampling is not independent, then:

$$VAR(\hat{Z}) = VAR(X) + VAR(Y) - 2.COV(X,Y)$$
If $COV(X,Y)$ + ve, $VAR(\hat{Z}) < VAR(Z)$

Thus, if we can induce positive correlation between the runs, then we end up with an estimator with a reduced variance. In essence, this approach gives good control of the set of values (it ensures, as far as is possible that all policies suffer the same bad sampling and then removes this bias by working with the difference). It gives some control over the sequence effect.

To gain the fullest effect of common random numbers, we need random number streams that have a large, complete period and in which a large (preferably unlimited) number of entry points is possible. If a simulation contains k sampling processes and there are n runs for each policy, then we need $k.n$ different random number seeds. For example, consider the harassed booking clerk example in which there are three clerks. In this case, eight seeds are needed, this being one each for the two arrival processes, one for each clerk's personal service and one for each clerk's phone conversation.

If eight such streams were available, then this would ensure, as far as it is possible that the sampling processes were fully synchronised in each run. The idea of synchronisation is to ensure that the same random number is used for the same purpose in each policy comparison. In fact, perfect synchronisation is rarely, if ever, possible in simulations in which the effect of the different policies is to change the sequence in which events may occur. In many cases, this change of event sequence will lead to the individual random numbers being used for different purposes. Thus, if the idea of the simulation is to try different queue disciplines, the effect of this will be to change the sequence in which customers are served. This in turn will prevent full synchronisation.

There is no guarantee that common random numbers will give complete control over the set effect because, in many random sampling algorithms, there is no one-to-one correspondence between random numbers and the samples. This is particularly the case in methods that rely on rejection approaches—which are surprisingly common. Nevertheless, it is hard to conceive of circumstances in which the use of common random numbers would lead to an increase in sampling variation. Thus, they can be generally recommended for those cases in which different policies and configurations are compared.

Although the use of common random numbers seems straightforward, this is not always the case in practice. This is because not all commercial simulation software packages allow the analyst full control over random number generation. Some packages only allow a maximum number of streams per run, some even permitting only a single stream per run of a simulation. Also, even in those cases in which the analyst may employ as many 'streams' as needed, it is important to realise that these are rarely proper streams. Instead, the analyst may specify as many seeds as required, with the hope that each will lead to an independent sub-stream (see Figure 12.4).

12.4.4   Control variates (regression sampling)

This is a way of using inside knowledge so as to control the sampling variation. It relies on our knowing at least something of how the simulation *should* behave, were the sampling to be properly controlled. It may be used to gain a better estimate of a single random variable, whereas common random number streams are used for comparison between policies and configurations.

Consider a single server queue with a known service time distribution. If the observed service time in the simulation is higher than the known mean, then the observed queue lengths should be higher than would otherwise be the case, assuming that other aspects of the model are performing normally. This information can be used to control the undesirable sampling variation by allowing for a 'bad' set of samples. In this example, the fact that the observed service time is too high is used to drag the queue length distribution back into its 'proper' position.

Using a single server queuing system as an example, suppose that Q is the random variable that represents queue length and that it takes values q. Defining the following variables:

μ_Q = True (population) queue length, and

$\bar{q}$ = Observed (sample) queue lengths in the simulation.

If the aim of the simulation is to estimate the mean queue length, an obvious way of estimating the mean queue length would be to use:

$\mu_Q = E(\bar{q})$.

But, instead, the estimator could incorporate the knowledge that we have about the relationship between queue lengths and service times:

$\hat{q} = \bar{q} - \delta(\bar{s} - \mu_s)$

where μ_s is the true (population) mean service time,

$\bar{s}$ is the observed mean service time in the simulation,

and δ is the control variate.

Hence, the original estimator of the mean queue length is to be 'dragged back' by some multiple of the difference between the actual and the expected service times. This multiplier, δ, is known as the control variate. The new estimator is unbiased, since:

$$E(\hat{q}) = E(\hat{q}) - \delta.E(\bar{q} - \mu_s)$$
$$= \mu_Q - \delta.(\mu_s - \mu_s)$$
$$= \mu_Q$$

Using the usual variance algebra:

$$VAR(\hat{q}) = VAR(\bar{q} - \delta.\bar{s})$$
$$= VAR(\bar{q}) + \delta^2.VAR(\bar{s}) - 2\delta.COV(\bar{q}, \bar{s})$$

Re-arranging this gives:

$$VAR(\hat{q}) - VAR(\bar{q}) = \delta^2.VAR(\bar{s}) - 2\delta.COV(\bar{q}, \bar{s})$$

If the variance is to be reduced, then the following condition must hold true:

$$VAR(\hat{q}) - VAR(\bar{q}) < 0$$
$$\Rightarrow \delta.VAR(\bar{s}) < 2.COV(\bar{q}, \bar{s})$$
$$\Rightarrow \delta < \frac{2COV(\bar{q}, \bar{s})}{VAR(\bar{s})}$$

This means that some value of the control variate δ must be selected so as to guarantee this. The usual suggestion is that such a value may be found via a simplified analytical model or from preliminary simulations.

This example has developed a control variate for the mean of a distribution, but a similar idea could be used for the other moments of the distribution and for more than a single distribution in a simulation. Any variance reduction induced by control variates is a result of gaining some control of the set effect by dragging the values in the set closer towards their 'true' values.

12.4.5 Antithetic variates

This is often recommended, but there is very limited evidence that it works very well. It is mentioned here for completeness. As with control variates, the approach is used when the aim is to gain a better estimate of a response variable for a single policy, unlike common random numbers, which are used for policy comparison.

Suppose that a simulation produces a response variable X and that two runs of the simulation produce estimates X_1 and X_2. An obvious unbiased overall estimator would be to use $Z = (X_1 + X_2)/2$, for which the variance is:

$$VAR\left[\frac{(X_1 + X_2)}{2}\right] = \frac{1}{4} VAR(X_1) + \frac{1}{4} VAR(X_2) + \frac{1}{2} COV(X_1, X_2).$$

However, in theory, it is possible to do better than this by introducing negative correlation between the two runs. If this can be guaranteed, then $COV(X_1, X_2)$ is negative, which leads to a reduced variance. In essence, the idea behind antithetic sampling is to correct for poor sampling. Thus, if a sample turns out to be 'too low', then its antithetic should turn out to be 'too high'. Taking the arithmetic mean of the two should drag the result back to some 'true' value. (The words 'too low', 'too high' and 'true' are in quotes, because when a system is simulated, the true values are usually unknown—for this is why the operation of the system is being simulated).

In practice, this method is implemented in a number of ways of which the most popular, suggested by Tocher (1963), is to take each simulation run and repeat it with a complementary, or antithetic, run. The first run, might use m random number streams that produce values $\{u_{m,1}, u_{m,2}, ..., u_{m,i} ...\}$ for all m. The second, or antithetic run, might use $\{1 - u_{m,1}, 1 - u_{m,2}, ..., 1 - u_{m,i} ...\}$. This will ensure negative correlation, at least in the input streams. This can be shown to be very effective in simple queuing simulations, but the practical problems with this approach stem from the fact that samples from different distributions are combined and the effect of this can be very hard to discern.

Page (1965) proposed a different antithetic procedure for a simple queuing problem in which he interchanged the random stream for service with the one used for arrivals to gain an antithetic run. Saliby (1980) analysed the variance that resulted from simulations of a simple queuing system using both approaches, concluding that Page's interchange of streams led to a greater reduction in output variance.

However, it is as well to be cautious in the use of antithetic sampling. Law and Kelton (1991) suggest a number of common circumstances in which the method might actually lead to an increase in output variance rather than to a reduction. The basic problem is the difficulty of ensuring that the deliberately induced negative correlation between the input variables finds its way through to the response variables. This is because most discrete simulations are complicated sampling experiments in which samples are dynamically combined. This results in complex transformations that make it hard to be sure what effect changes on the inputs will have on the outputs—that is why, in most cases, the simulation is being conducted. Whereas common random numbers can always be recommended, the same is not true of antithetic sampling.

12.5   DESCRIPTIVE SAMPLING

12.5.1   Basic idea

Descriptive sampling was proposed by Saliby (1980) and is similar to a selective sampling, suggested by Brenner (1961). It offers almost complete control of the set effect and partial control of the sequence effect. Kleijnen (1974) argues that selective sampling will always lead to biased samples. Saliby demonstrated that this is not true of descriptive sampling. Whereas the usual variance reduction techniques are attempts to staunch the flow of blood from damaged samples, descriptive sampling attempts to prevent these accidents from happening. It does so by separating the two functions of sampling into separate operations as follows:

(1)   Select values from the distribution so that full and proper coverage of its values is given and this will guarantee that the moments of the sample distribution are correct. Random numbers are *not* used for this purpose.
(2)   Place these values in a sequence and select from them at random, without replacement, using random numbers for this purpose.

12.5.2   Procedure

Consider a random variable X, with a known p.d.f. $f(x)$. Saliby's original approach relies on the use of inversion sampling (see Section 11.4.1) to generate samples x, from the distribution of X. The first stage is to determine the size (n) of sample that will be needed in the simulation. This is, of course, problematic, and it is better to err on the side of caution by selecting a sample size that may be slightly too large. This known sample size n is then used to divide the $(0, 1)$ range into n sub-intervals as follows:

$$U_i = n/2 + (i-1)/n \qquad i = 1 \ldots n$$

where $\{U_i\}$ are the midpoints of the sub-intervals.

The second stage is to take a full set of samples from the cumulative distribution, using the U_i values as shown in Figure 12.8. Thus,

$$\{x_i\} = F^{-1}(u_i) \qquad i = 1 \ldots n$$

Finally, random sampling without replacement is used to generate the random sequence in which the values are used in the simulation.

As an example, consider a negative exponential distribution with a mean of 10. If inversion sampling is used, then samples of X result from $x_i = -10*\log_e(u_i)$. Table 12.2 shows two sets of samples, the first from the usual method of random sampling, the second is from a set of 10 descriptive samples. It is clear that the descriptive sample gives a better estimate of the mean and standard deviation, despite its small size.

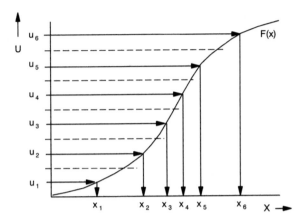

Figure 12.8 Descriptive sampling on the cumulative density function

Table 12.2 Descriptive sampling versus random sampling

Sample number	Random sampling		Descriptive sampling	
	U_i	$x_i = 10*\ln(U_i)$	U_i	$x_i = 10*\ln(U_i)$
1	0.53	6.35	0.05	29.96
2	0.81	2.11	0.15	18.97
3	0.29	12.38	0.25	13.86
4	0.13	20.40	0.35	10.50
5	0.39	9.42	0.45	7.99
6	0.35	10.49	0.55	5.98
7	0.01	45.05	0.65	4.31
8	0.30	16.09	0.75	2.88
9	0.71	3.42	0.85	1.63
10	0.34	10.79	0.95	0.51
Mean		13.75		9.66
SD_{n-1}		12.60		9.17

The practical problems in using descriptive sampling stem from two issues. The first is the need to specify the sample size in advance—which may be problematic in some simulations. One practical approach to this is to take the samples in stages. For example, the $(0, 1)$ interval might be divided into 1000 sub-intervals. Descriptive samples could then be taken by using the mid-points of the sub-intervals. If more samples are needed, a different point could be chosen in each sub-interval, leading to another 1000 samples and so on. There would, of course, be some waste, but the resulting output variance should be much lower than if random sampling had been employed. The second practical issue is that many distributions cannot be sampled by inversion, and this still remains an issue to be tackled, although Saliby (1990) makes some suggestions.

12.6   EXPERIMENTATION

12.6.1   Basic ideas

Many simulations are carried out so as to compare system configurations or policies for operating the system. The basic idea of this was shown in Figure 12.1 at the start of this chapter. The inputs that are controllable and which are thought to affect the system response are known as *factors*. These can be quantitative variables, e.g. the number of clerks serving in the theatre booking office. They might also be qualitative, for example the priority rule that determines whether personal enquirers are served before phone calls. The aim of the simulation may be to determine how many clerks are needed and what priority rule produces the best result.

Although it is normal to focus on the controllable factors in the simulation, one advantage of a simulation is that some uncontrollable effects can also be simulated. For example, the arrival rate of customers is not directly controlled by the theatre manager. Yet she may wish to find the clerk/priority combination that copes best with a range of arrival rates.

In the simplest possible experiments there are just two things to compare. If this is a single factor that can take two values, then these values are referred to as *levels*. Hence the simplest case is either two factors, both at one level, or one factor at two levels. In either case, the experiment is designed to assess which of the two produces the most favourable response from the model. Various approaches may be used to make this comparison, and care must be taken (as discussed) earlier if classical statistical methods are to be used.

The field of experimental design is one which has occupied statisticians for many years, since the pioneering work of Fisher (1951). There are many texts on this subject (e.g. see Cochran and Cox, 1957; Box and Draper, 1987). The mathematical statistics involved can seem very daunting, but the basic principles are simple enough. The aim is to ensure that any experiment is conducted in such a way that the comparisons made are fair and that sampling variation is properly accounted for when drawing conclusions from the results of the experiments. Careful design of an experiment takes time, but can save a lot of heartache and should actually save time in the long run. This book can only scratch the surface of the possibilities but for more detail see Kleijnen (1975), who discusses many of the ideas that are valuable in the context of discrete simulation.

It is important, as mentioned at the start of the chapter, to realise that there is an important difference between the experiments conducted by simulation analysts and those carried out by many other people. Much of the theory that underlies experimental design assumes that the experiment is some kind of black box and that the analyst has little or no inkling of what goes on within. Hence, the aim of the experimentation is to untangle the effects of the various factors that may be causing the distinctive behaviour of the system. In simulation experimentation, by contrast, the analyst has the great advantage of knowing what lies within the model. The model is not a black box; rather, it is a creation of the human mind and any inside knowledge may be used to good effect.

12.6.2 Factorial experiments

When an experiment must be designed to consider the combined effects of rather more than two levels or two factors, the common recourse is to a factorial experimental design. Such experiments are usually analysed by the analysis of variance, often shortened to ANOVA. Factorial experiments aim to compare the effects of each level of each factor with each level of each other factor being considered. In this way, the possible effects of the interacting factors and levels may be considered.

Suppose that a simulation experiment involves three factors, each of which may operate at any of three levels. This means that there are $3^3 = 27$ factor–level combinations to consider in the experiment. Because of the stochastic variation inherent in discrete event simulations, each factor–level combination must be replicated several times. Even if each factor–level combination were only to be replicated three times, this would lead to 81 runs of the model. In general, an experiment with n factors each operating at m levels and with k replications will need $n^m k$ runs if the experiment is to be properly analysed. Hence, such experimentation can clearly be a very time-consuming process. There is, of course, no particular reason why each factor should operate at the same number of levels.

In an experiment in which three factors were being considered, each at two levels, then this would be a 2^3 factorial experiment. If there are n factors at m levels, then this is described as an n^m factorial experiment. With three factors X, Y, and Z, such an experiment would aim to uncover the following:

- *The main effects*: these are due solely to the factors X, Y and Z as they are individually changed without altering the other factors. Thus, for example, these might include the effect of changing the number of clerks, whilst keeping everything else the same.
- *The interaction effects*: these are due to simultaneous change in one or more of the X, Y and Z factors. If two factors are changed simultaneously, this is known as a second-order effect. It is a third-order effect if all three factors are altered at the same time.

The analysis of variance attempts to examine the results of an experiment so as to unscramble these various effects. This unscrambling is not attempted by a form of magic, but by an attempt to split the total variation of the response variables into independent components. The intention is that each of the components should represent one of the main effects or one of the interaction effects. How these components are identified will depend on the assumptions that underlie the analysis of variance. As with most classical statistical analyses, the idea is to see if the effects that are detected in the components is significantly different from zero. That is, does the analysis support the view that the observed variation is due to the effect of the factors and their levels, or is it just due to chance variation?

Although it is often necessary to resort to the full panoply of the analysis of variance, this is not always the case. Indeed, the best starting point is to find some suitable way to plot and to tabulate the results. It may be that, from these plots and tables, it is very obvious what is going on. Failing this, then some resort to the proper analysis of variance may well be necessary.

12.7   THE ANALYSIS OF FACTORIAL EXPERIMENTS

12.7.1   Basic ideas

As discussed above, the idea of a factorial experiment is that it enables the investigation of the main effects and, most significantly, of their interactions. The principles of these experiments will be described here by using the simplest possible case, although exactly the same principles may be applied to more complex cases. In the simplest case, there are just two factors under investigation, and suppose that these factors are referred to as A and B. Suppose, too, that both factors operate at n levels and that each factor–level combination is replicated k times. Hence there are n^2 factor combinations to assess and each of these will be replicated k times, giving $n^2 k$ runs in total.

In this approach to experimentation, the starting point is an assumption about the ways in which these effects, main and interaction, are linked. The usual assumptions can be expressed in the following model:

$$Y_{ijk} = \mu + \alpha_i + \beta_j + \theta_{ij} + \varepsilon_{ijk}$$
Equation 12.1

That is, the overall response of the system is the mean response, plus the sum of three other elements. Thus, in this model, the effects represent the differences that are observed between the response variates and the mean response with different combinations of A and B. The details of the response variables and the other elements are as follows.

Y_{ijk} = the response variable, i.e. the result of factor combination A_i and B_j at its kth replication;

μ = the overall average effect of the factor–level combinations, i.e. the grand mean;

α_i = the main effect of factor A at level i, where $i = 1 \ldots n$;

β_j = the main effect of factor B at level j, where $j = 1 \ldots n$;

θ_{ij} = the interaction effect of the factor combination A_i and B_j;

ε_{ijk} = any variation in the response variable that is not explained by the sum of the other factors: this is known as the residual variation, or error term.

In order to make the analysis manageable, it is usual to make two more assumptions:

(1)   The residuals $\varepsilon_{i\varphi\kappa}$ are all independent Normal $(0, \sigma^2)$ variables: i.e. with mean 0 and variance σ^2.

(2)   The sum of each of the effects, main and interaction is zero, i.e.:

$$\sum_{i=1}^{n} \alpha_i = \sum_{j=1}^{n} \beta_j = 0$$

$$\sum_{i=1}^{n} \theta_{ij} = \sum_{j=1}^{n} \theta_{ij} = 0 \text{ for all values of } i \text{ and } j.$$

Table 12.3 Null and alternate hypotheses

Null hypotheses	Alternate hypotheses
$H_0(1)$: the interaction of A and B has no effect, i.e. $\theta_{ij} = 0$, for all i and all j	$H_1(1)$: $\theta_{ij} \neq 0$, for some values of i and j
$H_0(2)$: factor A has no effect, i.e. $\alpha_i = 0$ for all i	$H_1(2)$: $\alpha_i \neq 0$ for some values of i
$H_0(3)$: factor B has no effect, i.e. $\beta_j = 0$ for all j	$H_1(3)$: $\beta_j \neq 0$ for some values of j

12.7.2 Hypotheses

As with all statistical inference, it is important that the hypotheses under consideration are carefully defined. In this experiment, the aim is to detect the main and interaction effects, if they exist. It is usual to check the interaction effects first, because if these are significant then there is no point in checking just for the main effects. Hence, the null and alternate hypotheses are as shown in Table 12.3, in the order in which they will be tested.

12.7.3 Analysis

The aim of the analysis is to use the experimental data to attempt to fit parameters to the model shown in equation 12.1. This is usually done by least squares estimation, as in regression modelling. Thus, the aim is to find estimates of the parameters α_i, β_j, θ_{ij} and μ by minimising the following sum of squares:

$$S_E^2 = \sum_{i=1}^{n} \sum_{j=1}^{n} \sum_{k=1}^{m} (Y_{ijk} - \hat{\mu} + \hat{\alpha}_i + \hat{\beta}_j + \hat{\theta}_{ij})^2$$

Where the caret (^) over the symbols indicates that these are least squares estimates. It can shown that the error sum of squares S_E^2 may be partitioned as follows.

$$S_E^2 = S^2 - (S_A^2 + S_B^2 + S_{AB}^2)$$

where S^2 is the total sum of squares and S_A^2, S_B^2 and S_{AB}^2 are the sums of squares due to A, B and the interaction AB. These sums of squares will be used to provide estimates of the proportion of the output variance that is due to each factor and factor combination.

12.7.4 ANOVA table

Using normal algebra and calculus it is possible to derive the ANOVA table shown in Table 12.4, which shows how the sums of squares can be computed: in this table,

Table 12.4 ANOVA table

Source	Degrees of freedom	Sum of squares	Mean sum of squares
A	$n-1$	$S_A^2 = \sum\limits_{i=1}^{n} \dfrac{y_{i..}^2}{nm} - \dfrac{y_{...}^2}{n^2 m}$	$\dfrac{S_A^2}{n-1}$
B	$n-1$	$S_B^2 = \sum\limits_{j=1}^{n} \dfrac{y_{.j.}^2}{nm} - \dfrac{y_{...}^2}{n^2 m}$	$\dfrac{S_B^2}{n-1}$
AB	$(n-1)^2$	$S_{AB}^2 = \sum\limits_{i=1}^{n}\sum\limits_{j=1}^{n} \dfrac{y_{ij.}^2}{m} - \sum\limits_{i=1}^{n}\dfrac{y_{i..}^2}{nm} - \sum\limits_{j=1}^{n}\dfrac{y_{.j.}^2}{nm} + \dfrac{y_{...}^2}{n^2 m}$	$\dfrac{S_{AB}^2}{(n-1)^2}$
Error	$n^2(m-1)^2$	$S_E^2 = S^2 + S_A^2 + S_B^2 + S_{AB}^2$	$\dfrac{S_E^2}{n^2(m-1)}$
Total	$n^2 m - 1$	$S^2 = \sum\limits_{i=1}^{n}\sum\limits_{j=1}^{n}\sum\limits_{k=1}^{m} Y_{ijk}^2 - \dfrac{y_{...}^2}{n^2 m}$	

$$y = \sum_{i=1}^{n}\sum_{j=1}^{n}\sum_{k=1}^{m} y_{ijk}, \quad y_{i..} = \sum_{j=1}^{n}\sum_{k=1}^{m} y_{ijk}, \quad y_{.j.} = \sum_{j=1}^{n}\sum_{k=1}^{m} y_{ijk}$$

12.7.5 Hypothesis testing

The idea of the hypothesis testing is that it should indicate whether any of the factors have a significant effect on the response variable. As discussed in Section 12.7.2, the order in which the hypotheses are investigated is important and the usual procedure is to investigate the interaction effects first.

The null hypothesis, $H_0(1)$, is that the interaction of A and B has no effect, i.e. $\theta_{ij} = 0$ for all i and all j. This can be tested by computing a test statistic and then comparing its value to that produced by the F distribution as follows:

$$\text{Reject } H_0(1) \text{ if } \frac{S_{AB}^2/(n-1)^2}{S_E^2/n^2(m-1)} > F_{(n-1)^2,\, n(m-1)}$$

If $H_0(1)$ is rejected, that is, if there is a significant interaction effect, then there is no point is testing the other two hypotheses.

If, however, $H_0(1)$ is accepted, that is, there is no significant interaction effect, then the model of equation 12.1 simplifies to the following:

$$Y_{ijk} = \mu + \alpha_i + \beta_j + \varepsilon_{ijk}$$

Equation 12.2

The following test statistics may then be used to test $H_0(2)$ and $H_0(3)$:

$$\text{Reject } H_0(2) \text{ if } \frac{S_A^2/(n-1)^2}{(S_E^2 + S_{AB}^2)/n^2(m-2n-1)} > F_{(n-1)^2, (n^2m-2n-1)}$$

$$\text{Reject } H_0(3) \text{ if } \frac{S_B^2/(n-1)}{(S_E^2 + S_{AB}^2)/n^2(m-2n-1)} > F_{(n-1)^2, (n^2m-2n-1)}$$

In this way, it is possible to test whether the factors and their interactions have any significant effect on the observations of the response variable.

12.8 SUMMARY

This Chapter has introduced the fundamental ideas and methods that are used in planning and interpreting simulation experiments in which the output is one or more response variables. It pointed out that experiments on terminating and non-terminating systems must often be planned differently from one another and that run-in periods are commonly used in non-terminating systems for which a steady-state analysis is required. Three approaches to variance reduction were introduced alongside a discussion of the causes of sampling errors that lead to undesirable variation. Finally, the basics of the factorial design and analysis of experiments was introduced to show how they may be employed in the formal analysis of simulation experiments.

EXERCISES

1. Investigate the effect of random number streaming on the results from the harassed booking clerk program of Chapter 7.

2. Using a simulation program that you have available, investigate the effect of random number streaming on the simulation output.

3. Use descriptive sampling to take a sample of size 10 from a triangular distribution.

4. Using a spreadsheet, generate a long sequence (say 20,000) of serially correlated values. Investigate the batch sizes that would be needed to implement batching in an attempt to gain independent samples.

5. If you have a simulation program available in which the results are serially correlated, repeat exercise 5 on that series.

6. Find a simulation case study from the literature and critically review the simulation output analysis as it is presented in the case study.

REFERENCES

Box, G. E. P. & Draper, N. R. (1987) *Empirical Model-bulding and Response Surfaces*. Wiley, New York.

Brenner, M. E. (1961)   Selective sampling—a technique for reducing sample size in simulations of decision making situations. *J. Ind. Eng.*, **14**, 291–6.

Cochran, W. G. & Cox, G. M. (1957)   *Experimental Designs* (2nd edn). Wiley, New York.

Conway, R. W. (1963)   Some tactical problems in digital simulation. *Managem. Sci.*, **10**, 47–61.

Fisher, R. A. (1951)   *The Design of Experiments*. Oliver & Boyd, Edinburgh.

Fishman, G. S. (1973)   *Concepts and Methods in Discrete Event Digital Simulation*. Wiley-Interscience, New York.

Fishman, G. S. (1978)   *Principles of Discrete Event Digital Simulation*. Wiley-Interscience, New York.

Kleijnen, J. P. C. (1974/75)   *Statistical Techniques in Simulation* (2 vols). Marcel Dekker, New York.

Kleijnen, J. P. C. (1987)   *Statistical Tools for Simulation Practitioners*. Marcel Dekker, New York.

Kleijnen, J. P. C. & van Groenendaal W. (1992)   *Simulation: A Statistical Perspective*. Wiley, Chichester.

Law, A. M. & Kelton, W. D. (1991)   *Simulation Modeling and Analysis* (2nd edn). McGraw-Hill, New York.

Page, E. S. (1965)   On Monte Carlo methods in congestion problems: II. Simulation of queuing problems. *Ops. Res.*, **13**, 300–305.

Saliby, E. (1980)   A re-appraisal of some simulation fundamentals. PhD Thesis, Lancaster University.

Saliby, E. (1990)   Understanding the variability of simulation results: an empirical study. *J. Opl Res. Soc.*, **41**(4), 319–27.

Tocher, K. D. (1963)   *The Art of Simulation*. English Universities Press, London.

Part III

System Dynamics

13

Modelling feedback systems

13.1 FEEDBACK SYSTEMS

13.1.1 Hierarchical feedback systems: an example

Consider a company which produces spares and replacement parts for the motor trade. Suppose that it does not produce original equipment and is dependent on the large number of motor factors and retailers. Thus, the company has two groups of final consumers of its products:

(1)   Garages who fit the parts to their customers' vehicles;
(2)   DIY motorists who fit the parts themselves.

The company has no direct contact with either of these groups of consumers.

To make its products, the company buys in raw materials and processes them. Thus, it creates two distinct sets of stocks within its own boundary:

● Raw materials;
● Finished goods.

All of these stocks must be financed and will thus be subject to some control.

The finished goods are sold to motor factors who themselves hold stocks as wholesalers. The motor factors buy in large lots from the manufacturer and sell in smaller batches to the retailers or the garage trade. The DIY motorists buy in units from the retailers. This produces the overall hierarchical system shown in Figure 13.1.

DIY motorists enter a retail outlet to buy parts, and as the individual sales occur the retailer's stocks are reduced. In time, possibly as a result of a call from a salesman, the retailer places an order with the motor factor. As several such orders are met, the motor factor's stocks are also run down. Thus the motor manufacturer receives an order from the factor. In this way, the finished stocks of the manufacturer are depleted. Eventually, the effect is felt on the raw material stocks and so an order is placed on the raw material supplier. Most likely, the parts manufacturer operates a production plan which calls for production of particular parts in batches at regular time intervals.

Several things are apparent in moving up this chain of supply from the DIY motorist to the manufacturer. First, the batch sizes of stock replenishments increase. Thus, mistakes are more costly higher up the chain. Second, the purchasing decisions move further and further away from the consumers'

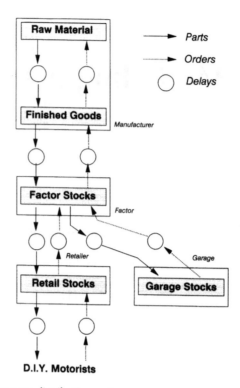

Figure 13.1   A motor parts distribution system

behaviour. Hence, both the cost and the risk of wrong action increase higher up the chain. A third feature is the presence of delays in the system. For example, the manufacturer does not respond to individual orders from factors by attempting to maintain a constant finished stock level. Rather, batches are made and added to the stocks at intervals. Similarly, the retailer may place weekly or monthly orders on the factor.

Suppose, for example, that the DIY motorists suddenly reduce their demand for parts. What happens?

(1)   The depletion of the retailers' stocks slows down. This occurs immediately.
(2)   Rather later, the factors' stocks are also higher than normal. If parts ordered from the manufacturer a month earlier begin to arrive in stock, then this makes things even worse. Eventually, the factors reduce their orders to the manufacturer. If things get too bad, they may stop ordering for some time.
(3)   Meanwhile, in the absence of market intelligence, the manufacturer may be blissfully unaware of all this. While the downturn in DIY demand is happening, the regular production plan of the manufacturer continues. Then suddenly, to the unaware manufacturer at least, demand dries up. This causes severe problems. Raw material stocks are too high and more supplies are already on order. Finished stocks are also mounting and there is no prospect of moving the stock. Thus, the manufacturer has either to reduce

production, which will create severe labour problems, or devise some means of shifting the stocks. One way might be to offer a special price promotion.

(4)   Remember that these problems hit the manufacturer some time after the original downturn in DIY demand. If their luck is bad, and sometimes it is, the price promotion may coincide with a resumption in DIY demand. The price promotions may inflate this demand still further. This causes frantic calls for deliveries at all levels in the hierarchy. Thus, there is a risk that the manufacturer may end up over-producing to meet this artificial demand. What happens next? That depends, but there is a clear risk of catastrophic overshoot in production.

Of course, this scenario is not entirely realistic. However, similar effects do occur in systems of this type. Small decisions at a low level can have much amplified effects further up the system. Such multi-level systems need to be modelled with the aim of exploring their stability and response.

13.1.2 Causal loop diagrams

These offer a simple way of mapping out the interacting elements of feedback systems. As will be seen in chapter 14, Forrester (1961) put forward a rather more complicated system of flow diagrams to aid system dynamics modelling. For present purposes the simpler causal loop diagrams will suffice. The idea is to show which factors cause other factors to change.

As a simple example, consider a thermostatically controlled domestic central heating system. This is shown in simplified causal loop form in Figure 13.2. Gas is burned to provide heat; heat input to the room causes the room temperature to rise; as the temperature rises, this trips a thermostat which cuts off the gas supply. If the temperature drops below some pre-set temperature, the thermostat causes the gas supply to be restored.

Notice the following conventions:

(1)   The direction of the arrow head indicates causality. For example, an increase in room temperature causes (via the thermostat) the gas supply to be cut off.

(2)   The sign at the arrow head indicates the effect of the causality. If an increase in one factor causes an increase in another, other factors remaining

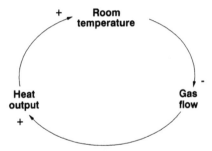

Figure 13.2   Causal loop for a central heating system

unchanged, then a plus sign is correct. If an increase in one leads to a decrease in another, other factors being unchanged, then a minus sign is called for. Sometimes both effects are possible and a question mark should be used. In the central heating example, increased heat output should lead to an increase in room temperature—hence a plus sign is shown.

Of course, the systems investigated by management scientists are much more complex than this simplified central heating system. The control function in particular is much more complicated and, most likely, is fairly diffuse. At one extreme, control may be exercised via simple programmed rules or procedures which are rigorously followed. For example, jobs of certain types may always be allocated to specified machines in a job shop. At the other extreme is the adaptive behaviour by which any organisation ensures its continued existence. This is characterised by conscious responses to changes in the organisation's environment which present both threats and opportunities. For instance, companies manufacturing clockwork watches around 1973 needed to be ready for the micro-electronics revolution. Some were not.

Hence, it would be wrong to regard organisations as machines or even as directly analogous to machines. Only low-level control is exercised by simple procedures. Thus, the causal links for organisational control are shown as dashed lines on the diagrams. This is to emphasise that control is usually exercised via policies which can be changed without affecting the causality of the 'material links'. Most likely, the purpose of the simulation is to explore the effect of current and alternative policies on the rest of the system. Dashed lines are also used to indicate information flows.

A good introduction to the use of causal loops and their value in qualitative analysis is given in Wolstenholme (1990) and a further example may illustrate their use. Section 2.3.1 described a simple deterministic simulation which used a time-slicing approach and which could be implemented on a spread-sheet. It described the recruitment problems of Big Al, a somewhat unsuccessful gangster. As well as considering the equations which govern Big Al's problems, it can be instructive to examine the causal loops which determine what is going on. Figure 13.3 shows the causal loops which drive Big Al's recruitment patterns. It shows what, to some at least, may be obvious from the description given in Section 2.3.1, that is, several negative feedback loops control the behaviour of the system. In particular, two deserve mention. The first controls the recruitment rate by measuring the gap between the current mob size and Big Al's target—the smaller the gap, the lower the recruitment rate. The second control comes from the arrest rate (the rate at which Big Al loses mobsters) and is directly related to the current mob size. To achieve his goal, Big Al will have to find ways of beating these two controls—either by making mob membership more attractive as the mob size increases or by keeping his men out of gaol.

13.1.3   Closed and open loops

A feedback system is one which incorporates a loop from the output to the input. In simple homeostats, this feedback path allows control to be exercised by

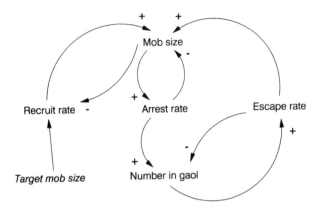

Figure 13.3   Causal loop diagram for Big Al's recruitment problem

comparing the difference between the output and some desired result. In negative feedback systems this difference, or error term, is reduced by taking appropriate action. This is how thermostatic control is exercised in domestic central heating systems. If the room temperature is below some desired level, then a heat source is used to increase it (i.e. to minimize the difference between the actual and desired temperature). When the error is zero, the heat source is withdrawn. Closed-loop systems have intrinsic control.

   Not all systems are closed in this way. Some central heating systems have no room thermostats and no automatic control on the radiators. Hence the system goes on burning fuel regardless of the room temperature until either the fuel runs out or someone turns the system off. Such a system is an open loop and has no intrinsic control. Feedback systems are closed loops and offer intrinsic control. Hence, causal loop diagrams of management systems always include closed loops. That is, ignoring input variables, it should be possible to follow the influence links in the direction of causality from any point in the diagram and return to the same point. Absence of such closed loops on a causal loop diagram indicates either that the diagram is wrong or that the system has no intrinsic control. The former is more likely.

   The analysis of mechanical, electrical and electronic systems is a major preoccupation of design engineers. Control theory offers a mathematical approach to the analysis of such systems. In many ways, the roots of system dynamics as propounded by Forrester are to be found in control theory and this is clear in the first text on the subject (Forrester, 1961). Indeed, Forrester recommends drawing flow diagrams to assist in system analysis and these diagrams use symbols familiar to control engineers. For example, control functions are represented by valves. Thus many of the concepts of control theory, though without the complex mathematics, spill over from control theory into system dynamics. These diagrams are described in Section 14.1.

13.2   ANALYSING FEEDBACK SYSTEMS

13.2.1   Level of detail

Discrete event models concentrate on the state changes and interactions of individual entities. This microscopic approach contrasts with the approach usually taken to the modelling and simulation of feedback systems. Here it is normal to operate at a much more aggregate level by concentrating on the rates of change of populations of entities. For example, if the distribution system of the motor parts manufacturer were being simulated it would not be sensible to follow each individual stock item through the system. Instead, a simulation model would most likely be used to analyse the changes in rates of demand and production in the system.

To build the model it would be normal to regard these rates as varying continuously through time. In some cases, this is a reasonable assumption. For example, suppose that the parts flowing through the system are cheap and common items such as screws. To all intents and purposes, the variable 'number of screws' is continuous, even though the figure '234.675 screws' has no meaning in the real system. For other systems (for example, the cases described in Chapter 15) any assumption of continuity requires careful consideration.

In order to model feedback systems for simulation it is important to concentrate on their structure rather than their content. The structure defines how the variables interact, the content is the meaning of those variables for the organisation. Two systems may have similar structures but quite different content. For example, a supermarket and the control room of a fire station may both be analysed in terms of their queuing structure. Both systems have customers who are served, but the meaning (and importance) of the customers differ. In the fire station the customers are calls awaiting response, whereas in the supermarket the customers are the shoppers. Causal loop diagrams are concerned with system structure. Coyle (1977) points out that the management scientist has to maintain two views of a system at the same time. To model it, the system must be seen in terms of its structure, but to consider making changes it is crucial to keep in mind the meaning of the variables. Only then will it be clear which changes are feasible. Thus, a rounded approach is needed.

13.2.2   Simulating feedback systems

Engineering students are familiar with the modelling of feedback systems by differential equations. Indeed, the design of servo-mechanisms is still a feature of many engineering curricula. Once such systems become realistically complex, then their direct analysis is often impossible. Various means are resorted to so as to get round this difficulty. One approach is to use analogue computers to simulate the behaviour of the system being studied. Such a computer employs a network of electrical components whose behaviour can be described by the same differential equations as the system of interest. Analogue computers allow continuous variables to be represented by continuous properties such as voltage and current. In one sense, therefore, analogue simulators offer a more accurate way of simulating feedback systems than system dynamics. The simulation is carried out by subjecting the selected electrical circuits to specified inputs and observing the behaviour of the model system. The components are then rearranged or tuned to design systems which perform in the way required.

A major difficulty with analogue computers is that they require a reasonable expertise in the design of electrical circuits—otherwise, the selection and assembly of the correct components is impossible. Another problem is that few commercial organisations possess analogue computers. However, most do have digital computers. An obvious development was therefore the production of digital computer packages which simulate analogue computers. To use the current versions of such systems, the analyst formulates the problem in terms of differential equations. These digital–analogue packages, such as SLAM (1972) and the later versions of CSMP, use standard integration routines to simulate the behaviour of the system of equations given certain lengths.

Rather than use such digital simulators of analogue computers, it is much simpler to use the approach taken in system dynamics. This approach allows simple systems to be simulated on straightforward spread-sheets. More complex models may need specialist software of the type discussed in Section 14.5.

13.3   SYSTEM DYNAMICS MODELLING

To analyse feedback systems in system dynamic terms it is normal (Forrester, 1961) to concentrate on three aspects of system structure:

● Delays;
● Levels;
● Rates.

The meaning of these is discussed in the sections below.

13.3.1   Delays

It is important to realize that information and materials (or whatever make up the 'stuff' of the system) are rarely transmitted and received instantaneously. To give a simple example, orders may be sent by customers to their supplier by ordinary mail, thus introducing a delay of at least one day. Similarly, a company may have good reason to increase its production by 30% but face a lead time of four weeks to do so because of the need to train more staff. Delays occur for all sorts of legitimate reasons and often these may be reduced at a cost. For example, a company with geographically dispersed distribution depots may choose to transmit information about stock levels by facsimile transfer rather than by using the normal mail.

Delays, of whatever type, can have profound effects within feedback systems. As a trivial example, most people have had the distressing experience of trying to control the temperature of a shower which has a manual mixing valve. Typically, such a valve mixes water from separate hot and cold sources. The mixed water then passes to the shower head and thence drops onto the person in the shower. Unfortunately, it takes time for the water to travel from the mixing valve to the shower head. Hence the familiar pattern of events unfold:

(1)   Bather enters shower area and turns on the water, but the water is too cold because the shower was last used some time ago;
(2)   Bather turns the mixer valve so as to increase the water temperature;
(3)   No immediate effect, therefore the bather turns the mixer valve further towards hot;
(4)   Scalding water now hits the bather who frantically turns the mixer valve to the cold side;
(5)   Water still too hot, so the bather turns the mixer valve still further towards the cold side;
(6)   Bather now hit by cold water! Therefore the bather turns the mixer valve towards hot, but with no immediate effect.

And so the process continues.

With stable water flows and an intelligent bather, the temperature oscillations decrease in amplitude until the right temperature is achieved. All this is because of a delay in a simple system. Figure 13.4 shows the temperature oscillations and their eventual damping. To avoid such oscillation, the answer is to reduce the delay. Thus, the temperature should be sensed as close to the mixing valve as possible. Hence, if a thermostat is to be used, it should be placed in the circuit immediately after the valve.

Let us return to organisational systems. The motor parts manufacturer (Section 13.1.1) has real difficulties in trying to control production runs and stock levels. As it stands, the system includes far too many delays; also decisions about the production rates are too far removed from the behaviour of the consumers. One objective of the manufacturer, if more control is required, may be to reduce the effect of these delays. That is, the manufacturer must be more in touch with the state of the market. This does not mean that the management must respond to every fluctuation in the market. However, they ought to be in a position to decide whether or not to react.

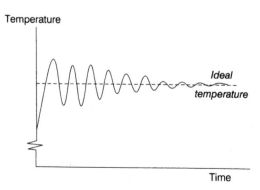

Figure 13.4   Temperature variations under a shower

Thus the consideration of delays is an important part of the analysis of feedback systems. Section 14.4 discusses how different types of delay are handled in system dynamics.

13.3.2   Levels

Organisational systems contain accumulations of one kind or another. In system dynamics these are usually called *levels*. The current conditions of the levels within a system correspond to the system state. Often, levels are clearly recognisable as such (for example, stocks of various types). Another example might be cash balances which are produced by inflows and outflows of funds. A slightly less obvious example might be a labour force with numbers of employees at different grades and experience. This too could be regarded as a level or accumulation within the system. Levels continue to exist (in principle, at least) even if all activity ceases (Forrester, 1961).

In modelling feedback systems it is important to identify the relevant levels of the system. Generally, these levels are subject to some control by the management of the organisation. By examining the levels within the system the system state can be understood and appropriate corrective action may be taken.

13.3.3   Rates

Activity continues in any dynamic system. This activity may be represented by the *flow rates* which control the levels. Thus, cash balances are affected by the rates at which money flows into and out of the organisation. The labour force is affected by the rate at which people are hired and leave. These flow rates vary continuously and must be represented in such a way as to capture this variation. Flows occur instantaneously but can be usefully measured as average rates over a period. If the period is made small enough, then the rate changes will appear to occur smoothly and will thus capture something of the continuous variation.

13.3.4   Policies

It should now be clear that the system dynamics method views feedback systems as interconnected sequences of levels and flows. Matter and information flow from one level to another. Thus, the levels are affected by the flow rates and the flow rates may be affected by the levels. As an example, a manufacturer's finished stocks are determined by at least two flow rates:

(1)   Despatch rate to customers;
(2)   Production rate of finished goods.

In turn, the production and despatch rates are affected by the level of finished stocks. Goods cannot be despatched if they have not been made. Thus, the despatch rate depends, in some sense, on the level of finished stocks. Similarly, if the finished stocks are too high, the management may decide to cut production.

Thus, in system dynamics terms, policies are explicit statements as to how levels affect rates and rates affect levels. In feedback systems, policies are expressed as decision rules stating what action is to be taken so as to achieve a given state. Hence, they might state the flow rate necessary to achieve (it is hoped) a certain level.

13.4   THE ORIGINS OF SYSTEM DYNAMICS

It ought to be clear that simulating hierarchical feedback systems calls for methods which are rather different from the discrete event approaches covered in Chapters 4–12. With such systems, the major concern is often with stability—that is, how does it respond to changes in its inputs? For example, what will happen if demand increases briefly and then settles down again? Or what effect would the doubling of certain stocks have on production rates in the short term? To answer these and similar questions calls for a simulation method which can cope with delays, with flows of information as well as 'material' and which lends itself to the study of transient phenomena.

System dynamics was first called 'industrial dynamics' from the book of that name by Forrester (1961). Despite its long history, in simulation terms at least, many management scientists are sceptical of its value. Possibly there are two reasons for this. First, *Industrial Dynamics* was an ambitious book, perhaps too ambitious. This is particularly seen in Forrester's claim that it presented a revolutionary approach to management. With hindsight, this does seem rather an exaggeration. Even at the time of publication, its mechanistic approach must have seemed a limiting factor to practising managers.

Another possible reason for the commonly found scepticism is that system dynamics is definitely not a highly refined and accurate tool. The aim is to explore the dynamics of feedback systems in terms of their stability and responses to external shocks. In many cases, the presenting instability may be so gross that exact analyses are not required. System dynamics presents a way of approximately simulating such systems. For the purist, the approximation may seem too great.

As mentioned in Section 13.2.2, the analysis of feedback systems via differential equations has long been the concern of engineers. System dynamics adopts a rather simpler approach in which the differential equations are replaced by first-order difference equations. As will be seen in Section 14.3, this results in an integration approach which needs to be used with some care, otherwise the results of a simulation could be misleading. Nevertheless, its simplicity can be a great asset in communicating with managers.

The idea of modelling socio-economic systems in feedback terms is not original to Forrester. Forrester gives credit to Tustin (1953) for considering in detail the analogy between servo-mechanisms and economic systems. Forrester's contribution was to provide a simple and systematic way of simulating such systems.

REFERENCES

Coyle, R. G. (1977)   *Management System Dynamics*, Wiley-Interscience, London.

Forrester, J. S. (1961)   *Industrial Dynamics*. MIT Press, Cambridge, MA.

SLAM (1972)   *A Simulation Language for Analogue Modelling*. ICL, UK.

Tustin, A. (1953)   *The Mechanism of Economic Systems*. Harvard University Press, Cambridge, MA.

Wolstenholme, E. F. (1990)   *System Enquiry. A System Dynamics Approach*. Wiley, Chichester.

14

System Dynamics Modelling and Simulation

14.1 INTRODUCTION

There are a number of tools associated with system dynamics that help modellers to simulate and understand how dynamic systems operate. In the early days of system dynamics, most models were developed using the DYNAMO system which is described in Forrester (1961). Since the mid-1980s there have been a number of significant developments in this area, mainly due to the widespread availability of MacIntosh computers and IBM PC compatibles running different versions of Windows. The tools, of which the best known is Stella/iThink (Richmond and Peterson, 1994) rely on graphical user interfaces to support model building and simulation. They thus parallel the development of visual interactive modelling systems (VIMS) described in Chapters 8 and 9.

This chapter shows how system dynamics models can be developed using this software and indicates some of the main pitfalls to be avoided. Before introducing these simulation and modelling tools, the chapter first shows how diagrammatic approaches may also be used to gain some insight. These require no higher technology than pencil and paper and yet are widely used in system dynamics.

14.2 INFLUENCE DIAGRAMS

Although verbal descriptions of dynamic systems can be helpful, many people find that diagrams are a useful aid to thinking about how these systems operate. Chapter 4 showed how the simple ideas of activity cycle diagrams can be used to tease out how discrete simulation entities interact. They may also be used as part of a process of automatic program generation, in which the diagram is read by an intelligent computer program that writes a computer program that will simulate the system represented in the diagram. These same ideas have also been used in system dynamics. The previous chapter introduced the idea of causal loop diagrams and this chapter provides more detailed approaches to system dynamics diagrams as a prelude to simulation.

14.2.1   Level rate diagrams

This first type of diagram was first introduced by Forrester (1961) in his original book on industrial dynamics. Figure 14.1 shows the main symbols that are used in these diagrams. However, note that Forrester's original diagrams had many different types of flow other than the two (material and information) shown in Figure 14.1. The symbols are defined as follows:

- *Levels.*   These are accumulations within the system, examples of which might be stocks, cash balances or number of people employed. These accumulations will persist even if all flows in the system drop to zero. They are an analogy with a tank of fluid into which liquid flows and from which it is drained. The level in the tank will vary, depending on the value of the in- and out-flows. If these flows are zero, or equal, the level will be static. Levels are similar, in concept, to the idea of system state in discrete simulation.
- *Flows.*   These represent the movement of material and information within the system through time. They are analogous to system activity, in that if all drop to zero, then the levels will not change—because there is no activity.
- *Decision functions.*   These represent the ways in which the material flows are controlled. The symbol on the diagram looks like a valve and, indeed, that analogy lies at their heart. Information passed to these functions causes the flow rates to be varied, which in turn affects the levels within the system. These decision functions are used to represent management policy in the system.
- *Delays.*   As discussed in the previous chapter, information (and material) may be delayed as it moves around a system. These symbols are used to represent different types of delay.
- *Sources.*   Some flows enter the system across its boundary. These exogenous flows come from sources.

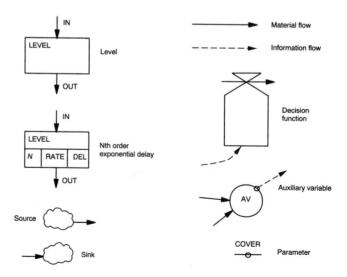

Figure 14.1   Forrester's flow diagram symbols

- *Sinks* Some flows leave the system across its boundary and their destination is shown as a sink.
- *Auxiliary variables.* These are used when some algebraic expression is needed when representing mathematical functions.
- *Parameters.* These are values used by the model (e.g. the number of weeks stock cover to be held in the system).

As an example of the use of level rate diagrams, consider the problem faced by Big Al in Chapter 2. Though Big Al wished to recruit *mobsters*, this is a simple exercise in manpower planning—people are recruited, some leave and some rejoin. In Chapter 2 this was simulated using a spreadsheet and the previous Chapter showed a causal loop diagram for its interacting factors. The method used in Chapter 2 to simulate it was very similar to the system dynamics method that will be introduced shortly. A possible level rate diagram is shown in Figure 14.2. This displays the information feedbacks that are used by Big Al in his vain attempt to recruit enough mobsters. The main 'material' flow is of potential, current and arrested mobsters. Information about the current mob size, the target mob size and the escapees is used to determine how many people will be recruited each period. Similarly, information about the current mob size is used to drive the arrest rate, and information about the number in gaol drives the escape rate.

14.2.2   Stella diagrams

As mentioned earlier, recent years have seen increasing use of system dynamics software that is based on graphical user interfaces (GUIs), of which Stella/iThink is perhaps the most widely known. Stella was originally developed for the Apple MacIntosh GUI, but is also available for Microsoft Windows-based systems. The full commercial version is usually known as iThink. As will become clear later, the Forrester DYNAMO approach requires the modeller to develop equations that represent the levels and flows within a system. The Stella/iThink approach (called the Stella approach from now on) is rather different. When using Stella, the modeller is presented with a GUI screen in which a palette of symbols is available. Using a mouse or other pointing device, the appropriate symbols are selected,

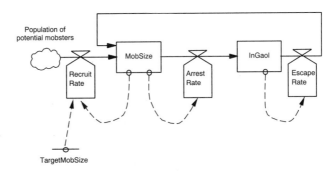

Figure 14.2   Big Al's problem: Forrester flow diagram

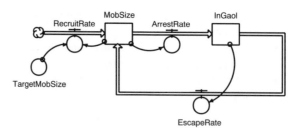

Figure 14.3 Big Al's problem: Stella diagram

placed on the diagram, and linked together. The Stella system is then able to read the diagram and can generate some of the equations automatically.

The symbols required on a Stella diagram are very similar to those of Forrester and can be seen in Figure 14.3, which shows a Stella flow diagram of Big Al's recruitment problem. As with Forrester's diagrams, levels are represented by rectangles—although they are known as *stocks* rather than levels. Two types of flows are used on Stella diagrams. Information flow is shown as a single line and material flow as a double line. Sources and sinks share the same symbols. No distinction is made, in Stella diagrams, between auxiliaries and parameters; both are represent by *converters*, shown as a circle. Stella diagrams have no special symbols for delays.

14.3   BEYOND THE DIAGRAMS—SYSTEM DYNAMICS SIMULATION

A system dynamics model is a set of difference equations whose variables change their value through time. The approach was developed by Forrester, who saw the analogy between physical control systems and the control systems employed in organisations. He provided an approach that is based on the one that most control engineers would use when trying to design or understand dynamic physical systems. The problem that faces such engineers is that, although they are often able to write differential equations that model how a dynamic system might behave, in many cases these sets of equations cannot be integrated directly. Instead, the engineer resorts to a numerical approach, usually with the help of appropriate computer software. Forrester provided a simplified version of this numerical integration in system dynamics.

14.3.1   Time-handling in system dynamics

In the terms introduced in Chapter 2, system dynamics usually employs a time-slicing approach. That is, as shown in Figure 14.4, within the simulation the values of the variables are computed at distinct points of time separated by an unvarying time increment. In system dynamics, this time increment is known as *DT* (written *dt* in Stella). The effect is to create linear piece-wise approximations to the smooth curves between each time point, as shown in Figure 14.4.

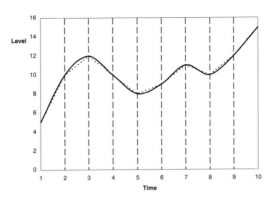

Figure 14.4   Time-slicing in system dynamics: linear approximations

As in all time-slicing approaches, the modeller must fix the value of *DT* in advance. If *DT* is too large, then the simulation will be too coarse and may miss important variation and transient effects. In addition, it should be noted that choosing too large a value for *DT* may cause the simulation to be very misleading in its dynamic behaviour—this problem is discussed later in Section 14.3.7. If *DT* is made too small, then this will lead to a model that runs too slowly (which may not matter greatly) but it may also require over-accurate estimates of the parameters of the model. This may, in turn, lead to excessive data collection and, therefore, of excessive cost. The usual advice is to choose a value for *DT* so that it is reasonable to assume that all flow rates in the model can be regarded as constant over that interval during the running of the simulation. If in doubt, make *DT* small.

14.3.2   Time-handling in DYNAMO

DYNAMO employed a syntax which now seems rather crude, but which was a major development in the late 1950s. It also has the advantage that it eases the task of checking whether a set of equations are dimensionally correct. Dimensional errors occur when the left and right hand sides of an equation have different units, and these are surprisingly easy to achieve! The syntax assume three consecutive points of time: *J*, *K* and *L*, each one separated from the next by *DT*, as shown in Figure 14.5.

System dynamics relies on two main types of equation that will be discussed in more detail shortly. These are *level equations*, in which the values of levels are computed, and *rate equations*, in which the rates are updated. The levels are computed at each time point *J*, *K* and *L*. The rates are assumed to be constant over the intervening intervals of length *DT*. Thus, if the inflow to a level exceeds its outflows, then the level will be higher at time point *K* than it was at time point *J*. Similarly, the level will fall if the outflow exceeds the inflow. A system dynamics

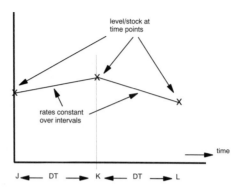

Figure 14.5   Time-handling in DYNAMO

simulation, expressed in DYNAMO terms, proceeds as follows:

(1)   Imagine that time has just left point *J*.
(2)   Increment time to *K*.
(3)   Compute the new values of the levels at time *K*, using the rates that apply over the interval *JK*.
(4)   Compute the new rates that will apply over the interval *KL*.
(5)   Re-label the time points so that *K* is now *J* and so that *L* is now *K*, and repeat the cycle until the simulation is complete.

14.3.3   Time-handling in Stella

Time-handling in Stella is rather simpler to describe, since there is no reference to *J*, *K* and *L*. Instead, the modeller must imagine any two arbitrary points of time that are separated by a time interval *dt*. As in the case of DYNAMO, there are two types of equations—those for stocks and those for flows, in Stella terminology. The simulation proceeds much as does a DYNAMO simulation. As time reaches some arbitrary point, the new values of the stocks are computed, then the new values of the flows. The flows are held constant over the next interval *dt* and when time reaches the next time point, the process starts all over again. This means that Stella equations are rather easier to read, but it also means that it is easier to make mistakes in the dimensions of the equations.

14.3.4   Level or stock equations

A typical level equation represents the 'physics' of a system and describes how a level or stock will rise or fall, depending on the values of its in-flows and out-flows. In DYNAMO format, the level equation for the number in gaol in Big Al's recruitment problem might be as follows:

$$INGAOL.K = INGAOL.J + DT^* (ARRESTRATE.JK - ESCAPERATE.JK)$$

Where:

$INGAOL.K$ = number in gaol at time K

$INGAOL.J$ = number in gaol at time J

DT = time increment

$ARRESTRATE.JK$ = arrest rate over the interval JK

$ESCAPERATE.JK$ = escape rate over the interval JK

Most level equations have a similar format and can be inferred directly from the diagram.

A corresponding stock equation in Stella might be as follows:

$$InGaol(t) = InGaol(t - dt) + (ArrestRate - EscapeRate) * dt$$

which ought to be self-explanatory.

14.3.5   Rate or flow equations

These equations show how information about the levels and about other flows are used to modify the flows. They can be used to represent the policies and control mechanisms that govern the changes in the levels. Whereas most level or stock equations can be directly inferred from the diagrams, which is what Stella does, this is not true of the rate or flow equations. Using the Big Al example again, a suitable DYNAMO rate equation for the arrest rate might be as follows:

$$ARRESTRATE.KL = MOBSIZE.K * 0.05/DT$$

Note that this is dimensionally explicit, in that the dimensions of $ARRESTRATE$ are people/time and, hence, the right-hand side of the equation must match these dimensions—which it does.

A Stella flow equation for the same policy might be as follows:

$$ArrestRate = MobSize * .05$$

Notice that, strictly speaking, this is dimensionally incorrect, since the dimensions of the left-hand side are people/time, whereas those of the right-hand side are just people. Stella rate equations imply that dt is somewhere on the right-hand side.

14.3.6   Big Al's problem—a Stella model

The diagram of Figure 14.3 was drawn using the Stella software on a PC running Microsoft Windows. The equations that underpin the diagram are shown below. Note that Stella automatically generates the stock equations, but the modeller must specify the flow equations since they specify how the flows will be managed so as to gain whatever control of the levels is required.

$$InGaol(t) = InGaol(t - dt) + (ArrestRate - EscapeRate) * dt$$
$$INIT \ InGaol = 0$$

$ArrestRate = MobSize * .05$
$EscapeRate = InGaol * .1$
$MobSize(t) = MobSize(t - dt) + (RecruitRate + EscapeRate - ArrestRate) * dt$
$INIT\ MobSize = 0$

$RecruitRate = (TargetMobSize - MobSize)/4$
$EscapeRate = InGaol * .1$
$ArrestRate = MobSize * .05$
$TargetMobSize = 50$

14.3.7   More on suitable values for *DT*

Although it may not be obvious at first sight, what is going on within a system dynamics simulation involves numerical integration. The usual method of achieving this in system dynamics is known as the Euler–Cauchy approach and it is implicit in DYNAMO. Stella, by contrast, allows the user to specify an integration method, although it provides Euler–Cauchy as the default. To illustrate the effect of integration methods, consider the following level–rate pair of equations:

$L.K = L.J + DT * (I.JK - O.JK)$
$O.KL = L.K/A$

where L is the level, I is the input rate, O is the output rate and A is a constant. The same pair of equations could be written as follows in Stella:

$L(t) = L(t - dt) + dt * (I - O)$
$O = L/A$

This pair of equations could be re-written as the following differential equation:

$$\frac{dL}{dt} = I - L/A$$

The Euler–Cauchy integration formula for this differential equation is as follows:

$L(n + 1) = L(n) + dt[I(n) - L(n)/A]$

where dt is the step-size and $L(n)$ represents the value of L at step n, the method being based on iterations through time, with an interval of dt.

Figure 14.6 shows the effect of different values of dt when using this Euler–Cauchy approach. It uses an initial value of 0 for L and I, with I rising immediately to a value of 4 and remaining there. Giving dt a value of 1 causes L to rise gradually and asymptotically towards the value of 4. Increasing dt to 2 and then to 4 causes the increase to be much sharper. But when dt is given a value of 8, the integration fails and oscillation sets in. In general, the Euler–Cauchy method is sensitive to the size of the integration step, dt, and also tends to propagate small errors which may be amplified as simulated time proceeds. Stella handles this problem by prohibiting its dt from exceeding a value of 1. In DYNAMO, small is definitely beautiful as far as DT is concerned.

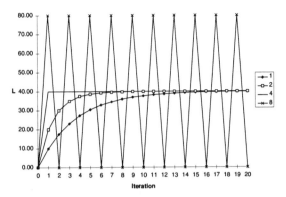

Figure 14.6   Effect of different values of DT in Euler–Cauchy integration

14.4   SIMULATING DELAYS IN SYSTEM DYNAMICS

An important feature of many dynamic systems is the presence of delays that make control of the system rather harder than might seem the case at first sight. The previous Chapter described how hard it can be to gain proper control of the temperature in a shower which has a simple mixer valve. In many organisational systems a number of different types of delay have been observed, of which the most common are as follows:

- *Exponential delays.*   These occur when part of a system takes some time to respond to changes in its input. The response is, in effect, damped, rather as a car's shock absorbers dampen the effect of the oscillations caused by its springs. This damping is usually very desirable, as it stops the system from over-reacting—but the damping does need to be properly considered. These exponential delays are covered in more detail later in this Section.
- *Pipeline delays.*   These are an analogy with a pipeline of known length into which material is fed and from which it flows once the material has passed through the pipe. In effect, these are delays of known duration. Examples might include delays due to postal systems or the delivery of goods. In effect, an input rate and output rate are separated by a level or stock, and the output rate is the input rate delayed by some interval. In Stella, these can be modelled by a special version of a stock known as a conveyor and the length of the delay is represented by its transit time.
- *Batch delays.*   These are analogous to ovens in which batches of items are placed, cooked for an interval, and then all released after some time interval. In Stella, these are modelled by a special form of stock known as an oven, with the time spent in the delay known as the cook time. Examples might include the delays caused by staff training, in which a class of recruits are all trained together for some time period and then released at the end of the period.

14.4.1   Exponential delays

Because the use of delays to dampen system responses is very common in organisational systems, special delays are provided for this purpose. In the case of DYNAMO, Forrester's level-rate diagrams use the special exponential delay symbol shown in Figure 14.1. Stella diagrams do not include such symbols, but use built-in functions to represent these delays. These exponential delays are usually defined by their order, common types being first-, second- and third-order exponential delays. The order of the delay gives some idea of the damping that it will exert on its input. Figure 14.7 shows explicit Stella diagrams for two exponential delays, a first-order and a third-order delay. As is clear, a third-order delay can be represented by a cascade of three first-order delays, with the output of one delay becoming the input of the next. The number of levels contained by a delay gives its order.

The Stella equations for the first-order delay shown in the top part of Figure 14.7 are as follows:

$$Level(t) = Level(t - dt) + (In - Out) * dt$$
$$INIT \ Level = 0$$

$$In = 10$$
$$Out = Level/Del$$
$$Del = 5$$

whilst those for the third-order delay are as follows; note that, in this case, the delay period *Del* is spread equally across the three levels, which has the effect of applying *Del/3* to each output rate:

$$Lev1(t) = Lev1(t - dt) + (In - Inter1) * dt$$
$$INIT \ Lev1 = 0$$

$$In = 10$$
$$Inter1 = Lev1 * 3/Del$$
$$Lev2(t) = Lev2(t - dt) + (Inter1 - Inter2) * dt$$
$$INIT \ Lev2 = 0$$

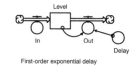

First-order exponential delay

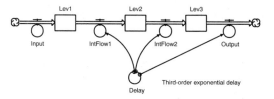

Third-order exponential delay

Figure 14.7   Exponential delays: Stella diagrams

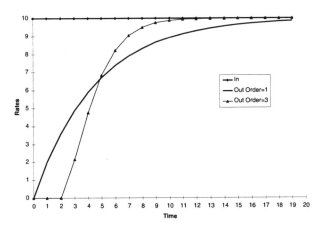

Figure 14.8   Exponential delays: step response

$$Inter1 = Lev1*3/Del$$
$$Inter2 = Lev2*3/Del$$
$$Lev3(t) = Lev3(t-dt) + (Inter2 - Out)*dt$$
$$INIT\ Lev3 = 0$$

$$Inter2 = Lev2*3/Del$$
$$Out = Lev3*3/Del$$
$$Del = 5$$

The effect that these delays have on the output can be seen in Figure 14.8, which shows the result of providing a step input of 10 to a system in which the initial values of the levels and of the output is 0. The first-order delay produces a response in which the output climbs asymptotically towards the value of 10, rising quickly at first and then slowing down. This exponential curve is what gives these delays their name. The third-order delay has rather more of an S-shaped response. Until period 3, nothing happens and then there is a very steep climb towards the value of the input.

14.5   COMPUTER SOFTWARE FOR SYSTEM DYNAMICS

As with discrete event simulation, so system dynamics models can be developed using a range of types of software. This chapter has already covered the basics of Stella/iThink and also of DYNAMO. In addition, the following may also be used.

14.5.1   General-purpose programming languages

As with discrete event simulation there is, of course, the option of writing a system dynamics simulation program from scratch in a general-purpose programming language such as Pascal, FORTRAN or C. It should be clear that this is not an overwhelmingly difficult task for someone who is fluent in such a language—indeed, it is easier than writing a discrete event simulation. However, using a general-purpose language is not really to be recommended in the light of the other available options.

In particular, system dynamics models benefit from having graphical output available in the form of plots of the variables of interest. These need not be created dynamically as the simulation proceeds, but should certainly be available at the end of the simulation. Providing such graphs is tedious in the extreme. If using a general-purpose language, therefore, the best option is to write the results of a simulation into a file which has a format which can be read by one of the graphics or spread-sheet packages. The latter packages may then be used to generate reasonable graphs with very little effort. However, they are not part of the simulation system itself and it can be tedious to have to leave the simulation repeatedly just to examine the graphs.

A further problem with using a general-purpose programming language is that the user will need to write procedures and functions to represent the standard system dynamics functions such as delays. If these are already available in a library then some time can be saved.

14.5.2   Spreadsheets

Spreadsheet programs such as Lotus 1-2-3 and Excel are ideal for carrying out simple system dynamics simulations—although they are not recommended for large-scale or complicated models. The basic procedure is to regard the rows of the spreadsheet as representing the time points in the simulation and the columns are used to represent the variables. Some care needs to be taken to ensure that the correct computation sequence is maintained, for example levels must be made dependent on the correct rates at the right time points. But other than that, the use of a spreadsheet is quite straightforward.

As with using a general-purpose language, spreadsheets do not contain the in-built functions found in specialist system dynamics software. Therefore, these need to be provided—probably by the use of appropriate spreadsheet macros—not difficult, but rather tedious.

Most spreadsheets have direct links into their own graphics routines, which means that the results of a simulation can be displayed immediately just by swapping to the appropriate graphs. This is another area in which spreadsheets score over using a general-purpose language for system dynamics.

One caveat about using spreadsheets must, however, be noted. There is a tendency for spreadsheet models of all types (which therefore includes system dynamics) to grow too large and to contain spaghetti-like links between cells. When a spreadsheet model gets into this state it is almost impossible to validate or verify and is probably best scrapped. If the system dynamics model is growing too complex then resort should be made to specialist software.

14.5.3   Specialist system dynamics software

DYNAMO and its successors

When the system dynamics approach was introduced by Forrester as industrial dynamics, it was implemented in the DYNAMO programming language. By contemporary standards. DYNAMO looks very crude, but it must be remembered that it was in use by the early 1960s. Pugh (1973) gives a definitive account of all the features of DYNAMO at that stage. DYNAMO is still available today and Richardson and Pugh (1981) provide a substantial introduction to its use. A version for use on IBM PCs and compatibles, Professional DYNAMO (Pugh Roberts Associates, 1986), is also available.

In the UK, the System Dynamics Research Group at Bradford University produced another language system, DYSMAP (Ratnatunga, 1980), which used a syntax which is very similar to that of DYNAMO. A summary of its features is to be found in Coyle (1977), who argues that it is preferable to DYNAMO. DYSMAP was intended for mainframe use and required a FORTRAN compiler. Coyle (1996) introduces COSMIC, a PC-based system dynamics package which has an optimisation extension, COSMOS.

A later version, DYSMAP2 (Dangerfield and Vapenikova, 1987) is specifically designed to run on IBM PCs and compatibles. DYSMAP2 has an interactive command processor which makes the whole process of experimentation much easier. Both DYSMAP2 and Professional DYNAMO make full use of PC graphics for display purposes.

Visual Interactive Modelling Systems for system dynamics

The 1990s have seen an explosion in the availability and use of VIMS for discrete simulation. There have been fewer, though parallel, developments in system dynamics. As described earlier in this chapter, Stella/iThink (High Performance Systems, 1994) is perhaps the most widely used system dynamics VIMS today. It is available on common operating systems and is relatively easy to use. A similar package is VenSim (Ventana, 1996).

As with all such VIMS, the diagrams tend to get very complicated once a system reaches a certain scale. Stella and similar systems approach this problem by providing a hierarchical structure in which part of a model may be replaced by an input:output block that contains all the stocks and flows, and which communicates with other blocks via its inputs and outputs. This allows the modeller to develop a model sector by sector, each sector being built and tested before being linked to other sectors. In this way, the parsimonious modelling style advocated throughout this book may be followed.

EXERCISES

1. Draw a causal loop diagram of the following system.

    A biscuit company sells its biscuits to retailers, most of whom demand a price discount which increases with the amount purchased. High discounts mean high sales, but lower unit returns for the biscuit company. On the other hand, low discounts lead to low sales and, sometimes, to no sales. Low sales result, therefore, in low market share, which makes retailers reluctant to stock the biscuit company's products. This leads the retailers to demand yet higher discounts if they are to stock the biscuits. High sales lead to lower unit costs in production and distribution.

2. Draw a causal loop diagram of the following system.

    Bailrigg Computer Services (BCS) provides an on-site maintenance service to customers who pay an annual fee that guarantees the repair of their computer systems within 24 hours on any weekday, apart from Bank Holidays. To this end, 50 service engineers are employed and all are equally skilled. Being a quiet part of the country, BCS have little or no labour turnover but this may be about to change. Nippon MegaCorp Computers (NMCC) are about to open their UK service centre in Bailrigg and will almost certainly try to entice some of the BCS engineers to work for them. Hence, Bill Ritchie, who runs BCS, thinks that he must plan for labour turnover by introducing a training school. His idea is as follows:

    > Each month he will recruit a number of trainee engineers who will enter a 6-month training scheme. At the end of the 6-month programme they must take a test and those who pass will join the staff of engineers. Those who fail may be found other jobs by BCS, but they will not join the staff of engineers. The problem facing Bill is, what recruitment policy should he adopt?

    He is inclined to record the number of engineers who leave each month and to use these figures to compute an exponentially smoothed forecast of the expected losses of engineers. In each month he will recruit enough trainees to replace this expected loss to NMCC, adjusted for the proportion of trainees who are expected to fail at the end of the training programme.

3. Develop a system dynamics model of exercise 2, using the following additional information.

    If, in any month, the number of engineers on the staff is 50 or higher, then he will recruit no trainees that month. He thinks that he might use a = 0.2 for his forecast, and he reckons that, each month, the number of engineers who leave BCS for NMCC will be Normally distributed with a mean = 5 and standard deviation = 2. He also expects that 0.8 of each monthly cohort will be successful in their training and will join the BCS staff of engineers.

4. Develop a causal loop diagram of the following system.

    The Sweat Shop is based in one of the Asia Pacific Tiger economies and employs craft workers who manufacture hand-produced articles that sell in the EU. Employment legislation is lax and this means that workers can be hired and fired at will. Working conditions are also rather poor and so the work is tedious and time-consuming. No proper work study has ever been conducted but some basic data can be imputed from the meagre records that the owner keeps.

    - He reckons that each worker can produce ten items per day.
    - The invoices suggest that each day he receives orders that are Normally distributed with a mean of 200 items and a standard deviation of 20. However, he suspects that this demand may soon increase, possibly doubling and becoming much more variable.

- Workers are readily available, but need some training (during which time they are unpaid). The training takes 5 days to complete. If he finds that he has too many workers then he sacks them. Being kinder than some owners he gives them 3 days notice, during which time they continue to work normally.

He prefers to keep about 5 days' demand for finished goods in stock and he has an unlimited supply of raw materials. His son is studying in the UK and, during his last vacation, installed a demand forecasting system based on simple exponential smoothing with an alpha value (smoothing constant) of 0.2. Anything more sophisticated will not be used.

The owner would like your advice about what hiring and firing policy to adopt, given that he prefers to have just the right number of workers to meet his demand for goods.

5. Develop a system dynamics model and simulate the system described in exercise 4.

REFERENCES

Coyle, R. G. (1977)   *Management System Dynamics.* Wiley-Interscience, London.

Coyle, R. G. (1996)   *System Dynamics Modelling: A Practical Approach.* Chapman & Hall, London.

Dangerfield, B. C. & Vapenikova, O. (1987)   *Dysmap 2 Users' Manual.* University of Salford.

Forrester, J. W. (1961)   *Industrial Dynamics.* MIT Press, Cambridge, MA.

High Performance Systems (1994)   *Stella II Technical Documentation.* High Performance Systems Inc., Hanover, NH.

Pugh, A. L. III (1973)   *DYNAMO Users' Manual.* MIT Press, Cambridge, MA.

Pugh–Roberts Associates (1986)   *Professional DYNAMO Introductory Guide and Tutorial and Professional DYNAMO Reference Manual.* Pugh–Roberts Associates, Cambridge, MA.

Ratnatunga, A. (1980)   *Dysmap Users' Manual.* University of Bradford.

Richardson, G. P. & Pugh, A. L. (1981)   *Introduction to System Dynamics Modelling with DYNAMO.* MIT Press, Cambridge, MA.

Richmond, B. & Peterson, S. *et al.* (1994)   *Stella II. An Introduction to Systems Thinking.* High Performance Systems Inc., Hanover, NH.

Ventana Systems (1996)   *VENSIM System Manuals.* Ventana Systems Inc., Belmont, MA.

15

Systems Dynamics in Practice

Note: The companies involved in these studies are given pseudonyms to protect their competitive positions. As well as changing their names, it has been necessary to disguise their products to make identification even more difficult. Both belong to multi-national organisations with turnovers in excess of $500 million per annum. All the divisions involved in these studies are located in the UK.

15.1 ASSOCIATED SPARES LTD

Associated Spares Ltd (ASL) make and sell parts for the domestic appliances and the motor trade. They supply original equipment and spares.

15.1.1 The problem as originally posed

In 1977, the general manager of the UK distribution division of ASL put it something like this:

> 'The economy seems to fluctuate by about 5% over a 5-year cycle. What I don't understand is why the demand at the central warehouse fluctuates much more than this. Mind you, we have so many products at different stages of their life cycles that I can't prove that this really happens. But I'm fairly certain that it does and it creates enormous problems for my business. Is there any way in which you can help?'

As is so often the case, the initial brief was rather vague and some effort had to be put into problem structuring. After visiting a number of retail outlets and extensive discussions it looked as though a system dynamics approach could be of some use. In particular, it could be used to identify the effect of the various decision rules used in the distribution division of ASL. It could also show the effect of changes in the market.

15.1.2   The multi-echelon system

Investigation revealed that a multi-echelon distribution system existed. Figure 15.1 shows how it operated. The parts were made in a number of plants throughout the UK and were held in a central warehouse. The UK had been divided into discrete geographical areas, each of which had its own regional warehouse. These received supplies from the central warehouse. Beneath the regional warehouses in the hierarchy were a large number of retail outlets, some of which were owned by ASL. Normally, the retail outlets ordered supplies from the nearest regional warehouse. In exceptional circumstances, urgent orders were despatched direct to the retail outlets from the central warehouse. ASL provided stock control advice for the retail outlets.

Thus, there were large aggregate flows of material and information in a system which included many feedback loops. Management put a great deal of effort into controlling the operation and hence there were a great many decision rules. A further complication was the existence of delays due to forecasting, despatch lead times, batching of orders, etc. Previous knowledge of similar systems suggested that fluctuations of the type suggested by the general manager were indeed possible. Hence system dynamics models were constructed with the aim of studying these dynamic responses.

Four models were eventually built. Three of these were separate models for the retail branches, the regional warehouses and the central warehouse. The fourth model was a combination of the earlier three.

15.1.3   The retail branch model

Construction of this model began with a very simple view of the system as shown in Figure 15.2. Later this was enhanced to include the real-life complications, that is, the analyst was consciously following the 'principle of parsimony'. Starting with this simple model, it was possible to introduce the client to the ideas of system dynamics and thus to gain his confidence. Via the influence diagrams, the analyst

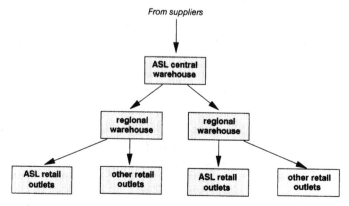

Figure 15.1   The ASL distribution system

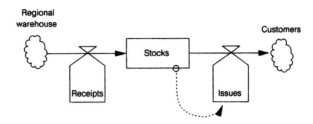

Figure 15.2   ASL simple retail branch model

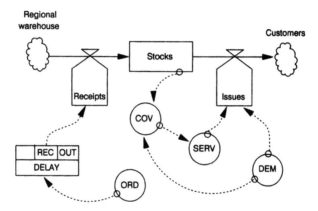

Figure 15.3   ASL first revision to simple retail branch model

and client were able to discuss the obvious shortcomings of the simple model and successive improvements were made.

All that the simple model of Figure 15.2 shows was that stock was created by the difference between receipts and issues in each branch. Obviously, these processes of receipts and issues needed to be modelled. Figure 15.3 shows the first stage in this modelling. Receipts result from the orders placed on the regional warehouse followed by a substantial delay. Issues (sales) stem from customers' demands.

However, there was also the problem of the mix of products in stock to be considered. Figure 15.4 shows the relationship which was found to exist between stock cover and service levels. Stock cover was defined as the total weeks of stock divided by average weekly demand. Thus, a stock equivalent to 6 weeks' demand meant that 83% of customers could be satisfied from stock. The link between issue rate and stock levels was established and built into the system dynamics model as a table functions.

There was then the order rate to investigate, and it was apparent that the following were important factors affecting order rates:

- Forecast demand (historical demand, current demand and the forecasting system);
- Expected lead-time usage;
- Usage between stock reviews;

% Service level

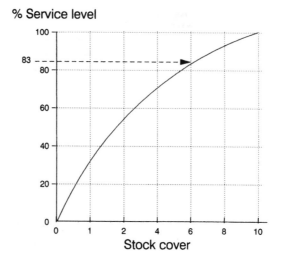

Figure 15.4   ASL stock cover

- Buffer stock held to compensate for demand fluctuations;
- Actual stock levels;
- Outstanding orders;
- Lead times;
- Supplementary orders.

The retail branches were controlled through entirely manual systems which involved a fixed review period. Sales forecasting was via simple exponential smoothing. The smoothing process had the effect of damping out sharp fluctuations (which is good). But it also introduced a delay between changes in demand and their reflection in sales forecasts (which is bad).

The manual stock control system used the sales forecast, modified to allow for delivery lead times, safety stocks and the stock review period. This led to a target stock level which was computed manually at intervals determined by the review periods. Expensive and fast-moving items were reviewed more often than the rest. Thus for some products, this introduced a delay of several weeks before changes in sales led to revised target stock levels. The difference between free and target stocks led to an order placed on the regional warehouse. The supplies, however, were only received after a lead time delay of several weeks. In the retail branch model this lead time delay was held constant, using the average delay experienced. Figure 15.5 shows the final model of the retail branches.

Figure 15.6 shows the effect of subjecting this retail branch model to a step increase of 5% on a previously steady demand rate. The immediate effect is a considerable decrease in stock levels caused by the sluggish response of the stock control system. The forecast of demand rises steadily until it reaches the new steady state after about 6 months. The orders placed on the regional warehouse display highly erratic behaviour. The order rate initially lags behind the sales rate and then overshoots after about 3 months. Eventually it falls to a new steady-state

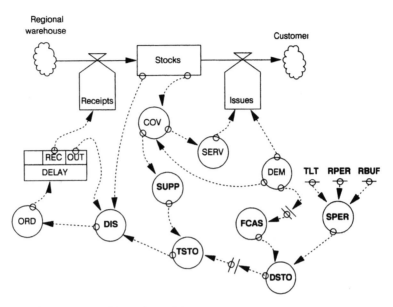

Figure 15.5   ASL final retail branch model

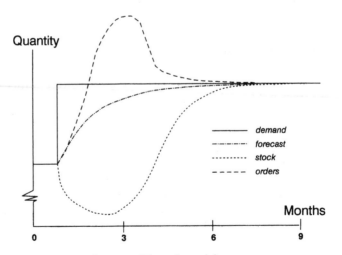

Figure 15.6   Step response of ASL retail branch model

level. Notice that for a period of about 4 months, the 5% increase in sales leads to an amplified response in the order rate to the regional warehouse.

Why should this happen? A number of reasons are apparent.

(1)   The various delays lead to an immediate fall in stock levels. This in turn leads to higher orders being placed on the regional warehouse.

(2)   In particular, the stock control system attempted to maintain a constant stock cover of *n* weeks' stock. Thus the increased demand means that stocks are built up, not just to replace the extra sales but also to maintain the stock.

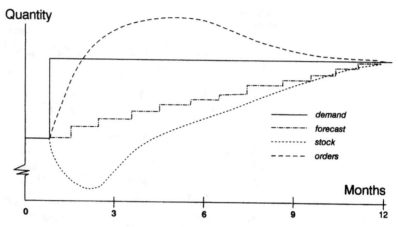

Figure 15.7   Step response of ASL regional warehouse model

Thus, a simple model of a retail branch brought considerable insight into the effect of demand fluctuations. The delays and the stock cover ratio led to amplification and the system took about 6 months to settle down. And this after only a 5% change in sales rates.

15.1.4 The regional warehouse model

At the regional warehouses, the systems were rather different from those in the regional branches. The stock control was achieved via a computer system which aimed to keep stocks between maximum and minimum levels. Thus the levels were continually monitored and replenishments were ordered as soon as the minimum level was reached. Back orders were also possible because unsatisfied orders from retail branches were held on a backlog file until supplies were received. The forecasting was based on a weighted moving average rather than exponential smoothing. Hence, although the overall structure of the branch and regional models were similar, the details were completely different.

Figure 15.7 shows the output from the model when previously steady demand is increased by 5%. As at the branch level, stocks initially fall and the order rate overshoots the increased demand rate but the different forecasting system leads to stepped increases in forecasts. Overall, the regional warehouse responds in a way which is qualitatively similar to the retail branch. However, the system takes over 12 months to settle down. The retail branch took about 6 months to settle down.

15.1.5 The central warehouse model

The management systems at the central warehouse were computer-controlled, although more sophisticated than in the regional warehouse. Orders from the regions were entered via data input terminals and interacted with the stock control systems to produce invoices, despatch notes and other paperwork. The demand forecasting used a double exponential smoothing system, allowed for seasonality in demand, identified outliers, etc. A full-scale production control and planning system placed orders on the factories as and when necessary. Overall, the systems were different from those employed at both branch and regional levels. Hence, the detail of the model differed from that of the earlier two.

Figure 15.8 shows the effect of increasing demand by 5% on the central warehouse after a previously constant demand. The demand forecast slowly rises to meet the new demand rate, and it takes over 12 months to do this because of the small constants used in the double exponential forecasting system. This forecasting system had been introduced to dampen out the effect of certain large customers placing orders only a few times each year. The rate at which orders were placed on the factories overshoots by a large amount. The stock levels have still not settled down after 12 months of simulated time. The general manager's suspicions were beginning to look correct.

15.1.6   The total system model

It was also important to model the interactions of these three systems. Although the retail branches may experience a 5% step change in sales, their demand on the next level of the system will be amplified and delayed. As well as this amplification, the phasing of the new rates may differ somewhat. Hence, the already unsatisfactory state of affairs may look much worse after aggregating the three models. Figure 15.9 shows an outline influence diagram of this aggregate model. To make the model more realistic, the lead time experienced by the retail branches were no longer assumed constant. Increased demand on the regional warehouse from

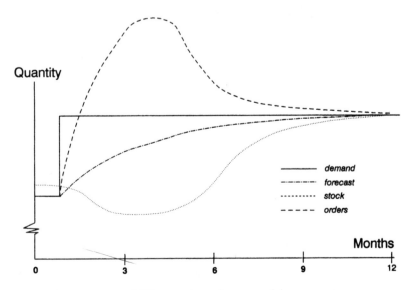

Figure 15.8   Step response of ASL central warehouse model

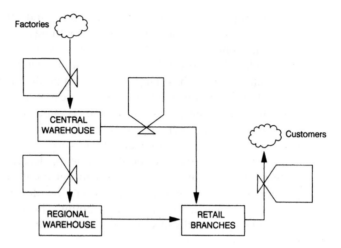

Figure 15.9   Outline of total ASL model

several retail branches would lead to a lengthening of the lead times. Similarly, service levels would change.

Figure 15.10 shows the result of subjecting the total system model to a step increase of 5% in sales at the retail branches. As might be expected from the three separate models, a familiar pattern emerges. The increase in customer sales leads to overshoot in the demands placed by the retail branches on the regional warehouses. In turn, these increases lead to greater overshoot in the orders placed from the regions on the central warehouse. Finally, the central warehouse places orders on the factories at a rate way above the 5% step increase in customer sales.

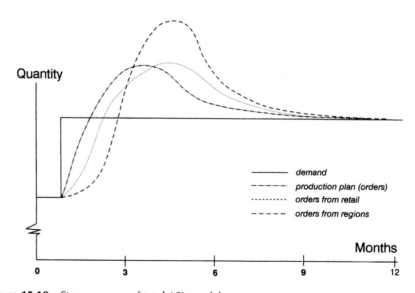

Figure 15.10   Step response of total ASL model

A 5% step increase in end user demand leads to the following maximum order rates within the system:

- Retail branch to regional warehouse: +8% maximum.
- Regional warehouse to central warehouse: +10% maximum.
- Central warehouse to factories: +23% maximum.

Thus changes in the market have been amplified up to four times within the system. The further away from the original change, the greater the degree of amplification. The various delays make such massive fluctuations inevitable because corrective action takes a long time to have any effect. There is also the risk that management may over-react if they see that their attempts to control things bring no immediate effect.

15.1.7   Some conclusions

The intuition of the general manager was clearly correct and he needed no persuasion of this for two reasons. First, most people love to be correct. Second, the stage-by-stage modelling had allowed him to keep continual contact with the progress of the study.

How could the operation of the system be improved? Many of the problems were caused by the interaction of the different systems found in the three levels of the hierarchy. Each of these systems made sense at its own level; put together, the effect was unfortunate. The first point is that the managers of the three levels were able to learn how their different policies interacted. It was clearly impossible to optimise the behaviour of the entire system; however, each manager could now be made aware of the difficulties faced by others elsewhere in the system.

Given that the project was commissioned by the manager responsible for the central warehouse, it is fair to ask what benefits he received. As mentioned earlier, his intuition was proved correct. Also, the models clearly showed the effects of the delays within the system and identified the important interactions. In this sense, the 6 months of part-time work which went into the project could be viewed as problem structuring. The manager and the analyst were now aware of the weak points of the system and could now examine ways of improving its performance.

From the initial study, a further 18 months of part-time work was commissioned. Detailed investigations of various possible improvements were carried out. These were as follows:

(1) Operate without regional warehouses;
(2) Cut down information delays so that central warehouse could monitor end-user demand rather than simply using demand data from the regional warehouses;
(3) Modify the forecasting systems;
(4) Operate a stock control system not based on stock cover ratios;
(5) Change the parameters of the existing stock control systems.

Implementation of some of these followed.

15.1.8 A postscript

ASL hit a cash flow crisis shortly after the final meeting of this project and traditional remedies emerged from the directors' desks. One suggestion was that a 5% cut in stocks across the board would free the required cash. Thus a golden opportunity arose to use an existing model to see what would actually happen.

What the simulations showed was that a 5% cut in target stock levels implemented simultaneously at all three levels would result in the following changes in actual stocks:

- A 6.7% drop at the central warehouse;
- A 10.7% drop at the regional warehouse;
- A 7.9% drop at the retail branches.

It would take the retail branches 4 months to reach this level whereas the central warehouse would take 6 months. For a substantial part of this 6 months, stocks would be rising at the central warehouse due to de-stocking lower in the system. This de-stocking would occur faster than schedules on suppliers could be cut.

Hence the directors were able to see that their notion of a 5% cut across the board would produce rather worse effects than anticipated. If stocks were to be rebuilt later, corresponding problems would arise. The 5% cut was not implemented.

15.6 DYNASTAT LTD

15.2.1 An expansion programme

Dynastat makes a range of electromechanical controllers for oil-fired heating systems. These devices use sophisticated electronics and are fitted to heating units for which Dynastat holds worldwide patents. Because of these controllers, the heaters use up to 15% less oil than competitive products. The rise in oil prices which occurred in the mid-1970s resulted in great increases in demand. At first, this increase was managed by using sub-contractors to produce some units. But it became clear that Dynastat was stretched to its limits and large-scale investment was necessary.

The board agreed an investment programming costing about $70 million with the aim of doubling the output of the Dynastat factories. While planning the programme it became obvious that a key problem would be the need for more skilled manpower. A particular difficulty was the Rockingham plant near London. In the past it had been difficult to recruit enough skilled workers, and it seemed as if this could be a severe brake on the expansion program.

15.2.2 The manpower problem

An analyst from the internal consulting group was asked to advise on this problem. At the first meeting, the personnel manager of the Rockingham plant said that he was convinced that the programme was impossible. His experience suggested that the skilled manpower targets were out of reach. As the meeting continued, it became clear that he had thoroughly analysed the recruitment potential—however, labour turnover seemed to have been forgotten. After a quick analysis of available figures, it became clear that the labour turnover for skilled workers was about 25% per annum (labour turnover being defined as the number leaving in a year divided by the average number of employees during the year). Later checks showed that 25% was typical for this type of industry.

In system dynamics terms, manpower can be regarded as a level fed by recruitment and depleted by labour turnover. Hence the simple model shown in Figure 15.11 was constructed. By using it, the recruitment rate to fill a specified number of jobs can be calculated. Remarkable as it may seem. Dynastat had previously been unable to relate labour turnover and recruitment to the expansion program. But before this simple model could be used, appropriate functions for turnover and recruitment were required.

15.2.3 Recruitment

One fear was that the current high level of economic activity would make it even more difficult to recruit enough skilled workers. Analysis of available data showed that the numbers of skilled workers recruited in the past was positively correlated with the health of the economy. The apparently good relationship is rather misleading, as it might suggest that recruitment is easier when the economy is booming. However, the reality is that more recruitment is necessary when the economy is booming and few recruits are needed when product demand is low. Hence some other way of modelling recruitment was needed.

A further complication was that Dynastat needed to model future recruitment rates and there was no guarantee that their economic cycles would coincide with that of the rest of the nation. Thus, the forecasts of hiring rates were produced by a combination of analysis and management judgement. To ensure consistency, the same forecasts of national economic activity produced for demand forecasting were used when predicting hiring rates and labour turnover. However, the forecasts were modified to allow for expected regional differences.

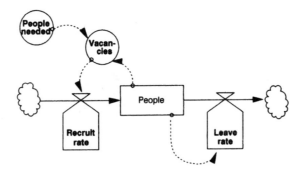

Figure 15.11   First simple Dynastat model

15.2.4 Turnover

Analysing historical leaving rates produced some interesting results. The leaving rate was very high immediately after joining Dynastat but was very low after 6 months. Thus, new recruits were highly likely to leave, but if they survived for 6 months then they were likely to stay for much longer. Hence for further analysis, the 'attrition curve' could be simplified by considering skilled workers to be either 'new' or 'established'. The modelling was made easier by the discovery that this simple model would suffice for all groups of skilled and semi-skilled workers in the factor. 'New' workers were found to have a turnover of 170% per annum and the 'established' turnover rate was about 10% per annum. These rates would not necessarily hold for the other Dynastat factories.

The effect of local employment levels on labour turnover was also investigated. It appeared that the leaving rate of 'established' staff was not affected; however, it had a great effect on the leaving rate for 'new' workers. This effect was incorporated within the model shown in Figure 15.12.

15.2.5 Some effects of this structure

If the model of Figure 15.12 is in a steady state, then the hiring rate must be positive, for the aim is to recruit enough workers to replace those who leave. However, there are delays in the system. As in most organisations, new workers were hired to fill existing vacancies—that is, no hiring action was taken until some workers had left. Hence, steady state is possible only if vacancies exist to drive the recruitment rate. This means that there would always be a shortage of workers in the factory if current policies were followed.

Without even simulating with the model, a further problem is apparent. The overall average turnover was 25% per annum, represented by 170% for 'new'

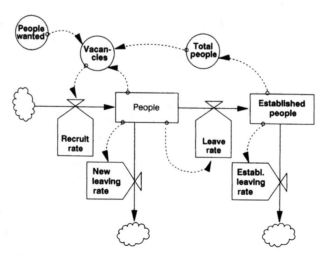

Figure 15.12   More complex Dynastat model

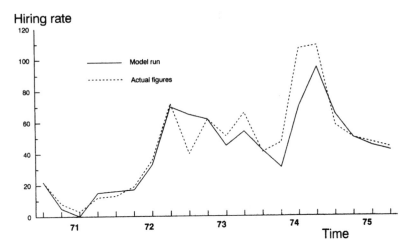

Figure 15.13   Dynastat initialising run

workers and 10% for 'established' workers. Suppose that Dynastat wish to increase the workforce from 4000 to 6000—a 50% increase. If the different rates are ignored, then the temptation is to recruit enough workers to fill the 25% overall turnover plus the 2000 extra. However, this is clearly wrong. There will be a turnover of 170% among the 'new' workers (if the economic conditions were unchanged) and thus the overall turnover will be much higher than 25% because the balance between 'new' and 'established' workers will have changed.

15.2.6   Validating the model

The principles of 'white box' validity (see Chapter 10) having been followed throughout model construction, a 'black box' check was now required. That is, could the model reproduce the past behaviour of the system? As the modelling occurred in 1977, the period 1971 to 1977 was chosen for this validation exercise. The results of initialising the model at January 1971 and running it until 1977 are shown in Figure 15.13. Statistical analysis confirmed that this adequately represented the actual system behaviour. Note, however, that this was not an entirely satisfactory check as the 1971 to 1977 data had been used to parameterise the model. However, some confidence was built up.

15.2.7   Simulation results

Figure 15.14 shows the results of the first run. It shows an enormous shortfall in available labour. This run assumed that previous policies were followed. The gap was so large that no conceivable increase in the hiring rate would close it. Hence attention was focused on the leaving rates and it was clear that reducing the 170% leaving rate of 'new' workers was crucial.

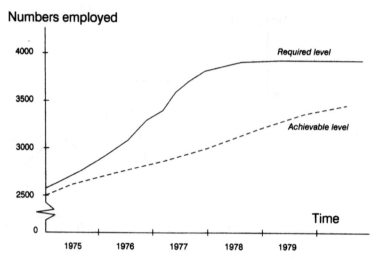

Figure 15.14   First Dynastat run

To do this, the model had to be made more detailed by sub-dividing 'new' workers. After some discussion and thought, it emerged that different factors caused workers to leave at various stages of their first few months at 'Dynastat'. These were as follows:

- FIRST MONTH: 'JOB SHOCK'
  Could be improved by better selection, induction, training, etc.
- MONTHS 2 to 6: 'CULTURE SHOCK'
  Could be improved by better supervision.
- AFTER 6 MONTHS: 'NORMAL ATTRITION'
  Affected by wage levels, the company image, motivation and other similar factors.

Using the model, the effect of improving these factors was investigated. Of course, for many of these the analyst had to rely on the judgement of the managers in order to incorporate appropriate functions into the model. Thus, the model was used to show the effect of improvements thought to be possible by the managers who would be responsible for their implementation. Some cross-checking of different opinions helped refine the process.

The complete model is shown in outline form in Figure 15.15 and the feedback links are obvious. Many factors were inter-related; for example, a high recruitment rate reduces the training available. This may affect the leaving rate of 'new' employees. A series of runs were used to investigate a range of actions which might reduce labour turnover. Examples were as follows:

- Improved job descriptions;
- Improved selection procedures;
- A more professional approach to recruitment;

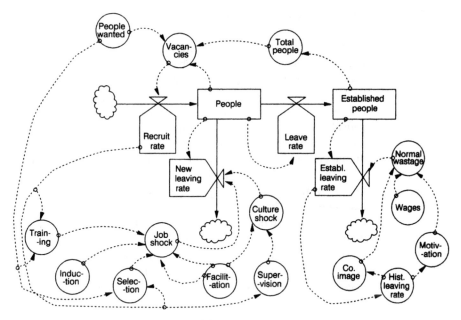

Figure 15.15   Complete Dynastat model

- Better training;
- Closer supervision;
- Retraining current workers.

As a result of these simulations, albeit based partly on the estimates of the managers, it was clear that the expansion plan was feasible.

15.2.8   Predicting length of service

It seemed likely that some recruits might be classified as 'high risk'. To check this, the records of several hundred past employees were examined for obvious indicators. This showed that a simple system of weighting factors such as age, marital status and previous job history gave a good prediction of length of service. This prediction could easily be calculated at the time of a recruitment interview and used sensibly with other factors.

This was expected to produce a tangible payoff by reducing the 'high risk' recruits. An individual leaving the company was estimated to have cost about $800 in recruitment and training. With an overall turnover of 25% and a labour force of 4000, turnover was costing about $800,000 per annum. Reducing overall turnover to 20%, even ignoring the expansion program, should therefore save about $160,000 per annum. This seemed a useful by-product of the simulation exercise.

15.2.9   The value of the exercise to Dynastat

As in the ASL case, the modelling was not very sophisticated and yet the benefits were high. The models were deliberately constructed in a parsimonious way. For example, the initial simple model of Figure 15.11 served to focus discussion on the leaving rates. This had not previously been a great concern to the company. Producing the results of Figure 15.14 led the management to give serious consideration to ways of reducing the turnover of 'new' employees. Indeed, the idea of 'new' and 'established' workers entered the everyday vocabulary of the managers concerned. That is, they began to think about the problem in new ways.

A further advantage stemmed from the apparently unscientific way in which much of the model was parameterised. Despite much data analysis, many parameters could only be estimated by using the judgements of experienced managers who would have to operate the new policies. Because of their close involvement with the model, no solution had to be 'sold' to them. Thus implementation was simply never at issue. Because simulation models, whether discrete or system dynamics, should be built in stages and can be shown as simple flow diagrams, this sort of commitment is possible. In this sense, simulation is not a last resort.

15.3   SYSTEM DYNAMICS IN PRACTICE

The ASL and Dynastat cases have been included for two reasons. First, they were successful exercises which led to distinct improvements within the organisations. Second, they illustrate important features of the use of system dynamics and of other simulation methods. These features are discussed below.

15.3.1   Simple models

Simplicity is not a virtue in itself, for over-simplification can clearly be disastrous. However, most analysts are beset by the desire to build all-inclusive models which are over-complicated. All management science models are simplifications. If a model could incorporate the full richness of the system being modelled then the model would be an exact replica of the system. This means that it would be just as difficult to control and, possibly, just as expensive to operate. Simplification is not disastrous, it is inevitable. Indeed, given that most management systems are in a constant state of flux, then an analyst would be totally occupied in keeping a replica up to date.

The approximations that make up the model need to be appropriate to the task in hand. Hence, in the Dynastat case, it was possible to consider the skilled workforce as a single homogeneous body. This was clearly a simplification, because not all the men and women would be equally skilled or equally productive. However, the model was not intended to reflect these individual differences, it was built to assess whether a sufficiently large labour force would be available to support an expansion plan. Given that the plan did not specify the precise set of skills required of the workforce and given that this was thought to be sensible, the model incorporated an appropriate level of complexity.

Chapter 2 has discussed the 'principle of parsimony'. It suggests the development of models which are initially simple and include only the grosser, structural features of the system. Refinements are made as and when necessary, although the overall structure remains unchanged.

15.3.2   Communication

Given that most management scientists operate in consulting roles to managers, their methods need to be appropriate to that role. A consultant who maintains little or no contact with the client group is unlikely to make much impact. Discrete simulation and system dynamics offer great opportunities for the type of communication which leads to implementation. The secret lies in the use of flow diagrams, parsimonious models and graphical output.

Flow diagrams, whether activity cycles or influence diagrams, are simple to understand. Hence, the management science model need not remain a completely black box to the client. By the sensible use of diagrams, the main structural features can be displayed, enabling the client to agree to them before detailed programming occurs. As the models are successively enhanced, much of this can also be displayed on the diagram. The Dynastat case illustrates this very clearly. The personnel manager had not thought to focus much attention on the question of the rate at which new recruits left the company. The flow diagrams showed the importance of this point and led to its incorporation into the study.

A further refinement mentioned in Chapter 8 is to add animated graphical output on a VDU as the programs run. This adds movement to the simplicity of the flow diagrams. Thus, the client is able to gain a stronger impression of how the model shapes up to the real system.

15.3.3   New thinking

This follows from the good communication produced by a simple approach to modelling. As an example, consider Dynastat, who gained three new insights from the system dynamics study. The first, as mentioned in Section 15.3.2, was the realisation that keeping workers at Dynastat was as important as recruiting them in the first place. With hindsight, this does seem rather obvious, but in the hectic time following the announcement of the expansion plan other aspects preoccupied the managers concerned.

The second insight was the distinction drawn between new and established staff. The analysis of labour turnover figures clearly revealed the existence of these two groups of workers. Obviously, the consideration of only two groups was a simplification—yet it provided enough reality to enable the managers to control their system more effectively.

The third insight stemmed from the second. It was the realisation, again after data analysis, that certain types of recruit were more likely than others to leave

Dynastat not long after joining the company. This led to the development of a simple screening procedure which identified the 'at risk' applicants. This again changed the managers' thinking about their recruitment practices.

15.3.4   Evolutionary involvement

Sometimes the client group may be able to specify exactly what they require of the analyst. Occasionally they are correct. More often, the call for help stems from a feeling that some improvement must be possible. In these cases, the modelling can only be exploratory at first. A feature of such exploration is the asking of sensible questions, 'What if we try to ...?' From the answers to these questions comes the development of issues which require detailed research. This exploration approach to problem structuring (Pidd and Woolley, 1980) is well illustrated in the ASL case. Here the successive development of different models for the various sectors of the company led to more detailed questions being asked. Thus, system dynamics modelling led on to the detailed program of work described in Section 15.1.7.

REFERENCE

Pidd, M. & Woolley, R. N. (1980)   A pilot study of problem structuring. *J. Opl. Res. Soc.,* **31**, 1063–1068.

Author Index

Subject Index